Operating the IBM PC Networks

Operating the IBM® PC Networks

Paul Berry

SYBEX®

Berkeley · Paris · Düsseldorf · London

Cover art by Kurt Fink
Book design by Ingrid Owen

Compaq is a trademark of COMPAQ Computer Corporation.
Corona and Corona-DOS are trademarks of Corona Data Systems.
FF and TallScreen are trademarks of Qualitas, Inc.
GRAFPLUS is a trademark of Jewell Technologies, Inc.
IBM, IBM Personal Computer, IBM PC/AT, IBM PC/XT, IBM PC-DOS, PC Network, Token Ring NETBIOS, and IBM Color Printer are trademarks of International Business Machines Corporation.
Intel is a trademark of Intel Corporation.
LOCALNetter is a trademark of Microsoft Corporation.
MS-DOS is a trademark of Microsoft Corporation.
Norton Utilities is a trademark of Peter Norton.
PCWrite is a trademark of Quicksoft.
Sidekick is a trademark of Borland International, Inc.
STSC is a trademark of STSC, Inc.
Systek 6000 Broadband Network, Sytek 6610 Network Server, and Sytek 6650 Network Translator are trademarks of Sytek Corporation.
TMS 380 is a trademark of Texas Instruments, Inc.

SYBEX is not affiliated with any manufacturer.

Every effort has been made to supply complete and accurate information. However, SYBEX assumes no responsibility for its use, nor for any infringements of patents or other rights of third parties which would result.

Library of Congress Card Number: 85-63777
ISBN 0-89588-307-4
Printed by Haddon Craftsmen
Manufactured in the United States of America
10 9 8 7 6 5 4 3 2 1

Acknowledgments

I am grateful to my editor, David Kolodney, for numerous suggestions and improvements and especially for his contributions to the structure of this book, and to Tanya Kucak for meticulous line editing. Rosemary Morrissey, Paul Neuman, and David Baker of IBM, Nancy Locke and Edward Cooper of Sytek, and Jerry Whitnell of Nestar Corporation helped by providing or explaining essential technical information. Dr. Harry Saal of Nestar introduced me to networks, and Dr. R.S. Langer of SYBEX encouraged my proposal to write about PC Network. Thanks also to the other people at SYBEX who helped make this book possible: David Clark and Olivia Shinomoto, word processing; Joel Kroman, technical review; Ingrid Owen, book design; Donna Scanlon, typesetting; and Jon Strickland and Laura Hurd, proofreading.

My greatest debt is to the real Sachiko (accent on the first syllable), who not only contributed her name and her computer to numerous examples but sustained and encouraged me throughout the research and writing of this book.

Table of Contents

Ten Planning the Network 201

Eleven Installing the Network 223

Twelve Automating with Batch Files 263

Introduction

This book is about PC Network, IBM's program for managing a local-area network of personal computers. The book addresses the various people involved in the day-to-day operation of a network, as well as those responsible for planning, installing, and managing it.

Networks

A network is a set of personal computers linked together so that they can share disk storage and peripheral devices such as printers. By installing a network, an organization transforms its various PCs from a collection of separate, isolated computers into a community in which machines—and the people that use them—can readily cooperate.

During the last few years experiments by many manufacturers have explored a variety of approaches to the physical link between computers, the types of computers thus linked, and the programs that manage communication between machines. Meanwhile, organizations seeking to reap the benefits of networking have faced a profusion of rival claims, products, standards, and capabilities. Although many of these products have been intended for the various machines in the family of IBM Personal Computers, until 1985 IBM itself had offered little or nothing to support a local area network made up of IBM PCs.

That situation changed when IBM introduced its own system for linking personal computers. IBM called it *PC Network.*

One Program, Two Systems of Transmission

The name *PC Network* embraces the set of programs that manage the network, although it has sometimes been used to refer to one of the systems of hardware on which the network software runs. This book covers the PC Network program operating with either of two kinds of hardware links.

The first hardware system, delivered in spring 1985, was the *broadband system,* which links computers by cables and connectors like those used for closed-circuit TV. The computers on the network transmit and receive data on two of the standard cable-TV channels.

The second hardware system, the *token-ring system,* was announced in fall 1985 for delivery in spring 1986. The token-ring uses cables and connectors that are part of the *IBM cabling system* proposed in 1982 and described in 1984. The central idea of this cabling system is that office buildings provide built-in data cables (which can even be telephone-style wires) so that a broad range of computers and other devices can be connected simply by plugging them to the nearest data outlet.

The program called PC Network works with either the token-ring or the broadband system. To the person at the keyboard of a PC on the network, it makes no difference which hardware system is employed. This book applies equally to both; where it is necessary to distinguish between them (for example, in Chapter 11, Installing the Network) the two systems are called the *token-ring version* and the *broadband version* of PC Network, respectively.

Requirements

The PC Network software is designed to run with the operating system PC-DOS version 3.10 or later. The necessary network adapter card can be installed in any of the models of the IBM Personal Computer having sufficient memory, except the PC Jr. A machine on the network which is to provide services to other machines must have a fixed disk, and is usually a PC/XT or PC/AT.

The PC Network hardware and software will operate on compatible machines of manufacturers other than IBM (for example, Compaq). Some machines, for example the Corona PC, may require their own versions of the operating system, corresponding to PC-DOS 3.10, but not PC-DOS itself. It's advisable to ask the manufacturer whether a particular make and model will accept the network adapter, the PC Network software, and the operating system required.

To Whom this Book Is Addressed

In a network, there are many roles, some played by different people and some by the same person at different times. This book addresses different roles in different chapters. Which parts you read may depend on which roles you play.

- **Network User:** You take advantage of services offered by other machines, but you aren't involved in providing those extra services. Chapters 1 to 6 are for you (although you may want just to skim Chapter 3).
- **Network Server:** You operate a machine which provides services that others use. Like the users, you need Chapters 1 to 6; you also need Chapters 7 to 9 which specifically discuss the management of machines playing the role of server.
- **Network planner or administrator:** You have reponsibility for planning and setting up a new network. The first part of the

book gives you background on what the people using the network will be doing, and chapters 10 and 11 tell you specifically how to plan and install the hardware and software. Appendix B discusses differences between the token-ring and broadband systems; Appendix C lists further sources.

- **Network support person:** You have ongoing responsibilty for keeping the network running smoothly, responding to the needs of some of the users, and adjusting the network to meet the load and needs that develop. You'll need to be familiar with Chapters 1 to 11, but you'll find additional useful material in Chapters 12 and 13. Chapter 14 adds a perspective on how some features visible in PC Network today fit into some long-range developments in the DOS operating system.
- **Everybody:** Appendix A provides a glossary of technical terms related to PC Network, and Appendix B adds a non-technical discussion of the principles that underlie the token-ring and the broadband versions of the network. Appendix C lists further sources of information.

Part I and Part II

This book is in two parts. Part I, Using PC Network, is concerned with daily operations of a network that is already established. Part II, Planning, Installing and Maintaining PC Network, is concerned with setting up a new network and also adjusting it after it has been started.

If you don't yet have a network, of course, you'll have to set one up before you can use it. Nevertheless, there's good reason to put the chapters that deal with planning and installation in Part II rather than in Part I. First, people who aren't involved in installation can go straight to what they need for daily operations, without having to wade through installation instructions. Second, those of you who are about to do the installation should first read through the chapters on daily operations, so you have a clear idea of what people will be doing with the network you are planning and installing. There are decisions required during planning and installation that you can't make without an appreciation of what's involved in using and operating the network.

A Note about Capitals

In the early days of computing, computers didn't know about lowercase letters. At the computer, you had to write *FORTRAN* (for example) because there wasn't a way to say *Fortran*. Some writers needlessly perpetuated this oddity of early computers even after their keyboards and printers had plenty of lowercase letters to use. A page with lots of words in CAPITALS has always made me feel that someone is shouting at me, so I've tried to avoid that here, or at least to tone it down. The IBM Personal Computer recognizes both lowercase letters and capitals but the DOS operating system doesn't distinguish between them. It lets you write either way, but ignores the capitalization in what you write. (Inside, it converts the names of commands and files to caps.)

Where I have shown the names of files, or the names by which the network identifies people or computers, I've tried to capitalize them as if they were English: mostly lowercase, but with the first letter capitalized. (I've left DOS as DOS because it's the initials of three words.) Computer commands are often made from English verbs. Where those occur in the text I've capitalized them, not because the computer requires capitals (it doesn't) but to distinguish them from ordinary English words of the same spelling. Where I've reproduced displays generated by the computer, I've preserved the capitalization of the actual display. When you're typing instructions to the computer, you can capitalize or not, as you find convenient.

A Note about Pronouns

A network is used by many people, and the same people at different times play different roles. Most of this book is addressed to "you," by which I mean you the reader who is playing the role I'm talking about at the moment. In different chapters or paragraphs, you applies to different people. I trust I've made clear to whom each section is addressed. But if you find a paragraph that says you and your reaction is "Not me!" please forgive my habit and skip to a part where "you" means you.

One more point—English is constructed so that whenever you or I refer to some third party and that third party is just one person, we have to identify that third person's sex. Of course gender has nothing to do with computing. But people feel bad about being called "it," and I feel grammatically guilty about sentences such as "Each user has their own file." So I've restricted myself to just one third-person singular pronoun. I mean it to refer to anyone, regardless of sex. I realize that some network administrators, or programmers, or computer users are really male.

Part I

Using PC Network

PC Network's Powers and Possibilities

One

This book is about using the IBM program called PC Network to manage a local-area network of personal computers.

The PC Network program works with a network of IBM PCs that are linked either by the IBM *token-ring* network (introduced in 1986) or by the IBM *broadband* system (introduced in 1985). The behavior of PC Network is the same in either case; this book applies equally to both.

What Is a LAN?

A local-area network (or LAN) is a set of personal computers (now universally called PCs) linked so that they can exchange information and share resources. In particular, they can share disk storage and peripheral devices such as printers. A network may also permit computers to share a *gateway*—a link to external sources of data, to another network, or to a large host computer.

How Local Is "Local"?

A LAN is called a *local-area* network because the physical link between the computers has a limited range. Usually, it serves a small- or moderate-sized company or a department within a large company. You may hear the term *local-area network* applied to networks whose range is a few yards, a mile or two, or even more. For networks that go beyond that, the term *wide-area network* is used; they may span many miles or even encircle the earth.

The distinction between local-area and wide-area networks rests mainly on the form of the physical link between them. LANs use very high speed two-way links that are effective at short range, but have not been economically feasible over distances greater than a few miles. LANs usually offer service confined to a small- or moderate-sized company or a department or division within a larger organization. The number of computers they connect ranges from two to two hundred or so, rarely as many as a thousand; around two dozen is a common size.

Each PC Still Does Its Own Work

There are some things that participating in a LAN doesn't change. The various users of a network continue to work independently on their respective machines. Each of the PCs still does its own calculations; the data it works on must still be physically present in its own memory while processing takes place.

That's probably the key distinction between a time-sharing system and a LAN: a time-shared terminal provides the control for calculations that take place somewhere else, at a host computer. By contrast, a LAN provides storage or printing or communication facilities to a PC that still does its own calculations.

The network's contribution is to permit programs, data, and messages to be transferred between PCs rapidly and easily. (And, of course, when a PC exploits a gateway, it may function as a terminal on another system and still do calculations of its own.)

Although the principal use of a network is to share resources such as disk drives, files, or printers, those devices are connected to the network only indirectly. It's the *computers* that are linked. Each device is connected to a PC, but the PCs talk to each other.

What Is PC Network?

The program called PC Network is an operating system for a network of IBM Personal Computers. It doesn't itself provide any of the application programs you want to run. Rather, it provides the framework in which you run other programs.

Scale of PC Network

Networking has benefits even for two or three PCs, but the maximum number that can be served is far higher. A ceiling is imposed by the capacity of the network adapter cards and the capacity of the cable. Even at its most limited, using telephone-type cabling for the token ring or the standard broadband translator and cabling kits, the network can support 72 PCs, spread in a radius of about 500 feet for the token ring and about twice that far for broadband.

With data-grade cabling, the maximum number of PCs on the token ring rises to 260 in a 1000-foot radius or split among several smaller areas spread over a greater distance. With custom cabling and a substitute frequency translator, the broadband version can support as many as 1000 PCs within a radius of more than a mile.

No single machine can be simultaneously in contact with all the others. For most purposes, one machine offering services over the network can serve no more than 25 different PCs at one time.

A Network Operating System

A functioning network is built up from the hardware (such as cables and adapter cards) that provides the physical link between machines and the software that manages communication along those links. But to operate effectively, a network needs more than these links. Presiding over the physical channels of communication, to coordinate and exploit their use, the machines need a system to manage the network as a whole. That's what PC Network is for.

The software that manages the network has to work closely with the operating system of each machine. In many ways, it acts as an extension of the operating system. However, it is specialized to deal with issues peculiar to networking—issues that don't arise when a machine is independent and self-contained.

Although IBM doesn't list PC Network as an operating system, that's what it amounts to. PC Network works closely with DOS and exploits some new features that have been provided in DOS starting with version 3.10. PC Network is thus a major enhancement of DOS. (IBM introduced both PC Network and DOS 3.10 in spring 1985.)

Things a LAN User Can Do

PC Network permits the people who use a group of PCs to share storage space on *fixed disks* (also called *hard disks*) and to share the use of printers attached to machines that have fixed disks. For example, you may have a PC that has neither a fixed disk nor any sort of printer. But once you connect your PC to a network, while continuing to work at your own machine, you can:

- Import data stored in another PC.
- Use programs stored on the fixed disks of other computers, without keeping any copy of your own.
- Send data from your own machine to another for storage.
- Read and write in what amounts to your own private files, even though they are really located on the fixed disks of other machines.
- Have your output printed on any of the available printers, even though they're really attached to other machines.

Advantages of Installing a LAN

There are many advantages in this sort of arrangement. Here's a preview list of some of them.

Smaller Machines Get Some of the Powers of Big Ones

In particular, a machine that has no fixed disk of its own can still offer you many of the conveniences of having one by sharing the use of disk space on one or more other machines. Similarly for printers.

Everybody Can Share the Use of Specialized Equipment

If a department has one high-speed printer with wide paper, another with narrow paper, and also a letter-quality printer, everybody on the network can send output to whichever is appropriate. (PC Network includes software for managing printer queues; you could also arrange something similar for other special peripherals, such as a plotter.)

Programs and Data Can Be Stored as One Master Copy for Everybody

When the company or department has a collection of programs that many people use, there's no need for each user to have an individual copy on diskette. A few machines—or perhaps just one—can store them all. That avoids the clutter of separate copies for every user, and it simplifies the job of making sure that the one master copy has the current release. (*Note:* Proprietary software usually requires a *site license* when it is used this way.)

Data Can Be Very Simply Transported

In an office, data must often be passed from one user to another. When the machines are separate, this usually means copying the data to a diskette and carrying the diskette to the person who needs it next. The network makes it possible to transmit the data directly, or simply to store it in a place where all the interested parties can have access to it directly.

Backup Can Be Institutionalized

It's important to protect data from mechanical failure or inadvertent erasure. Concentrating storage in a relatively few fixed disks, each serving many people, makes it easier to regularize and institutionalize the task of making and keeping backup copies.

Network PCs Can Share a Communications Link to a Host Computer

One of the PCs participating in a network may have installed within it an adapter card that permits it to connect to a communications link (for example, a phone line). When a link to a remote computer is shared among members of a local-area network, it is called a *gateway*. As a PC gateway, IBM offers the Asynchronous Communications Server (program 1642003). One of the PCs on a network installs the program, which drives two serial ports on the machine. Any of the PCs on the network can request to use one of those ports to sign on as a terminal or remote station on the host computer.

Network PCs Can Act as 3270 Terminals

IBM markets an SNA (system network architecture) gateway as a separate product called PC Network SNA 3270 Emulation. It permits PCs on the network to act like the 3270 terminals often used for work on time-shared host machines. The PCs that use the gateway are linked by the same network hardware as PC Network. They may switch between 3270 emulation and other network activities, but they can't do both at once. These gateways are really outside the scope of this book, but are briefly described in Chapter 11.

Characteristics of PC Network

Whether PC Network is used to manage PCs linked by the broadband system using coaxial cables or by the newly introduced token-ring system, the following is true of either:

- Each PC must have a card called a *network adapter* installed inside it. There's one for the broadband system and a different one for the token-ring system.
- Each PC must run the PC Network program to manage its participation in the network. The program is the same for either system. The token-ring system requires an additional program called NETBIOS, whose functions in the broadband version are built into the adapter card.
- Each PC must have a cable that runs from its network adapter to a multiway connector and from there directly or indirectly to all the other PCs. (The cables carry minute voltages; there's no risk of fire or shock from them.)
- Each multiway connector serves a cluster of up to eight PCs. (However, you may not see the connection box; it may be installed out of sight, leaving visible only the jacks for the individual PCs.)
- It doesn't matter which PC is plugged where on the network. A PC is identified not by the geographical point at which it is connected, but by a name it establishes for itself. You can unplug a PC and connect it at a different point on the network, and it makes no difference at all.

Networking May Be Largely Invisible and Automatic

Depending on the way you use your PC and the sort of software you run, you may or may not be aware of the network. You may choose to maintain control yourself and write the commands that connect your PC to the network. Alternatively, you can embed those details in programs that automate the task—programs that are executed automatically when you start your machine or when you start certain jobs. Once the auto-start procedures have been set up, you may use the network regularly yet hardly notice it's there. This book includes what you'll need to know to set things up for yourself or to ask for when someone else is setting things up for you.

Decentralized, Cooperative Processing

PC Network represents a change in the balance between stand-alone machines and large central computers. Historically, there have been two major patterns. On the one hand, there were independent stand-alone computers. On the other hand, there were large time-sharing mainframes supporting many terminals but with all storage at a central place.

Some designs for networking PCs have adopted a central strategy like that of time-sharing. They have one large, specialized server unit to which all the PCs are connected. The thrust of their development is to make that central service bigger, faster, or more reliable.

PC Network is not centralized. It tends to be more diffuse. So far, IBM has not offered dedicated high-performance servers for it, but relies on services offered on a part-time basis by general-purpose machines, which often continue to do local processing as well. A major service (for example, use of fixed disk space) may be offered by several different servers, perhaps to various overlapping subsets of users. Even if IBM offers specialized servers, it seems unlikely that they will be exclusive or operated in a centralized way. Already, specialized servers such as the Sytek 6610 can be used within PC Network's decentralized style of control.

This rather flexible, floating style of offering network services seems to me a forerunner of things to come. Today, to the users of a small network, it may not make much difference or may even seem a needless complication. But in the long run, as interconnections between machines become more commonplace, surely this is the pattern that must emerge. You won't have everybody tying in to one enormous central source. It's more likely each computer—and each computer user—will have more services available from different sources and will shift casually among the different offerings.

How Do Token Ring and Broadband Affect PC Network?

Token ring and *broadband* are names for two different ways of providing the physical link between computers. Either can be used to form a network of PCs; the program called PC Network operates on either. (IBM has sometimes used the term *PC Network* to denote the physical broadband links that were the only means of transmission when the PC Network program was introduced in spring 1985. To avoid confusion, in this book *PC Network* always refers to the program, and not to either of the cabling schemes on which the program runs.)

Two Systems of Linkage, One Set of Rules

There are many different systems for transmitting data at high speed. The two systems IBM uses for linking PCs are the token-ring network and the broadband network. Those are shorthand ways of labeling the two systems by naming each after a few of its many attributes.

The two systems differ in the type of cables they require and the ways in which traffic between the various machines is regulated electronically. Inside, at the level of the hardware, these systems are quite different, but they have been carefully designed so that their rules for transmitting data are exactly the same. For most purposes, neither the person using the computer nor the program running on it can tell which physical transmission is in use. (That's a bit like the situation when you use the telephone: you can dial a long-distance call and have no idea whether your voice is carried by cable, by surface microwave, or by satellite.)

For those who are interested, Appendix B contains a general description of the two systems. If you're planning a new network, it is important to consider the alternatives, especially the consequences of using one form or the other. However, to use PC Network once it's installed, you don't need to know what's in that appendix.

LAN-to-LAN Bridge Connects the Two Types of Network

An individual PC equipped so it can connect to a LAN normally has just one network adapter. Either it can plug into a token-ring network or it can plug into a broadband network. It is committed to one or the other. All the PCs that participate in a network have to have the same type of cables and adapter. However, it's possible for two different networks, one based on token ring and the other on broadband, to be linked by a single PC that acts as a bridge between them.

IBM program 6467036 is called Token-Ring Network/PC Network Interconnect Program. The PC that acts as bridge must be dedicated: that is, it can't handle anything else while it's doing that. The bridge PC contains both an interface card for the token-ring network and an interface card for the broadband network. When it sees traffic on one network destined for a computer on the other, it relays the message. That permits PCs on one network to "see" PCs on the other. The two networks appear to their users as one big network.

The Servers and the Served

The PCs that participate in a network play several roles. The most important distinction is between the roles of *server* and *user.*

When your PC is playing the role of server, you offer some of its facilities so that other computers on the network can use them. When your PC is playing the role of user, it makes use of facilities offered by others.

Any PC with sufficient resources can offer to share them with others. For most purposes, a server must have a fixed disk drive. Any number of the PCs on a network can play serving roles. Serving isn't necessarily limited to just one disk server or print server. As the number of PCs grows, no one server could meet the demands of all the others, so the number of servers grows too. Moreover, there are advantages to having multiple servers even when your network is small.

The same PC can play both roles at the same time: it can simultaneously provide resources to others and use services that others provide.

Four Configurations

Each PC can run the PC Network program in any one of four possible configurations, with varying powers and requirements for disk storage and main memory. There are three levels of *user* configuration, and one configuration called *server,* which includes all the powers of the user configurations. The four are described in Chapter 2.

Human Roles in a Network

The various roles that the PCs play in the network have counterparts for the people that operate them. And just as the network of PCs requires an operating system, so do the human users. They need someone to set up ground rules, see that conventions are established and shared, coordinate demands, and even mediate disputes about such things as priorities or allocations of network resources. I call that person the network administrator. You won't find that term in the IBM manuals that describe PC Network, but I think it's essential that someone play that role and that the community of human users recognize that person's authority. Chapters 10 and 11 discuss several things she will need to do.

Role of the Human Operator of a Machine That Plays Server

When you're the person who operates a machine that regularly acts as a server on the network, you inevitably take on some duties related to your machine's role. These duties are likely to tie you to a single machine. For one thing, you have to be there to start the machine to make it available to others (unless perhaps you establish ways to keep it running unattended). You are likely to receive a fair number of messages from users inquiring about details they need to know in order to make effective use of the server machine. If your machine is offering printers, you may have to intervene to manipulate the *queue* (waiting list) of jobs to be printed. Also, there's the mechanical work of maintaining the printer, supplying paper, changing ribbons, stacking output. If your machine shares disk files, you may be involved in keeping backup files and sometimes in restoring old files from them.

Role of the Human Operator of a Machine That Plays User

If your work makes you a user but not a server, the existence of the network may change your style of work in a quite different direction. Because the network can provide you extensive storage, you're less likely to do your everyday work from diskettes. With access to any of the printers on the network, you become indifferent to the physical location of printers—and may prefer to avoid them. In fact, you may very well "float": that is, have no fixed machine of your own. You can sit at any available machine on the network and—without carrying a packet of diskettes—have access to the same files and the same printers as usual. In this regard, you become more like the user of a time-sharing terminal.

Clusters of Users

The pattern that emerges as a network grows is one of overlapping subgroups. For example, a network of 20 PCs might include four that regularly act as servers. Any user can in principle make use of anything offered by any of the servers, or even make use of all of them at once. But for most of the work most of the time, the users are clustered. These aren't (necessarily) physical clusters of geographic neighbors, but logical clusters of people with common patterns of work. The people who share an interest in a particular application mostly use a particular server, where the programs or data that they need reside. Occasionally, as they need something else, they make use of shared resources on another server.

You might compare servers to grocers in a small town or village. Each provides several services. Shoppers can go to any of them, but usually pick just one or two for most of their wants. If everybody decided to go to the same one at the same time, there'd be serious overcrowding. But most of the time they don't.

Consequences of Distributed Serving

Decentralization has its pros and cons. For the community as a whole, one striking advantage is that one of the servers can fail without idling everybody until it's repaired. No single machine becomes a bottleneck through which all must pass or on which all rely.

Having several machines acting as servers implies having several people able to assist in the server role. Avoiding excessive reliance on a single human server is quite as important as avoiding reliance on a single machine.

Offering and Using Shared Resources

A machine that plays the role of server can make offers to share various parts of its resources. Each offer may refer to either a directory or a printer.

A directory is a collective name for a set of files within a disk. Directories are organized into a tree-structured hierarchy (described in more detail in Chapter 11). A directory may itself contain directories (and each of those may contain directories, too, indefinitely).

When a server offers a directory, the user who takes up the offer has access to the files in that directory and also to the files in any subdirectories that the offered directory may contain. Each disk has a master directory that has no name of its own (other than the name of the disk drive on which it is mounted) and is referred to as the *root* directory of the disk. Offering to share the root directory amounts to offering the entire disk. Offering to share any other directory amounts to offering part but not all of a disk.

When a printer's services are shared among several users, the various pieces of text that each wants printed are sent to the computer that manages that printer. The computer saves the text in a *spool file,* and later (as a background job, which runs while the computer continues to do other work in the foreground) transmits the text from the spool to its printer. Thus, each computer that offers a shared printer must have a queue manager; it's built into the PC Network software.

Redirection: How PC Network Interprets Old Programs in New Ways

A major issue for the designers of a network is to find a general way of treating names so that you can equally well run programs that were written for the network and programs that weren't. At the moment, there are far more programs designed for stand-alone machines than designed expressly for a network. The strategy IBM has adopted is *redirection.* In practice, that means:

- You (or the program you are using) may refer to shared resources as if they existed on your own machine. (Naturally, that's what programs that don't know about networking are doing anyway.)

- The DOS operating system looks at a table of network names that you've previously established. When the operating system sees a reference to a printer or disk file that is really located somewhere else, it redirects that command to the proper place. The processor in the network interface card automatically takes care of transferring information to or from the remote device.

The great advantage of redirection is that it permits you (but doesn't require you) to use the network in the same way as you use your own machine. In particular, you can make use of the network to run programs that were written before networking was invented and that contain no explicit reference to the network.

Voluntary Cooperation in a Network

The work of a network depends on the collaboration of each of the participating PCs. Each PC remains an independent machine, with its own keyboard and its own operator. If a PC's operator doesn't choose to run the PC Network program, that machine can neither offer its services to others nor make use of services that others offer. (There's one exception: a connected machine that isn't running PC Network can temporarily dedicate itself to serving one PC Network user.) Nor can a PC that isn't running the PC Network program send or receive messages.

Resources are available to a network only when they've been offered from the machine where they're actually located, and only as long as its operator leaves the offer in effect and that machine keeps running. Until a PC offers to make some of its resources available to the network, those resources remain strictly under its own control. If the operator decides always to run PC Network and always to offer resources to the network, those can be included in an Autoexec.bat file so that they're carried out automatically each time the machine is started.

The Network Is an Alliance of Equals

In a network there is no "head" computer. None of the computers has power over any of the others. All association and exchange is voluntary.

The PC Network program merely provides a means by which the computers can readily cooperate to send and receive data. Resources are effectively shared not because the network itself makes sharing work, but because of common conventions in the programs run by the various machines, which ultimately come down to conventions adopted among the community of human users of the network.

Public vs. Private Use of Shared Resources

Some resources that a server offers are naturally public: for example, a collection of application programs that everyone in the department uses. The server routinely offers these all the time on a read-only basis. When PC Network is installed on a server machine, it creates a directory called Apps (for application programs), and within Apps, a separate subdirectory for each application that is to be generally available. Then, all the server has to do is offer Apps. Each user who wants to use one of the public applications has only to request to use Apps, and thereby gain access to all the applications.

Other resources are essentially private. For example, the same server may offer each member of a department a private directory in which she may read or write at will. As you'll see in Chapter 11, when PC Network is installed on a server machine, it prompts the person doing the installation to supply a list of the names of users. For each name supplied, it creates a directory. It routinely offers to share each of those private directories.

Collaboration Depends on Corresponding Names

The convention that links each user/server pair is a shared vocabulary of names. The server offers to share a resource and gives it an arbitrary name. A user requests to use something having that name. The correspondence of names is what links them.

Each PC Names Itself

Each of the PCs participating in a network adopts a name for itself. The name is quite arbitrary. But since communication works only when computers know each other's names, it's essential that the community of users agree on the names, or at least on the names of the computers that will offer services to others.

When a PC adopts a name for itself (for example, Server2), that means it will be on the lookout for network communications addressed to Server2. The act of selecting that name (at the time you start PC Network) doesn't notify anyone else that it has adopted that name, nor do others have any means of asking the network software "What names have others adopted?"

PC Network maintains no central directory of names. Each PC records only its own name or names. The network regulates names in only one way: when a PC proposes a name for itself, the network software verifies that no other PC now on the network has claimed that name (and rejects a name that it finds already in use).

The PC Network program doesn't itself provide a means to coordinate or enforce the naming conventions used in a network. The people who use the network do that. Thus, successful operation of a network depends on common conventions and procedures established by the group of people who use it. They do that as a human group, acting outside the services offered by the PC Network program.

An Exchange with No Phone Book

To understand both the problems and the advantages of the way computers communicate through PC Network, you might think of it as a telephone exchange—with some startling differences. To begin with, PC Network uses names of up to 15 characters rather than seven-digit numbers. To identify a machine or person, you need to know only one name. Names are usually simple and easy to remember. However, to reach a specific resource, you have to know two names: the name for the machine where the resource is located and the name under which the resource is offered. Using a resource is like dialing its two names. In this exchange:

- Anybody can call any resource—but you have to know *both* names.
- Each resource can have many names, at its owner's discretion and changeable at will; the resources can be given both obvious names and obscure ones.
- There is no phone book or information service: everything is unlisted.

This analogy helps make two points clear. First, when you offer a service that you want others to use, you have to adopt a name for it that others can remember, refrain from changing that name, and publicize what it is. (When you install PC Network on a server, you can ask it to print what amounts to a "phone list" for each of the people who will use it.)

Second, when you want to offer a private service, you adopt a name for it (and, optionally, a password) that you reveal only to those you wish to use it. If you're worried about it leaking out, you pick a name that is hard for others to remember if they glimpse it casually, and you change it frequently.

An Offer to Share Is Voluntary and Can Be Revoked

As the "owner" of the PC where a resource is physically located, you control whether and when that resource is local (available only to programs running on your machine) or shared (available to the network).

You can do that independently for each separate resource: for example, for each directory within a fixed disk or for each printer (if you have more than one).

Temporary Suspension of Some Network Functions

After you've started the network in one of its four configurations, you can temporarily suspend one or more or the general functions that the network provides. For example, when you have printers that are shared with the network, you can suspend all printing or the work of a specific printer. It's possible to cause similar pauses in receiving messages, using network resources of others, and so on. Such a pause may give you a respite to make adjustments or temporarily regain local control of a resource shared with the network. There's a corresponding command to end such a suspension.

For such temporary suspensions, the IBM manual uses the word *pause;* IBM treats it as if it were a transitive verb in phrases such as "pause the printer."

Messages between PCs on the Network

Precisely because the network depends heavily on cooperation between the human users, it includes a facility for sending and receiving messages. PC Network's built-in message facility is convenient for brief, more or less immediate, messages between users. It's a way users can converse briefly to coordinate their work. It's handy for such things as a broadcast note saying *Printer will be down for service between 2 and 3* or a private note to ask an individual *Jack, what's the name of the file with the new draft of your proposal?* The message facility is not a full-fledged electronic mail system; however, the resources of the network permit installing electronic mail as an application.

Cooperative Applications

Networking opens up a class of applications that didn't really exist before on personal computers. These are *multiuser cooperative applications.* To make clear what they are, first consider what they are not: they aren't independent.

In *independent* applications, each user of the network—even though sharing use of the physical resources—still works independently, on a private copy of the program, in a private segment of the storage space. Users of such applications refer to the same files as other users in only one way: to make a private copy. The master file remains unchanged in the public storage area.

When independent users store data in the shared space, each is using her own private segment of the public storage and not really sharing it with anyone else. Thus, while a user may *read* from a common public file, in an independent application she can *write* only to a file over which (at least for the moment) she has exclusive control. When different users at the same time use disk space on the same machine, they are really writing in separate parts of the shared storage. In those instances where they actually write to the same file, they take turns at temporary exclusive use—a sort of serial monogamy of files.

By contrast, using a *cooperative* application, several different users can update portions of the same file at the same time.

Electronic mail is a common example of a cooperative application. It's usually implemented with a central directory showing for each message which people on its "to" list have received it. You want a central directory for that purpose so that a message can be delivered to a recipient who wasn't on the network at the time it was sent, and so that messages can still be delivered when the sender is no longer active.

In similar fashion, an order-entry system may permit several different users all to post orders at the same time. Each user has to be able to update the same inventory data base.

Clearly, you don't want people to write in the very same location in a file at the same time and thereby lose data. Conversely, you don't want to have everybody else locked out of access to their mail while one person decides what to read. This requires fine tuning: a way to hold access to just the relevant part of the file, without tying up the rest.

Detailed File Interlocks in DOS 3.10

DOS 3.10 permits an application program to exercise precise control over access to a specific segment within a file without tying up the whole file. This sort of thing is referred to as *record locking* or *field locking,* in contrast with the cruder step of *file locking,* which ties up the whole file when anyone is updating it. Such a facility is needed only when you have multiple users, so it becomes relevant only when you're using a network. (Although, strictly speaking, it's a DOS facility, not part of PC Network itself.)

As the use of networks becomes widespread, you can expect a certain amount of new software that takes advantage of cooperative control. In the early stages of the development of networks, few application packages had been written to exploit cooperative use. Private work in private segments of the shared space will continue to be the major style of work on a network, just as it has continued to be even in time-sharing systems with elaborate provisions for concurrent access to files.

The other advantages of networking still apply to independent work on a network.

Starting and Restarting the Network

Two

PC Network is decentralized. Starting the network means starting the PC Network software on your own machine. You do this so you can trade services with people who have started (or will start) the network on their machines. There isn't a head computer or central server that starts the network for everybody. Starting is something each person does individually, each on her own machine. As far as you're concerned, the network is operational whenever you've started the network software on your own machine, and the operators of the machines with which you interact have started it on theirs.

There are several ways to start the network, and options you can select or alter when you do. At start-up, your machine's name on the network is determined, and also its configuration (or level of participation) in the network. This chapter deals with three ways of starting PC Network on your machine, plus a procedure for establishing how it will start in future. The four are as follows:

1. The NET command. You can start the network by typing the command NET, which invokes a start-up menu that asks you to specify your choices. When you've specified them, the command starts the network, and displays PC Network's main menu. If this is the first time you're starting the network, this is probably the method with which to begin.
2. The NET START command. You type this command at the DOS prompt. You have to supply with it the various parameters that govern the network configuration you wish to use.
3. Start automatically when you turn on your machine. This is simpler yet—but you can't do it until your disk has an automatic-start command stored in the file Autoexec.bat. If someone—say, the network administrator—has prepared such a file for you, all you have to do is turn on the power (or reset the system with Ctrl-Alt-Del) with the disk in place. If you're doing it yourself, it's easiest to start the first time with method 1. After that, you can set up an automatic start for subsequent occasions.
4. Set up an automatic-start command. The network menus include a provision to save the current state of the network so that you can start it automatically at subsequent occasions when you start DOS. This generates an Autoexec.bat file automatically.

Alternatively, you can write such a file yourself or edit one generated by the network menus.

Menus versus Commands

Just about any of the instructions you can give to PC Network (including the instruction to start the network) can be handled either by indicating a selection from a series of menus or by typing a command. A command is a brief sentence starting with the word NET.

There is a fairly direct correspondence between what you can do with commands and what you can do with menus. When you aren't familiar with the commands, it's often easier to use the menus than to look up the appropriate commands in a manual. The menus lead you step by step through the various choices.

However, as you grow familiar with the menus, they get a bit tedious. Each menu asks you for very little, so it may take a sequence of three, four, or even five screens to pin down an action that, as a command, can be stated in a few words. For that reason, I discuss the menus and the equivalent commands together, so you can see what's equivalent to what, and (when you find it comfortable) gradually switch from menus to commands.

Where to Type Commands

You can type a network command either from the DOS prompt or from the command screen within the menus. Once PC Network has actually started, you can switch from any network menu screen to the command screen by pressing F2, and there enter a network command. Thus, when you're working in the menus, you can write a command anytime without having to leave the menus. (Curiously, many of the menu screens remind you that pressing F1 gets you help, but don't mention that pressing F2 gets you the command screen.)

Stopping the Network

There's no command to stop the network (although there are commands to pause and resume). Causing a pause in network operations is covered in Chapter 9. A pause occurs when you temporarily disable some or all of the network facilities, but PC Network remains resident on your machine and resumes its former roles when you signal it to do so.

PC Network is designed to be a *resident* program. Once you start it, it becomes an extension of your machine's operating system, continuously present whether or not you're actually using it. You may want to include the network in your start-up routine at the beginning of your working day. Once you've started PC Network, you go about your business in the usual way. If what you are doing requires the network, PC Network goes into action automatically (for example, to bring in for you a file stored on another machine). It remains present and ready to respond to a message if one comes in from elsewhere. Similarly, it remains ready to respond to your signal when you invoke the network menus by pressing the network-request key (assuming you've started PC Network in a configuration that supports those features).

Because PC Network is a resident program, you can start it only once in a work session. Once you've started it, there's no way to turn it off; it remains active until you turn off the power or reset the computer with Ctrl-Alt-Del. (To make sure that you don't do that by accident, once PC Network has been started, it intercepts Ctrl-Alt-Del and asks you to confirm that you really mean it.)

Four Levels of Participation in the Network

Whenever you start the network, you start it in one of the four configurations mentioned in Chapter 1. The *server* configuration permits others to use your fixed disk or printer. Alternatively, you can select one of the three different kinds of *user* configuration: *messenger, receiver,* or *redirector.*

The Hierarchy of Network Roles

The four configurations form a hierarchy. Each of the three higher levels includes all the capabilities of the levels below it. Figure 2.1 shows the powers of each, the resources required to start it, and the amount of main memory it consumes under standard conditions. (Chapter 13 discusses some fine-tuning considerations that affect performance and the amount of memory required.)

Duration of Your Choice of Configuration

Whichever configuration you choose remains in effect throughout the session. That is, although you can readily change the details of which resources you share or use, you can't change your initial selection of server, messenger, receiver, or redirector. It remains in effect until you turn the power off or reset by Ctrl-Alt-Del.

NET: Starting the Network and Entering the Menus

At the DOS prompt, type NET with nothing after it, and press Enter. When you've already started the network, this takes you to the main menu (see the last section of this chapter). When you have not yet started the network, this takes you first to a series of screens in which PC Network prompts you for information it needs in order to start the network, and then to the main menu.

Here is the start-up sequence, step by step.

Step 1. At the DOS prompt, type NET. This takes you to a full-screen IBM logo.

Step 2. At the IBM logo, press Enter. (The program won't accept any other response.)

Step 3. At *Starting the network,* you'll see the prompt *Please type in a network name for your computer* (see Figure 2.2). Type it in the space provided and press Enter.

A name may have up to 15 characters. The name you specify here is the name by which the network will identify your machine. Note that

Redirector

Abbreviation:	RDR
Requires:	320k disk drive, at least 128k memory
Consumes:	28k main memory
Powers:	Use network disks, directories, or printers offered by others. Send (but not receive) messages.

Receiver

Abbreviation:	RCV
Requires:	320k disk drive, at least 192k memory
Consumes:	47.4k main memory
Powers:	Those above *plus:* Receive messages. Save incoming messages in a log file.

Messenger

Abbreviation:	MSG
Requires:	320k disk drive, at least 256k memory
Consumes:	138.3k main memory
Powers:	Those above *plus:* Forward incoming messages to other machines. Adopt additional names to receive incoming messages. Use network-request key.

Server

Abbreviation:	SRV
Requires:	320k disk drive, fixed disk, at least 320k memory
Consumes:	186.2k main memory
Powers:	Those above *plus:* Share your disks, directories, or printers with the network.

Note: Although the network menus and manuals mention sharing both disks and directories, these are not different actions but alternative ways of looking at the same thing.

In addition, the token-ring version consumes 46k for token-ring NETBIOS and 7k for the adapter handler.

Figure 2.1: *The four network configurations*

when you're a server, you want a name for your *machine* (because others will be using it), but when you're a user, it's more useful to have a name for *yourself* (usable on any machine) than for the machine at which you are sitting. When you are acting as server, you have to use a name that is known to the people who will make use of the services you offer. When you expect to be strictly a user of services offered by others, it doesn't matter what you call your machine, provided it doesn't conflict with other names used on the network. To avoid conflicts with other users, the network administrator may want to approve the machine name you adopt.

Step 4. To decide which of the four configurations you want to start, the menus ask a series of yes/no questions. Figure 2.3 shows the first question on the screen.

- *Share your printer? disks? directories?* If you reply yes to this, PC Network deduces that you must be a server and takes you directly to step 5. But if you say no, the program asks the next question.
- *Add usernames, forward messages, and use the network request key?* If you say yes to this, PC Network deduces that you must be a messenger and takes you directly to step 5. But if you say no, the program moves to the next question.

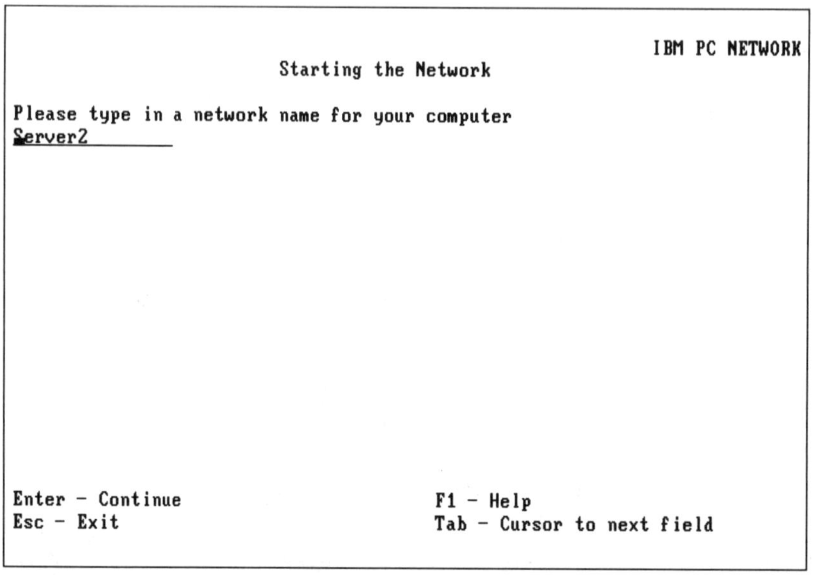

Figure 2.2: *Menu screen prompting for computer name*

- *Receive and save messages?* If you say yes to this, you must be a receiver, and if you say no you must be a redirector. Either way, the program has now identified which of the four configurations you want, and takes you to step 5 (see Figure 2.4).

Step 5. *Change defaults for starting?* If you reply no, PC Network leaves the default values unchanged (but doesn't tell you what they are) and moves to step 6. If you reply yes, it shows you the default value and the range of possible values of some of the parameters involved in starting the network. It permits you to set values other than the defaults, but doesn't require you to change anything. The number of parameters you'll see (and can change) depends on which configuration you've selected (see Figure 2.5).

The values that you select apply only to the session of PC Network that you're about to start. They are not saved in your Autoexec.bat file until you subsequently run through the screen *Save your network setup.*

Watch out: There are more start parameters than this screen shows; several others that may affect your capacity or performance on the network are not visible from within the menus. If you're just starting out and not using the network heavily, the values of those parameters may not matter. But keep in mind that later on it may pay to do more precise tuning of the way your machine participates in the network. This is discussed in Chapter 13.

```
                                                         IBM PC NETWORK
                        Starting the Network

Please type in a network name for your computer
Server2

To start the network you have to choose how you want to use the
network.  Type Y (Yes) or N (No) for the following and press Enter :


N  Share your printer? disks? directories?










Enter - Continue                               F1 - Help
Esc - Exit                                     Tab - Cursor to next field
```

Figure 2.3: *First menu screen for starting the network*

Step 6. After you've run through the screens that specify a setup, PC Network asks you to confirm that you want to start the network in the configuration that your answers have implied. It shows you a screen that lists the types of things you'll be able to do. The screen looks something like Figure 2.6. I've superimposed italic headers to show the name of the configuration implied.

The Starting Bugle

When you assent to the question *Do you want to do these tasks?* the program starts the network. The process takes a few seconds; to assure you that something is indeed happening, it first prints the message

    Network starting . . .

and then sounds four widely separated beeps. That done, it takes you to the main menu.

Starting the Network by the NET START Command

If you don't want to go through the menus, you can start the network from the DOS prompt (if you haven't already done so) by the

```
                                                          IBM PC NETWORK

Please type in a network name for your computer
Server2

To start the network you have to choose how you want to use the
network. Type Y (Yes) or N (No) for the following and press Enter :


Y  Add usernames, forward messages, and use the network request key?

N  Change defaults for starting?




Enter - Continue                          F1 - Help
Esc - Exit                                Tab - Cursor to next field
```

Figure 2.4: *A question regarding default parameters following the last of the questions to identify the configuration (which remains visible on the screen)*

NET START command. On the same line with the words NET START, you must supply the following:

- The configuration in which you want to start the network on your machine.
- The name you propose for the machine.

For example, to start your machine in the server configuration with the name Server2, you type:

NET START SRV Server2

Menu Screen: Change Defaults for Starting the Network

Parameter name	Label shown on the screen	Default	Min	Max
Asks the following in all configurations:				
ASG	Number of devices to be used?	5	1	32
Asks the following in server and messenger configuration only:				
MBI	Size of message-waiting buffer?	1600	256	60000
USN	Number of additional names that will be receiving messages?	1	0	12
Asks the following in server configuration only:				
SHR	Number of devices to be shared?	10	1	150
PRB	Size of buffer for printing?	512	512	16384
RDR	Number of network computers that will be using your devices?	10	1	25

Note: The menu screen doesn't show the remarks in italics, nor does it show the parameter names (at the left). You need to know them when you start the network by a command or when you modify the Autoexec.bat file to tailor your network parameters more precisely. They're included here so you can match the choices you get via the menus with the options you have when you write out a command. The phrase *number of* (names, devices, computers) means the maximum allowed during the session.

Figure 2.5: *Summary of options in menu screen for changing defaults when starting the network*

Names for the Four Configurations

In identifying the configuration, you can either write out its name in full or use a standard abbreviation. The names and abbreviations are given in Figure 2.7.

Name for Your Machine

This may be up to 15 characters and must be unique on the network (that is, not already in use either as someone else's computer name or as someone else's message alias). See the discussion of choice of names for users and servers earlier in this chapter.

Following the configuration and the machine name, you may (on the same line) specify values for any of 18 different parameters that govern the size of various tables and buffers used by the network. For

```
                                                          IBM PC NETWORK
                 Starting the Network  (continued)

You will be able to do the following:           RDR    RCV    MSG    SRV

  - Send messages to other computers             x      x      x      x
  - Use network disks, directories, and printers x      x      x      x

  - Receive messages from other computers        ___    x      x      x
  - Allow saving of messages in a save file      ___    x      x      x

  - Use the network request key to interrupt     ___    ___    x      x
    your work and use the network program
  - Receive messages for other names             ___    ___    x      x
  - Transfer messages to other computers         ___    ___    x      x

  - Share your disks, directories, and printers  ___    ___    ___    x

Y  Do you want to do these tasks?

    Enter - Start the network                F1 - Help
    Esc - Previous menu
```

Figure 2.6: *Screen to confirm your choice of network configuration before starting the network*

SRV	Server	Disk, directory, or print server
MSG	Messenger	Full user configuration
RCV	Receiver	Restricted user configuration
RDR	Redirector	Minimum user configuration

Figure 2.7: *Abbreviations and full names of network configurations*

example, MBI is the buffer for incoming messages. To set it to 4000 bytes, you include in the command the parameter /MBI:4000. The command just shown would then appear thus:

```
NET START SRV Server2 /MBI:4000
```

All 18 start parameters are discussed in detail in Chapter 13. In this chapter, six commonly set parameters are listed. (They're the same six you can set from within the menus.)

Capitalization

As in DOS commands generally, capitalization is ignored. It doesn't matter whether you write NET or net. Similarly, capitalization is ignored in the machine name. As far as PC Network is concerned, Server2 and SERVER2 or even sERVER2 are all the same name.

Start Parameters

The parameters you may use with NET START include ASG, MBI, USN, SHR, PRB, and RDR.

ASG: Maximum Number of Network Devices

This sets the maximum number of network disks, directories, or printers you can use at one time with the NET USE command. (That includes printers that are in fact on your own machine if you have offered them to the network and use them through the network.) Once you reach the maximum, you can't add another without first deleting one of those already in use. Minimum: 1. Maximum: 32. Default assumed (if you omit this parameter): 5.

MBI: Size of Message-Waiting Buffer

In the server or messenger configuration, you can have PC Network hold incoming messages in a buffer so you can read them later in the same session. (This facility is described in Chapter 5.) If you start the network in either the server or messenger configuration, the buffer is created (whether or not you actually elect to have messages buffered). The MBI parameter controls the amount of main memory set aside for the buffer. Minimum: 512 bytes. Maximum: 60,000 bytes. Default assumed (if you omit this parameter): 1,750 bytes.

USN: Size of Additional-Name Table

In the server or messenger configuration, PC Network permits you to receive messages addressed to other names in addition to the name of your computer. To do this, it maintains a table of the additional names. The table includes aliases that you select yourself as well as names under which messages addressed to other machines are being forwarded to your machine. (Additional names and forwarding names are described in Chapter 5.) If you start the network in either the server or messenger configuration, the table is created (whether or not you actually elect to receive messages under another name or someone else forwards messages to your machine).

The USN parameter controls the amount of main memory set aside for this name table. You specify that by the number of names; each name takes 600 bytes. Minimum: 0 additional names. Maximum: 12 additional names. Default assumed (if you omit this parameter): 1 additional name.

SHR: Number of Your Devices You Can Share

In the server configuration, you can offer to share disks, directories, or printers with the network. PC Network maintains a table that matches your machine's DOS names with the network names by which other users will refer to them. The SHR parameter limits the number of entries in that table. Each entry takes 350 bytes. (Notice that if you offer the same directory twice but with different names, access levels, and so on, that's two entries, not one.) Minimum number of entries: 1. Maximum: 150. Default assumed (if you omit this parameter): 10 entries.

PRB: Size of Buffer Used by Print Server

In the server configuration, you can offer to share printers physically connected to your machine. PC Network spools to your fixed disk each of the jobs submitted to your printer. When it prints jobs from the spool, it transfers them first from the fixed disk to a buffer in main memory, and from there to the printer itself. The parameter PRB sets the size of that buffer. Whenever a job is larger than the buffer, the print server has to break it into a series of separate transfers. The larger the buffer, the less frequently that is required; having a large buffer may reduce pauses while the print server goes back for more.

The parameter is the number of bytes of a print job transferred to the buffer at one time. The storage required in main memory is *twice* that amount. Minimum value for the PRB parameter: 512 bytes. Maximum: 16,384 bytes. Default assumed (if you omit this parameter): 512 bytes.

RDR: Number of Different Computers Using Your Devices

In the server configuration, PC Network maintains a table showing the computer names of all the computers that are using it—that is, that have successfully executed the NET USE command for a resource on your computer. The parameter RDR sets the maximum number of names in the table *in addition to* your own computer's name. Minimum number of additional computer names: 1. Maximum settable in the menus: 25. Default assumed (if you omit this parameter): 10. (A value as high as 29 can be set, but not in the menus, and only if you also set minimum values for SRV and USN; see Chapter 13.)

Outcome of a NET START Command

If PC Network can start the network according to your NET START command, it acknowledges with the message:

```
Command executed successfully
```

But if PC Network isn't able to start the network, you see a message beginning with NET followed by a number and a brief text. The IBM *User's Guide* contains an annotated list of these messages, which sometimes proves helpful.

Reporting the Values of the Start-Up Parameters After the Network Has Been Started

Curiously, PC Network gives you no way to do that. If you're typing the NET START command manually from the keyboard, you'd better remember what you did. (The omission is surprising. Writing one of the NET commands with nothing following it usually gives you a status report. That works for NET USE or NET SHARE, and several others, but not for NET START.)

Starting PC Network Automatically

You might expect that starting PC Network on your machine would always require one of the two procedures described above: the NET menus or the NET START command. In fact, starting up usually takes no more than your assent when at start-up the computer asks you:

```
Do you want to start the network? (Y/N)
```

Automatic Start-Up

Every time your computer is started, the DOS operating system automatically executes whatever instructions it finds in the file Autoexec.bat. (This is a general DOS service, not specific to PC Network.)

You can get PC Network to generate such a file for you by selecting the menu option *Save your network setup.* It's discussed later in this chapter. Possibly someone else has already done that for you. In that case, as you turn on the power, or reset the computer with Ctrl-Alt-Del, DOS asks you whether you want to start the network. You have only to answer Y or N (for yes or no), and press Enter.

As DOS works through the Autoexec.bat file that PC Network set up for you, it first asks you whether you want to start the network. If you reply yes, the computer starts the network according to the instructions in Autoexec.bat. But if you reply no, it skips over them, and goes on with other instructions routinely executed at start-up (which, as explained later in this chapter, are stored in a file called Autouser.bat).

Watch out: The question *Do you want to start the network?* is a bit misleading. It really means *Do you want to start the network according to the instructions previously saved?* That is: Do you want to start the network in the particular configuration specified there (server, messenger, receiver, or redirector)? Do you want to start the network with the particular values of various start-up parameters specified there (number of names, size of tables, etc.)? Do you want to start the network with those particular offers to share your equipment or use equipment belonging to others? Replying yes to the message *Do you want to start the network?* amounts to saying yes to all those questions.

When the setup previously saved *is* what you want today, you can start the network just as it was then merely by answering yes.

When the previously saved configuration was OK, but you want to change the details of which devices you offer or use, you can reply yes, start the network the way it was, and then change the details regarding disks, directories, or printers. But once the network has started, you can*not* change its basic configuration or parameters.

When you want to start the network in a configuration different from the one specified in the file Autoexec.bat, or with different values for any of the start-up parameters, you *must* answer no. When you reply no, DOS doesn't start the network, but continues with whatever other standing instructions are stored in your file Autouser.bat. Later on, you can start the network yourself (according to the steps to be described in a moment).

Messages Displayed While the Network Starts

The Autoexec.bat file that PC Network generates for you includes the command ECHO ON, which means that DOS displays the commands as it does them. You'll see a line beginning with NET displayed for each command, followed by a message confirming that the command has been carried out successfully or indicating a reason why it has not been possible to carry it out.

When your Autoexec file has started the network for you, it goes on to execute whatever was in your file Autouser.bat and finally leaves you at the DOS prompt. Proceed with your work. When you want to use a network menu, press the network-request key (Ctrl-Alt-Break), or (if you started a configuration that doesn't support the network-request key) just type NET at the DOS prompt.

Saving the Network Setup for Automatic Use Thereafter

One of the network menus is called *Save or cancel your network setup.* When you select that menu and then elect to save the setup, PC Network takes a snapshot of your current use of the network and saves it in your file Autoexec.bat (see Figure 2.8).

When you've typed the number that indicates your choice and pressed Enter, you are returned to the main menu, on which is displayed (as appropriate) one of the following messages:

Network setup saved

or

Network setup canceled

```
                                                              IBM PC NETWORK
                         Save or Cancel Network Setup

    1. Save your network setup

    2. Cancel your current network setup


    1  Choice







    Enter - Continue                          F1 - Help
    Ctrl-Home - Return to Main Menu           Esc - Previous menu
```

Figure 2.8: *Menu to elect to save the network setup*

Effect of Saving the Network Setup

When you save a network setup, PC Network rewrites your Autoexec.bat file. What it writes there will take effect the next time you start the operating system (when you turn on the power or press Ctrl-Alt-Del). The new instructions contain the commands that, when executed, reproduce your current network setup.

The next time you start DOS, it will as usual run through the commands stored in Autoexec.bat and encounter the commands that PC Network put there. These commands cause it to ask whether you want to start the network. If you say yes, it will run through the rest of the batch commands that it wrote when you elected to save the setup. These cause it to try to do the following:

- Start the network with the same configuration you now have, the same computer name, and the same values for optional parameters.
- Offer to share the resources you are now sharing just as you are now sharing them.
- Request to use the resources you are now using just as you are now using them.
- Request to receive message for any additional names for which you are now receiving messages.
- Save your incoming messages in the log file you are now using for that purpose.
- Request a pause in any functions that are now paused.

(However, if you are at present forwarding messages to another machine, PC Network assumes that is a temporary affair and does *not* record it in Autoexec.bat.)

Look Before You Save

Before you save the network setup, it's prudent to review your network situation. (Procedures for reviewing your current use of the network are described in Chapter 4.) By reviewing the way you're using the network now, you can make sure that you really do want, at future start-ups, to attempt to reconstruct things just as they are now. In particular, you should review resources belonging to other machines that you are presently using, and ask yourself: Will I want to use those network resources next time? Will those network resources be available to me next time? If not, it may be better to end your use of them before you save the network setup. That way, you'll avoid starting your next sessions by making a request to use something you don't need, or that won't be available then.

Saving the Network Setup Is Equivalent to Recording the Commands You Might Have Typed from the Keyboard

The Autoexec.bat file that PC Network created in response to your request to save the network setup consists of a NET START command and such other NET commands as are needed to reproduce your situation. Figure 2.9 shows a file that was generated for a machine called Server2 playing the role of server.

Inside the Autoexec and Autouser Files

PC Network's strategy for automatic start is to set up two files. PC Network pretty much takes over for itself the file called Autoexec.bat. It moves things that you might formerly have stored there into a file that it calls Autouser.bat. In effect, Autouser.bat becomes a second file of commands that are also executed automatically at start-up. Each time you save the setup or cancel the setup, PC Network rewrites Autoexec-.bat. It leaves Autouser.bat alone, however.

```
: *** Network Batch File ***
: ***
ECHO OFF
PATH C:\NETWORK
YNPROMPT Y N 39 Do you want to start the network (Y/N)?
IF ERRORLEVEL 1 GOTO A
ECHO ON
NET START SRV SERVER2 /SRV:5 /MBI:1600 /SHR:10 /SES:18
NET SHARE FAST=LPT1
NET SHARE LETTERQ=LPT2
NET SHARE APPS=C:\APPS /R
NET SHARE DATA=C:\COMMON\DATA85 /RWC
ECHO OFF
GOTO B
:A
PATH \
:B
ECHO ON
AUTOUSER.BAT
```

Figure 2.9: *Autoexec file generated by saving the network setup*

Autouser.bat isn't a name that DOS automatically recognizes. So PC Network gets DOS to execute the command stored there by making the last line of Autoexec.bat the command Autouser.bat. (It's OK for one batch file to invoke another, but it has to be the last thing it does, because control does not return to the originating batch file afterwards.)

To recognize an Autoexec file that it has produced, PC Network always makes the first line:

```
: ***Network Batch File***
```

When you ask PC Network to save the network setup, it has to decide whether you're already established as a two-file user. Its test is twofold: Do you have a file called Autoexec.bat that starts with

```
: ***Network Batch File***
```

and Do you have a file called Autouser.bat?

When the answer to both questions is yes, PC Network writes a new Autoexec.bat (with Autouser.bat as its last line) and leaves your Autouser.bat unchanged.

When the answer to both questions is no, PC Network renames your existing Autoexec.bat so that its new name is Autouser.bat. Then it writes a new Autoexec.bat. (If you didn't have an Autoexec.bat to rename, it creates a new Autouser.bat containing nothing but DATE and TIME. These are the standard DOS commands for setting your computer's clock at system start-up. If your machine can keep track of time while turned off, you can delete the references to DATE and TIME by editing Autouser.bat.)

And if the network finds that you do have an Autouser.bat but your Autoexec.bat does not start with

```
: ***Network Batch Files***
```

it decides something is wrong and sends you a message saying it can't save the setup.

Commands That Must Be Executed *Before* the Network Starts

There are some actions that can't be pushed into Autouser.bat because they must be executed before you start the network. For example, for reasons that are explained in Chapter 9, if you're running a print server, it may be important to set up the printer before you start the network. You'd like the necessary command to appear in the first part of Autoexec.bat. There's a way to do it.

To accommodate commands that must be executed before the network is started, PC Network permits you to insert extra lines at the front part of Autoexec.bat. It leaves these initial lines unchanged, but may rewrite all the lines that come later. The dividing line is a line containing only asterisks (preceded by a colon and a blank, so DOS doesn't try to execute the asterisks). Figure 2.10 shows an Autoexec.bat in which, using a standard text editor, several lines have been inserted ahead of the line that's all asterisks.

Notes on the Sample Autoexec File

PC Network writes its commands in all caps. In Figure 2.10, the user-inserted lines are shown in lowercase. But that's just to increase the contrast for the human eye; DOS is indifferent to case.

```
: *** Network Batch File ***
echo off
prompt $d$a $t$h$h$h$_$p$g$a
verify on
path c:\network
ynprompt y n 19 Set printer? (y/n)?
if errorlevel 1 goto c
copy \apps\text\start.prt prn /b
:c
: ***
ECHO OFF
PATH C:\NETWORK
YNPROMPT Y N 39 Do you want to start the network (Y/N)?
IF ERRORLEVEL 1 GOTO A
ECHO ON
NET START SRV SERVER2 /SRV:5 /MBI:1600 /SHR:10 /SES:18
NET SHARE FAST=LPT1
NET SHARE LETTERQ=LPT2
NET SHARE APPS=C:\APPS /R
NET SHARE SHIKOKU5=C:\SACHIKO *
NET SHARE U7844920=C:\PAUL *
NET PAUSE PRDR
NET PAUSE PRINT=LPT2
ECHO OFF
GOTO B
:A
PATH \
:B
ECHO ON
AUTOUSER.BAT
```

Figure 2.10: *Autoexec file with user-inserted commands*

The user-inserted lines make use of the command YNPROMPT. It's provided as part of PC Network, in the directory named Network. The numeric parameter that appears with YNPROMPT is the number of characters in the prompt message.

The example also illustrates the use of an obvious network name (Apps) for a widely shared directory. By contrast, the directories intended for the individuals Sachiko and Paul are offered with the obscure names Shikoku5 and U7844920.

When PC Network generates an Autoexec file, it always represents passwords by asterisks, so the passwords must be inserted by hand each time the network is started. Sad to relate, the program doesn't suppress display when you set a password.

If you edit an Autoexec file and write in the passwords explicitly (instead of using asterisks), the resulting file works correctly. However, the next time you save the setup, in the course of rewriting Autoexec, PC Network replaces the passwords with asterisks.

Effect of Canceling the Saved Network Setup

If you elect to cancel, PC Network removes from your file Autoexec-.bat the commands that ask *Do you want to start the network?* and all the commands related to starting the network. It keeps no record of them. During this purge, the program leaves unchanged any statements you may have inserted *ahead* of the statements that start the network. Here's how it decides which ones to leave in: it retains everything up to a dummy line that contains only:

```
: ***
```

The line of stars, inserted when PC Network created Autoexec.bat, marks the boundary between what the program leaves in and what it deletes.

Finally, the program makes sure the last line invokes Autouser.bat. Such a canceled Autoexec.bat may be seen in Figure 2.11. Next time you start DOS, it won't start the network and won't ask whether you want it started.

```
: *** Network Batch File ***
: ***
AUTOUSER.BAT
```

Figure 2.11: *Autoexec.bat resulting from canceling network setup*

The Main Menu

The main menu is the hub from which almost all journeys through the PC Network menus start, and to which almost all return. The main menu has two forms: one in the server configuration, and another that is common to the three user configurations. Figure 2.12 merges what are really two separate screens to show the choices side by side.

Watch out: You have to respond by entering a number indicating which menu you want to see next. If you sometimes play the role of user but other times play the role of server, note that things are grouped differently in the two versions of the main menu. Moreover, the same action is sometimes elicited by different numbers in the two menus.

The main menu gives you more than one route to get to some activities. For example, a report headed *Network devices you are using* summarizes your use of network printers and disks or directories. You can reach it equally well from the menu headed *Network status tasks,* from *Printer tasks* or from *Disk or directory tasks* (or by executing the command NET USE).

Once You've Started

Once you've started PC Network, you may use it to set up your use of resources available through the network or to offer your own resources to others. That done, you leave the network's menus and go about your business. From time to time, you may want to switch back to the menus either to send or receive a message or to alter the way you offer or use network resources. But you rarely stay long in the

```
                                                    IBM PC NETWORK
                   Main Menu - Task Selection

(Server machines)                       (User machines)

1. Message tasks                        1. Message tasks
2. Printer tasks                        2. Printer or print queue tasks
3. Disk or directory tasks              3. Disk or directory tasks
4. Print queue tasks                    4. Network status tasks
5. Network status tasks                 5. Pause and continue tasks
6. Pause and continue tasks             6. Save or cancel the network setup
7. Save or cancel the network setup
```

Figure 2.12: *Server and user forms of the main menu*

menus, unless perhaps you are operating a server kept busy by requests that require your attention.

The Network-Request Key

In either the server or messenger configuration, you can use the network-request key. No single button on your keyboard is the network-request key; rather, you press three keys simultaneously: while holding down Ctrl and Alt with your left hand, press Break—also known as Scroll Lock—with your right hand.

PC Network interprets the key combination Ctrl-Alt-Break as a signal to interrupt whatever you're doing and enter the menus. You may be within an application or at the DOS prompt. The key combination immediately suspends your application and takes you into the network menus. When you've finished with the menus, you are returned to whatever you were doing when you signaled the network request.

Ordinarily, pressing the network-request key takes you to the main menu. But if you do it in response to a message-waiting signal, PC Network takes you straight to the message editor/viewer (see Chapter 5).

Watch out: PC Network isn't the only resident program that offers handy request keys. For example, Borland's Sidekick offers a similar convenience. It's possible for such programs to contradict or paralyze each other. For example, if you start Sidekick (at least in the versions distributed in 1985) before you start PC Network, when you subsequently go to the PC Network menus your system may become catatonic, which you can overcome only by turning the power off. Starting Sidekick on your machine after you've started PC Network doesn't seem to have the same unpleasant effect.

Leaving the Network Menus

From most PC Network menu screens, Ctrl-Home takes you directly to the main menu. From there, Escape takes you back to where you came in. That is, if you started from the DOS prompt, that's where you return. But if you started by pressing the network-request key from within an application, you return to the application.

Offering Your Machine's Resources

Three

This chapter describes how you offer to share resources of your machine with other computers on the network. The chapter after this one describes how you take up such offers made by others and how you start to use their resources. If you aren't in a position to offer resources to others, you should skip to the next chapter or just skim over this one to get some idea of the sorts of things that other machines may offer to you.

Review of Some General Principles

Each instance of sharing involves two actions. First, someone has to *offer* to make a resource available. After that, other people can *accept* that offer.

To offer to share a resource, you must have started PC Network in the *server* configuration. If you have already started the network in some other configuration, you can't make an offer to share; you'll have to reboot and then restart the network with your machine as a server. (The only exception: the command PERMIT, discussed in Chapter 7, doesn't require you to be a server.)

By executing the command NET SHARE (or making the appropriate menu selections), you can offer to make a resource available to the network. By executing the command NET USE, some other machine accepts that offer and becomes able to use the resource.

If you regularly offer to share resources on your machine, the details of your standard offers are usually included in your machine's automatic start-up, defined in the file Autoexec.bat. The network menu option to save your network setup revises that file for you, so that the offers to share that are currently in effect will be made automatically each time you start your machine in the future.

What You Can Offer to Share

Two kinds of things can be shared: *printers* and *disk storage.*

When you share the use of your printer—that is, a printer that is physically connected to your machine—your computer sets up and manages a waiting list, or *queue,* of print jobs. Printing becomes a background task for your machine, to which it devotes part of its processing time while also doing other things. Printing will no doubt also become a background task for you; inevitably, there are things to do in managing the physical operation of the printer or managing the printer queue. Chapter 9 is devoted to managing the print queue.

When you share the use of disk space, what you offer is the use of a *directory.* A directory is usually part of a disk, not the whole thing. However, if you offer the *root* directory of a disk, that amounts to offering the use of the entire disk. (If you aren't familiar with DOS tree-structured directories, you can find a general review of the concept and the way it's used at the end of Chapter 11.)

The user who accepts your offer may choose to establish a *network path* to the directory on your machine, calling it by a two-level name composed of your machine name and the name under which you offer your directory. Alternatively, the user may choose to treat the shared space as a *virtual disk drive* on her own machine. Then the same physical space appears to you as a directory within one of your disks, but to the user at the other machine it appears to be an entire disk; she refers to it by a drive name (A, B, C, etc.). (At present, network users most frequently treat a shared directory as a virtual drive, because most programs and even many DOS commands don't yet handle network paths. But that will change with time.)

When you make space on your disk available to the network, DOS manages the access to it, both for your local use and for network use. When in the course of your own work you refer to a directory that you have offered to the network, you continue to refer to it by its name on your machine (rather than by the name under which you've offered it to the network).

SHARE Must Precede USE

PC Network won't let a machine undertake to use something unless its "owner" has first actually offered to share it. The offer has to come first. If your machine is the only server on the network, you have to start your machine and it has to make its offers *before* any of the other machines can make use of its resources. So usually, you incorporate the offers to share into your file Autoexec.bat, and you arrange to have your machine execute the offers automatically each time it's started.

PC Network doesn't limit a network to just one server. Far from it. A major advantage of PC Network's cooperative design is that many machines may play the role of server. Each may serve the entire community or may be used by just some subset within it. Moreover, the servers may also be users. No one is limited to playing one role exclusively.

Since servers may make their offers at different times, wherever there are multiple servers, the rule should be:

- Servers make their offers as *soon* as possible.

But

- Users take up their offers as *late* as possible; that is, only when actually needed.

This point is developed in the next chapter, on using shared resources. Basically, it means that while offers to share should be in the Autoexec.bat file, requests to use generally should not.

Offers Are Never Published

When one machine undertakes to make a resource available, it does not announce that to the network. Nor does it make available for potential users a table showing what it has offered. Instead, network applications assume each of the users of a shared resource has some prior basis to expect that an offer has been made. Basically, that's an agreement between the people who make up the network or a decision reached by the people who manage the network. It is not negotiated or enforced by the network itself.

You could think of it like this: when your machine offers a resource to the network, it's as though it secretly resolves to itself, "If someone were to ask me for this, I would agree."

Most Offers Are General

You don't offer a resource to a particular person or machine. You just offer to make your resource available. The offer can be taken up by anyone who knows the name you chose for identifying what you offered. The offer can be taken up by any number of machines. (Well, not quite any number: it's limited by the parameter SHR, discussed in Chapters 5 and 13).

If you want to make an offer that can be accepted only by certain people, there are several techniques by which you can restrict the offer. They are discussed later in this chapter. For example, you can change from day to day the network name by which you identify the resource that you offer (and provide the needed name only to those entitled to use it). In addition, you can require of each user that at the time she requests to use the resource, she supply a password of your choosing.

In your offer to share a resource, you can*not* specifically identify the machines or persons to which you make the offer. There is just one exception: the command PERMIT makes an offer specifically to *one* machine. It is discussed in Chapter 7.

Most (But Not Quite All) Offers Require a Fixed Disk

Just to start the network in the server configuration, you must have a fixed disk. Then, to execute NET SHARE to offer a resource to the network, you must have a fixed disk.

In general, you must have a fixed disk before you can offer to share anything. There is one exception: anyone, with or without a fixed disk, can execute the command PERMIT to make a disk or directory (but not a printer) available to another machine.

Limits on Sharing Imposed When You Start the Network

Certain parameters specified at the time you started the network as a server set limits on the use of your machine by others. These are discussed further in Chapter 13. If you need to change them, see Changing the Default Parameters, in Chapter 2. If you want to look into limits set by start-up parameters, skip forward to Chapter 13. Take a look at Figure 13.1 to see whether one of the parameters listed there is something you should investigate. It lists parameters that may make a difference to the server. Note that you can set new values for these *only* when you start the network. Some of the parameters require substantial memory space, to the extent that being a major server may make it difficult or impossible to run your own jobs on the server machine at the same time.

If you will be offering to share a large number of personal directories with different individuals, it is essential to increase the number of distinct devices or directories you can offer. That is controlled by the start parameter SHR. Its maximum is 150, but its default value if you don't reset it is only 5.

If you will be sharing for a wide audience, it is essential to increase the number of different computers that can simultaneously use shared resources on your machine. That's parameter RDR. Its default value is 10, and its maximum is 25. (Notice that the maximum doesn't mean that your network is limited to 25 people, or even that your machine is limited to 25 different users. It means that no more than 25 of them may use your machine at the same time.)

Using the Menus to Make or Withdraw an Offer to Share

If you're not already in the menus, get to the main menu by either pressing the network-request key (Ctrl-Alt-Break) or, at the DOS prompt, typing NET. Then you have to decide whether you're offering printers or offering disks and directories, since they're handled by different screens.

Offering to Share Disk Space

Proceed as follows:

1. At the main menu, select *Disk or directory tasks.*
2. At *Disk or directory tasks,* select *Start or stop sharing your disk or directory.*
3. At *Start or stop,* select *Start.* PC Network displays a screen on which you can fill in details of your offer; see Figure 3.1.
4. Fill in the details.

Filling In the Form

Fill in the name by which the directory you are offering is known to DOS on your machine. Based on what you write, PC Network constructs and records the complete path. As usual, if you don't include the drive name or show the root directory, DOS interprets your reply in the context of the current directory and drive. To avoid misunderstanding, it's good practice always to be explicit: state the path completely; include both the drive name and the initial slash that indicates the root directory. For example, not just *Accounts\Recv\Dept8* but *c:\Accounts\Recv\Dept8*. The directory thus identified is the directory to which your users will have access. However, they won't be able to tell what its DOS name is. They'll refer to it by the network name you specify in the next field.

Tab (Not Return) to Get to the Next Field

When you press Return, PC Network assumes you're finished with the entire screen. If you mistakenly press Return to get to the next field, PC Network protests that you haven't filled in the other fields yet (by saying *NET104. Required field missing*).

Pick a Network Name

The name you write here is arbitrary. It can be anything you want (up to eight characters), provided you haven't already used the same name in another outstanding offer. This is the name the users will have to know in order to take up your offer. It's your responsibility (or the network administrator's) to see that the people who need to know this name are told what it is.

```
                                                         IBM PC NETWORK
                     Start Sharing Your Disk or Directory

DOS name for disk or directory
     c:\Sachiko

Network name for your disk or directory
     Shikoku5

Password for disk or directory (Optional)
     Kudasai

Other users can
1. Read only                  4. Write/Create/Delete
2. Read/Write                 5. Read/Write/Create/Delete
3. Write only

5  Choice

     Tab - Cursor to next field
     Enter - Continue                        F1 - Help
     Esc - Previous menu                     Ctrl-Home - Return to Main Menu
```

Figure 3.1: *Screen for offering to share disk space*

When you use the menus to offer to share a directory, you must provide a network name for it. This is also referred to as the *short name* for the directory. (As you'll see in the description of the NET SHARE command later in this chapter, when you write the command yourself you also have the option of offering just a path, without a network name.)

Pick a Password—If You Want One

The password is optional. It may have up to eight characters (no blanks). If you write something in the password field, when a user takes up your offer to share she'll have to supply the same characters you write here. It's your responsibility (or the network administrator's) to see that the people who need to know the password are told what it is.

The password you specify remains in effect throughout the current session, but not longer. It's possible to save the network setup so that the rest of your offer is made automatically each time you start the network (described in Chapter 2). However, if you do save it, PC Network records that you used a password but not the password itself. It records your offer with an asterisk replacing the actual password. Each time it executes that command (that is, each time you start the network), it prompts you to set the password from the keyboard.

Passwords can be tiresome when used inappropriately. Use them sparingly. For directories that are universally available or have read-only access, passwords may be more nuisance than they're worth. Notice that you can get a fair amount of security simply by using an unpublicized network name for your directory. A password doesn't really offer a new level of security, other than the requirement to set it anew each time the network is started.

Pick a Level of Access

In the last field, you indicate by a number which of five possible levels of access you grant to files in this directory. The level you choose applies to all files within the directory. (If you want to set a level of access for just one file, it has to be in a directory by itself.)

The level of access you set applies to all users who take up this offer to share. (If you need to offer the same directory but with a different level of access, make a separate offer to share the same directory, giving it a different network name and password as well as a different level of access.)

On the menu screen, PC Network not only lists the five alternatives, but also fills in the answer 5 for you. If you want something different, replace the 5 by the number that indicates your choice. *Watch out:* This may be convenient, but it isn't safe. Because it supplies a 5 by default, unless you take steps to contradict it, PC Network gives your users the most general level of access. You'll probably need on occasion to give read-only access to some directories. If you press Return before you've filled in this field, you'll have granted more access than you intended.

What the Levels of Access Mean

The level of access governs the actions that your users (or their programs) are permitted to take with respect to files in the directory that you're offering. The letters in the abbreviation indicate whether an activity is permitted. The meanings of the terms are summarized in Figure 3.2.

Whether a user's program is actually permitted use of a file depends not only on the level of access that you here assign to the directory that contains it, but also on the way the program requests to use the file.

DOS 3.10 supports shared access to files. That's an important issue for a PC connected to a network, but one that didn't arise before networking was introduced. A request to use a file may indicate whether the program seeks to use it exclusively (denying access to others) or permits others to have various levels of access at the same time. A request for shared use indicates which activities must be denied to other programs. For example, a program may specify that it wants to open the file to read and write and that other programs requesting access must be

1	R	Open an existing file to read from it.
2	RW	Open an existing file to read or write.
3	W	Open an existing file to write but not read. If the program that uses the file elects to write from the beginning, it may overwrite all or part of the former contents. It may also elect to write only at the end, appending the new material to what's already there.
4	WC	Like W, but may also delete an existing file or create a new one.
5	RWC	Full access: read, write, create, delete.

Figure 3.2: *Levels of access to files in a directory*

denied permission to write. (The rules for shared access are summarized on page 6-121 of the DOS 3.10 *Technical Reference.*)

A great many programs date from the era before networking, so include no provision for what DOS should do in a network environment. DOS treats such programs as if they permit sharing only when files are opened for read-only access, and as if they seek exclusive access under all other circumstances. Such programs can have concurrent access to a file in a network directory only when you specify read-only access for its directory *and* they specify read-only in their requests to open it. By contrast, programs written to take advantage of the network may agree to shared read/write access, and (using the DOS SHARE command) may set up tables that dynamically control access to segments within the file.

Completing the Offer

When you've filled in the fields, press Enter. To indicate that your offer has been made successfully, PC Network does two things:

- Writes the message *Disk or directory now shared on network*
- Makes blank the fields you just filled in

Don't be disturbed that the information you wrote just vanished. That's PC Network's way of telling you it's ready for you to write an offer to share another directory. You may decline by pressing Escape.

When there's something wrong with your offer, PC Network displays an error message at the bottom of the screen. The information you supplied remains visible; you can tab back (Shift-Tab takes you back to a previous field) and use the Insert or Delete keys to correct what you wrote. Or you can just abandon the offer by pressing Escape.

Using the Menus to Withdraw an Offer

Later on, you may want to withdraw an offer to share. Here's the route through the menus:

1. At the main menu, select *Disk or directory tasks.*
2. At *Disk or directory tasks,* select *Start or stop sharing your disk or directory.*
3. At *Start or stop,* select *Stop.* PC Network displays a screen on which you can supply the needed information.
4. Fill in the network name of your shared directory. (Note: Use the network name that you assigned when you offered to share it, not its DOS name on your machine.) You can see such a screen in Figure 3.3.

PC Network acknowledges that you have withdrawn the offer to share by displaying the message *Disk or directory no longer shared on network.* Then it returns the network-name field to blank and waits for you to withdraw another offer. You can decline by pressing Escape.

Withdrawing your offer to share may cause problems for someone who is already using the directory you shared. When the user next tries to refer to it, or when DOS next checks on the state of network resources, DOS will display a message at the user's machine telling her *Network name was deleted* and perhaps identifying the file involved. If someone is using the directory, PC Network warns you about this by asking *Device or directory in use on the network; Are you sure?* If you are sure you want to do that, you can go ahead; the program has already supplied you with a Y as your suggested answer, and you have only to press Enter. You may instead change the reply to N. Perhaps you'll want to check to see what machines are in fact using that directory, or whether they actually have files open. (See the section on displaying what you've shared, later in this chapter.)

Offering to Share a Printer

The procedure is essentially the same as offering to share a directory, but slightly different questions apply, and so the form PC Network gives

```
                                                              IBM PC NETWORK
                 Start or Stop Sharing Your Disk or Directory

     1. Start sharing your disk or directory

     2. Stop sharing your disk or directory


     2  Choice

Network name for your disk or directory
     Shikoku5






     Tab - Cursor to next field
     Enter - Continue                           F1 - Help
     Esc - Previous menu                        Ctrl-Home - Return to Main Menu

■
```

Figure 3.3: *Menu screen to withdraw an offer to share*

you to fill in is slightly different. Here's the route from the main menu:

1. At the main menu, select *Printer tasks.*
2. At *Printer tasks,* select *Start or stop sharing your printer.*
3. At *Start or stop,* select *Start.* PC Network displays a screen on which you can supply the needed information. It's shown in Figure 3.4.
4. Fill in the details. In particular, supply a network name for your printer.

Offering to Share a Printer Means That You Too Have to Use It as a Network Device

When you share a printer known by one of the DOS reserved names PRN, LPT1, LPT2, or LPT3, you can no longer treat it as a local device on your machine. You have to treat it as a network device, just as the other network users do. (This rule applies to printers but not to directories: you can still refer directly to a directory on your machine even after you've shared it with the network.)

To make the process easier for you, as soon as you offer to share a printer whose DOS name is one of those four names, PC Network

```
                                                          IBM PC NETWORK
                        Start Sharing Your Printer

DOS name for printer
     LPT1 (LPT1, LPT2, ...)

Network name for your printer
     Fast

Password for printer (Optional)

     ________





     Tab - Cursor to next field
     Enter - Continue                      F1 - Help
     Esc - Previous menu                   Ctrl-Home - Return to Main Menu
```

Figure 3.4: *Menu screen to offer to share a printer*

automatically does the following:

1. Makes an additional offer to share the same printer, assigning to it another network name formed by putting the underline character ahead of its regular name. For example, suppose you have offered to share LPT1 under the name Fast. PC Network then makes an additional offer to share LPT1 under the name _LPT1.

2. Makes a request on your behalf to use the network name _LPT1, assigning it the name LPT1 for use on your machine.

It does both of these automatically, without any special action on your part, and without notifying you that it has done so. However, the offer to share _LPT1 and the request to use _LPT1 show up in the reports of network devices you are sharing or using.

The effect of these maneuvers is that now when you (or your program) use the name LPT1, output is no longer directed straight to your printer. Instead, it's redirected to _LPT1, which is the network name for your printer. Your output is handled by the network print-queue manager, just like output from anybody else on the network.

A network name is not normally permitted to begin with the underline character. PC Network uses it solely for this special offer that diverts your own printing to the print queue on your own machine. No other machine can take up that offer, since it can't request to use a name beginning with that character.

Using Menus to Withdraw Your Offer to Share a Printer

The procedure is exactly parallel to the procedure for withdrawing the offer to share a directory. Here's the route through the menus:

1. At the main menu, select *Printer tasks.*
2. At *Printer tasks,* select *Start or stop sharing your printer.*
3. At *Start or stop,* select *Stop.* PC Network displays a screen on which you can supply the needed information.
4. Fill in the network name of the printer.

PC Network acknowledges that you have withdrawn the offer to share by displaying the message *Printer no longer shared on network.* Then it returns the network-name field to blank and waits for you to withdraw another printer. You can decline by pressing Escape.

Withdrawing your offer to share may cause problems for someone who is already using the printer you shared. When the user next tries to use your printer, or when DOS next checks on the state of network resources, DOS will display the message *Network name was deleted* at the user's machine and perhaps mention its name, to indicate that the device she was using is no longer on the network. When someone is using the directory, PC Network warns you about this by asking: *Device or directory in use on the network; Are you sure?* If you are sure you want to withdraw your offer, you can go ahead; the program has already supplied you with a Y as your suggested answer, and you have only to press Enter. You may instead change the reply to N. Perhaps you want to check to see what machines are in fact using that directory or whether they are actually transmitting to the printer. (See Chapter 9, on managing the printer, or the section on displaying what you've shared, later in this chapter.)

NET SHARE: The Command to Make, Withdraw, or Report Offers

You can offer to share a disk, directory, or printer by the command NET SHARE. You can also use the command to withdraw an offer after it has been made or to summarize current outstanding offers.

To use the command, you need to be at the DOS prompt. Alternatively, from within the menus, you can press F2 to get a command screen (which supplies the word NET for you). The parts of the NET SHARE command are illustrated in Figure 3.5.

Examples of NET SHARE

To offer your directory \Perstext\Letters on drive C with the network name Mailfile, read-only access, and password Uzbek, enter:

```
NET SHARE Mailfile=c:\Perstext\Letters Uzbek /r
```

To offer the same directory under the same conditions but without a network name, enter (with your drive C as default):

```
NET SHARE \Perstext\Letters Uzbek /r
```

To offer your printer LPT1 with the network name Fast and no password, enter:

```
NET SHARE Fast=LPT1
```

An offer to share a printer *must* include a network name for it.

Offering to Share a Directory Without a Network Name

You can offer a directory by stating a path only, with no network name. In that case, you also omit the equal sign. The path may *not*

NET SHARE	*Shortname=Device:Path Password /Param /d*
Shortname	Up to eight letters. The network name under which you offer the directory or printer. Required when offering a printer, but optional when offering a directory; if used, it must be followed by =.
Device	DOS name on your computer for the printer you are offering, or for the drive on which the directory you are offering is located. If you include a drive name, you must have a short name and an = sign before it and a colon after it. (However, in NET SHARE, you may or may not write a colon after a printer name.)
Path	Path to the directory you are offering. This is empty when you're offering a printer or an entire disk. When there's a drive name and colon, the path begins immediately after the colon, with no blank between them. The path should start with \.
Password	Optional. Up to eight characters, separated from the rest of the command by blanks. If you write an asterisk for the password, each time the command is executed, *PC Network* prompts you to supply a password from the keyboard.
Param	Optional, but may be included only for a disk or directory. Set off from the rest of the command by blanks. One of: /R /W /RW /WC or /RWC. Default: /RWC.
/d	Only to indicate that you are deleting (withdrawing) an offer made earlier.

Figure 3.5: *Syntax of NET SHARE*

include a drive specification. (It's assumed to refer to whatever your default drive is at the time you make the offer.)

For example, the following example offers to share the directory called Perstext\Letters on what is now your default drive with read-only access:

```
NET SHARE \Perstext\Letters /r
```

Whether you elect to use a network name or to state a path has no effect on what the user can do. Either way, the user can elect either to adopt the path you offer or to treat it as a virtual drive on her own machine.

Multiple Offers of the Same Path

As far as PC Network is concerned, offering the same path with two different access levels constitutes two different offers. In order to map the user's request to one particular path, when you offer the paths, you not only give the users different access rights, you also give the paths different passwords. The user gets the access right that goes with the password she uses.

All this comes up because, when you go to delete one of these offers, you have to include the access right in the delete statement so PC Network can tell which offer you're deleting.

Benefits of Assigning a Network Name to a Directory You Share

Including a network name for a directory that you offer to share has some conveniences for you and for the users who accept the offer.

- To the users, the advantage is that they can arrange with you a private network name unrelated to the real name on the fixed disk—which helps assure individuals of private access to it.
- To you, the advantage is that you can, if need be, attach the network name to a different directory.

Here are two examples of leaving a network name the same while you change what it refers to. Suppose you have a directory of programs that your users read. You want to introduce new versions of the software. You install the new versions in a new directory. When you're ready to switch, you offer the new directory under the network name formerly used for the old version. All users are automatically transferred to the new version. But the old directory is still there. If some want to stick with the old version, you can invent a network name that will connect them to that version instead of the new one.

Or suppose that each month you create a directory for the month's billings. Several users need to see the current directory, but not the old ones. You pick a network name—for example, Current—and attach it each month to the appropriate directory. The users don't have to change what they do; they're always linked to the appropriate directory.

The /d Parameter Deletes an Offer to Share

The NET SHARE command can also be used to withdraw an offer to share. You write a shorter version of the command by which you made the offer, and include with it the parameter /d (for *delete*).

When you include /d, here's how you identify the device or directory whose sharing is to be deleted. If you've offered it with a network name (or short name), refer to it by the network name when you delete it.

If the directory you're withdrawing was offered as a path (with no network name), include the path in the same way as it appeared in the request to delete. And if it was one of a set of multiple offers of the same path, differentiated from one another solely by their access rights, include the access right in the request to delete.

Never include a password in a request to delete (even if the offer to share used a password).

An Aside: Seeing Your Own Directories as Virtual Drives

In general, each user who takes advantage of your offer to share disk space will see a directory that you offer as a virtual drive on her own machine. You may find it useful to treat your own directories the same way. For example, you might want to do that while testing on your own machine a program that others will use over the network. You can do that with the DOS command SUBST (which stands for *substitute*). Its syntax is very like NET USE, described in the next chapter.

At the DOS prompt, you type SUBST followed (on the same line) by a drive name (followed by a colon), a blank, and then the complete DOS path to a directory.

The drive name must be a letter of the alphabet from A up to the last letter specified by *last drive* in your file Config.sys. (When you install PC Network, it usually sets the last drive to N, but you're free to change that to some other value.) The drive name must be different from the drive mentioned in the path. DOS won't stop you from using the name of a real drive, but be aware that if you do that, you won't be able to make use of the real drive, since references to its name will be redirected to the path you define.

The path is the complete path to a directory that exists on your machine. You can't use this to refer to a path you're using through the network.

To refer to your directory c:\Apps as if it were your drive N, the command is:

```
SUBST n: c:\Apps
```

Terminating Use of a Substitute Drive Name

To end a substitution, at the DOS prompt write SUBST followed (on the same line) by the name of the virtual drive (with a colon) and the parameter D, like this:

```
SUBST n: /d
```

Displaying a Report on Resources You've Offered to Share

There are several ways to request this report. The report itself is the same, regardless of how you request it.

From the DOS prompt, or at the command screen within the menus, the command is simply NET SHARE, with nothing after it.

From within the menus, select *Display devices you are sharing.* You can reach that from any of the following menus:

- Printer tasks
- Disk or directory tasks
- Network status tasks

Figure 3.6 shows such a report generated from within the menus. (The version generated directly by the NET SHARE command lacks the caption and the instructions about function keys, but otherwise appears the same.)

Network Names and DOS Names

The display has one entry for each distinct offer you've made to share a device or directory. An entry may fit on one row, or it may require extra rows if the path name or list of users is longer than can fit on one row.

For each entry, there is a DOS name, describing where the device or directory is on your machine. If your offer included a network name (or short name) for the device, that's shown in the field headed Network Name. In Figure 3.6, you can see the network names Fast and

Daisy (which have here been given to printers), and Apps, Shikoku, and U7844920 (here given to directories).

For each entry that has a network name, the DOS name is either the standard DOS name of a printer or a drive name followed by a colon and a complete directory path.

Where you offered a directory *without* a network name, the network-name field is blank. In the field for DOS name, the path appears *without* a drive name. In Figure 3.6, there are two such offers, both of them to share \Perstext\Letters (with different access rights). These offers must have been made via the NET SHARE command (since in the menus, there's no way to offer a directory without a network name).

Meaning of the Status Field

The first column of the report shown in Figure 3.6 contains the status of each resource you are offering. For a directory, it shows the access parameter (R for read-only, W for write-only, RW for read/write, WC for write/create, RWC for read/write/create). Access codes are described earlier in this chapter.

Paused Status

It's possible to cause a *pause* in the services you've offered. During the pause, your offers to share directories and printers remain open, but all activity is suspended. Users who attempt to access any of the directories you have shared, or to submit jobs to the print queue on your machine, find they are temporarily unable to do so. Pausing is not specific to a particular device or directory, but to a general function (such as serving, handling messages, and so on). Pausing is described in Chapter 6.

If you have paused the sharing of devices and directories, each row affected by the pause shows the word *paused* as its status, overriding other displays in that column as long as the pause remains in effect. (Although your display of devices you're sharing reports the pause, the display that your users see when they ask for a report on what they're using does not report which ones are paused.)

System Status

In Figure 3.6, the status of the names _LPT1 and _LPT2 is shown as *system*. That means PC Network made these offers automatically, when you offered to share printers LPT1 and LPT2. At the right, the figure shows that these printers are in use by Server2. From that, you can deduce that Server2 is the network name of the machine that made the offers and generated the report.

When you offer to share a printer with the network, PC Network really offers it twice: once to everybody else on the network, and once in a special offer just for you. That's so you too can use your own printer as a network printer and redirect your private output to the network print queue. This automatic extra offer uses a network name formed by attaching an initial underline to the standard DOS name of the printer (for example, _LPT1 for LPT1). Since the network won't transmit a name that begins with an underline, only your machine can accept this offer.

Names of Users

The rightmost field in Figure 3.6 shows the machine names of machines that have accepted your offers to share. For example, the figure shows that your offer to share the directory to which you gave the network name Apps has been accepted by machines called Lieu, Barry, and Sachiko. No one is using the printer you called Daisy at the moment, so the user field for it remains blank.

Note that the user field only tells you which users have established a redirection to the directories you've offered. They *may* be using files on your disk, but you can't tell from this report whether they actually have

```
                                                                  IBM PC NETWORK
                             Display Devices You Are Sharing

Access/  Network             DOS
Status   Name                Name                    Names Using the Device
--------------------------------------------------------------------------------
         FAST                LPT1                    SACHIKO  PAUL     BARRY
                                                     SERVER1
SYSTEM   _LPT1               LPT1                    SERVER2
         DAISY               LPT2
SYSTEM   _LPT2               LPT2                    SERVER2
  R      APPS                C:\APPS                 LIEU     SACHIKO  BARRY
  RWC    SHIKOKU             C:\SACHIKO              SACHIKO
  RWC    U7844920            C:\PAUL                 PAUL
  R                          \PERSTEXT\LETTERS       BARRY
  RWC                        \PERSTEXT\LETTERS       PAUL
                              -- End of share list --

--------------------------------------------------------------------------------
     PgUp and PgDn - Scroll list
     Enter - Redisplay list                         F1 - Help
■    Ctrl-Home - Return to Main Menu                Esc - Previous menu
```

Figure 3.6: *Report of devices and directories you are sharing*

any files open at the moment. For that, you need the NET FILE command, described in the next section of this chapter.

Who's Using Files in the Directories You've Offered?

Perhaps just because you're curious—but especially if you're about to shut down your machine, withdraw your offer to share, or pause the server function—you need to know who's using the disk space you've offered to the network. You may also need to intervene if one of the users has inadvertently tied up a file that others need.

The NET SHARE command, described in the preceding section, tells you what devices or directories you have offered and what machines have accepted your offers. However, it doesn't tell you whether they actually have any files open at the moment. You can get that from the NET FILE command.

Reporting Files Currently Open

While NET SHARE summarizes for you the devices or directories you have offered to share and tells you which machines have accepted, that still doesn't tell you whether users have files open at the moment. There are two reasons you might want to know:

- You need to have your server pause or close it down. You need to know which users are active so you can decide whether to proceed or to warn them and ask them to close down what they're doing.
- Some of your users are complaining that they can't get access to a file they need because another user has exclusive access and isn't letting go.

The command NET FILE gives you the needed information and the power to intervene to free a held file, if need be. There is no menu for NET FILE, so you must use it either from the DOS prompt or, in the menus, by pressing F2 to get the command screen.

The command NET FILE can be used either to report on a specific file or to list all open files. If you know what file you want to ask about, the command NET FILE is followed by the name of one file on your machine. For example, to discover what machines now have open the file called c:\Dept8\Mailpool\Active, you write:

```
NET FILE c:\Dept8\Mailpool\Active
```

Figure 3.7 shows a possible report when the file is open.

Interpreting the Report on an Open File

The first field shows the complete DOS name for the file. That's the way the file's name appears on your machine, not the way it may appear to network users.

The next two fields show the machine names of users that have the file open, together with the number of locked segments they have requested. This shows a number other than 0 only when all the users who have opened the file did so by requesting shared access, and some of them have requested exclusive use of a specific segment within the file.

As mentioned in the discussion of access levels earlier in this chapter, to a program that doesn't use the shared access mechanism, DOS gives exclusive use of any file except a file offered as read-only. If one user has exclusive access to a file in that manner, that may indeed be what's preventing others from gaining access to it, but that isn't what's meant by *Locks* in the report. Since such a file does not request to lock individual segments within the file, it's reported as having 0 locks.

When the file you asked about is not open, PC Network sends the message *NET066: File not open.*

Asking about All Open Files

When you use the command NET FILE with nothing after it, you get a report of *all* files that are open. It includes files opened for any reason

```
                                                                IBM PC NETWORK

Name of Open File              User            Locks    User              Locks
-------------------------------------------------------------------------------
C:\DEPT8\MAILPOOL\ACTIVE       SACHIKO             0    BARRY                 1

End of lines; Strike a key to exit
■
```

Figure 3.7: *NET FILE report on a single file*

by anyone. That includes files that the print server on your machine has opened in order to manage the print queue, and files that you've opened locally without going through the network (in your private use of the server machine). For a file in either of those last two categories, the user field of the report shows your machine's network name. Figure 3.8 shows a report generated by nonspecific use of NET FILE.

In Figure 3.8, you can see not only files opened by the network users Sachiko and Barry, but also two files opened locally, identified here by the machine's network name, Server2. The file \Dept3\Letters\May1 has been opened by the operator of the server machine. It has nothing to do with the network, and it exists in a directory that has not been offered to the network.

The file \Network\PQ039.Spl has been opened by the PC Network print spooler, presumably to store a job in the queue for subsequent printing. The name indicates that it is job 39.

Forced Closing to Resolve an Access Conflict

A user seeking access to a file on your machine may be rebuffed because someone else is using it in a way that doesn't permit them both to work concurrently. This problem is more likely to occur when the users are running programs that were written for stand-alone machines and presume exclusive access to the files.

```
                                                                IBM PC NETWORK

Name of Open File            User           Locks    User              Locks
------------------------------------------------------------------------------
C:\PAUL\TEXT\CH01.NET        PAUL             0
C:\SACHI\DATA\BIOSTAT        SACHIKO          0
C:\APPS\TEXT\PCWRITE\        BARRY            0
RULER.DEF
C:\NETWORK\PQ039.SPL         SERVER2          0
C:\DEPT3\LETTERS\MAY1        SERVER2          0
End of lines; Strike a key to exit




     Enter - Continue                       F1 - Help
     Esc - Previous menu                    Ctrl-Home - Return to Main Menu

NET file_
```

Figure 3.8: *NET FILE report on all open files*

Suppose two users both wish to open a file located in a directory to which you have given read/write access. Unless their programs provide for file sharing, the first person to open the file gets exclusive access to it. The next user who seeks access to that file gets the message *Sharing Violation error,* followed by some indication of whether the problem occurred while reading or writing, and the drive involved.

Programs differ in the way they handle locks. Some try to minimize the time that a lock is in effect; they lock the minimum segment necessary and unlock it as soon as that part of the process is over. Others just grab the file for the duration of a work session. That's likely to be true of programs not really written with networking in mind. Even when the program is expressly designed for shared use, it's still possible for a user to suspend it—for example, by using the network-request key to bring up the PC Network menus—and thereby leave a lock in place when nothing is happening.

Sooner or later, someone will open a file in a way that prevents others from having the access they want, and inadvertently leave it that way. The other users' programs may go into an indefinite wait or (depending how they're programmed) may report the problem with varying degrees of grace. At that point, frustrated would-be users may send you messages to find out what's going on.

Displaying NET FILE for the file in question should show you who's using it. You may then be able to solve the problem by a reminder to the individual who has it open.

Failing that, you can force the file to be closed. This is a rather drastic action, so you'd better be sure it's really necessary.

To close a file, you write the command NET FILE followed by the complete DOS name of the file to be closed, and then the parameter C. PC Network asks *Are you sure you want to close the file? (Y/N)* but guesses that you are (since it supplies the suggested answer Y).

If you assent, PC Network closes the file. From the command screen of the menus, PC Network doesn't give you any message specifically saying it has done so. At the DOS prompt, it sends the usual message *Command completed successfully* that concludes any network command.

After you've closed the file, it becomes accessible for a new use. When the user who formerly had it open continues her work, she gets an error message. (She may not get the message instantly. For example, if she's reading from the file, DOS may have buffered the next segment in anticipation of a request to read it, so she won't notice that the file has been closed until the operating system really has to return to it for more data.)

Using Shared Resources

Four

This chapter describes how you enable your computer to take advantage of resources offered over the network by computers that are playing the role of server.

Perhaps You Won't Need to Know How

It's possible to store most of the steps to set up your machine on the network in a file of instructions that are executed automatically when you start your machine. If that has already been set up for you, all you need to do is reply Y (for yes) when your computer asks *Do you want to start the network?*

It's also possible to write the batch file that starts an application so that it automatically takes the steps needed to make network resources available to it. (Two approaches to doing that are described, one later in this chapter and the other in Chapter 12.)

Nevertheless, you may want to look at what follows for an explanation of what's going on behind the scenes. You may want to read it just out of curiosity, or to get an idea of how you can adjust the procedures to suit your changing needs—or out of self-defense, so you'll know what to do when something goes wrong.

If you're not so fortunate as to have it all done for you—or if you prefer to do these things yourself—this chapter goes into the details. It starts by reviewing some general principles regarding the way you use facilities offered by others over the network.

What the Servers Offer

A resource offered over the network by a server machine may be:

- A printer attached to another machine
- A directory of files, occupying all or part of a disk on another machine

The PC Network menus speak of *disks or directories* on the network. Those aren't two different things, but two ways of looking at the same thing. When a server offers to share disk space, the server always offers a directory, which is usually just part of a disk but could occupy the entire disk. When you take up the offer, you may treat the directory that the server offers as if it were a disk.

Public Network Directories

A server machine may be set up with a master copy of each of the programs widely used by your group or department. You don't need to keep a copy yourself. Your machine reads the program files from the server machine each time it needs them.

The usual arrangement is for the server to make available a single large directory of application programs. The server machine can call that directory anything, but the IBM *User's Guide* suggests the name *Apps,* and that seems a useful convention to follow. When you're using the server's Apps directory, the usual arrangement (but not the only one possible) is to make it appear to you as an extra disk drive on your machine—what is called a *virtual disk.*

When the Apps directory is installed on the server machine, it is divided into subdirectories, one for each major application or group of applications. Once you start using the server's Apps directory, the subdirectories of Apps appear to you as directories within your virtual disk. In addition to the various application directories, they include a directory for DOS commands and another for PC Network commands. Since the server machine makes available to you its copies of programs used by DOS and PC Network, your machine can operate with only a minimum number of DOS and PC Network commands stored locally. After you've started the network, that eliminates the need to keep a DOS or PC Network diskette in your disk drive.

What's Needed to Let Your Machine Make Use of a Server

To make it convenient for you to use a shared directory such as Apps, there are two things your machine has to do:

- Accept the server's offer to share the directory and establish a drive name by which your machine will refer to it. In PC Network terminology, you are said to *use* the server's directory. You can establish use from a menu screen or by executing the command NET USE.
- Tell DOS to include the new directory in its list of places to look for a program. In DOS terminology, that's called establishing an environment, and it's done with the PATH command. Once a path has been established, you can execute a program just by writing its name, without having to mention that it's on the server machine. As this chapter explains, there are various ways to establish the appropriate path.

Access Rights

The machine that offers to share a directory specifies the *access right* you will have when you use it. The access right is a broad limitation on the sorts of things you can do to any file within the directory. (The five possible access rights are described in Chapter 3.) The major distinction is between read-only directories and directories in which you are free to make changes:

- *Read-only.* Such directories are used to store files that you can use but not alter, such as programs or perhaps reference data.
- *Full access.* Within such a directory, you can read existing files, write new information in them, delete them, or create new ones. The directory acts like an extension of your own machine.

Under some conditions, two different users can make use of the same network file at the same time. That's always permitted for read-only files. Programs that make use of the shared-use conventions introduced with DOS 3.10 can also request various forms of shared write access. Programs that don't use those facilities (usually because they were written for stand-alone machines, before networking was introduced) can share access only to read-only files. For such programs, DOS treats all other requests for access as requests for exclusive use. That means that while one person has the file open, DOS won't let anyone else open it.

Private Network Directories

A server machine may set aside a separate directory for your individual use. While you're using it, it usually appears to you as another disk drive on your own machine. In reality, it is a directory occupying part of the fixed disk of the server machine. That's achieved by the following steps:

1. The operator of the server machine (or the network administrator) creates on the server machine a directory for your use. It is a separate directory, not a subdirectory under Apps. She probably gives it a name that helps her remember what it's for. The name your directory has on the server machine doesn't matter to you; you can't see the name, anyway.
2. The server machine offers to make your directory available to the network. The offer doesn't name you specifically, but no one else knows that the offer has been made. Since an offer lasts no longer than the time the server machine is running, the server has to make the offer again each time it is started. The server machine is usually set up to make such offers automatically.
3. As part of its offer, the server assigns a *network name* to your directory. The network name for a directory is also called its *short name;* it may have up to eight characters. The network name under which the server offers your private directory is something that should be agreed privately between you and the network administrator and/or the operator of the server machine. It's like an unlisted phone number: the network has no directory in which you or other users can see this name. It's a good idea to make the network name something that you can recall easily but is obscure to anyone else (your first-grade teacher's name, your mother-in-law's zip code; you get the idea). By agreement with the server, you may also set up a *password,* in addition to the short name.

4. You request to use the network name that the server has offered. Usually (but not necessarily), as part of your request you state the *drive name* by which the directory will be known on your machine.

The process by which you take advantage of the resources offered by servers is what the rest of this chapter is about.

Share Must Precede Use

PC Network won't let you use something unless someone has first actually offered it. The offer has to come first. You can put your requests to use resources in a file that is executed automatically when you start your machine—but if you do that, you have to be reasonably sure that the server will have started and made its offers before you try to start your machine. If you can't be sure of that, you may want to separate starting from using: start the network automatically when you start your machine, but delay your request to use a specific resource until later.

A Potential Path

When you take up the offer to use a network resource (either through the PC Network menus or by the command NET USE), you are establishing a link over which communication can travel when you need it. From then on, you go about your business. As your computer encounters references to the shared disk space or printer, it automatically redirects those references to the server. If you don't make any such references, there's nothing for your computer to redirect. What you have done is set up a path that *may* be used.

Duration of Your Use of a Network Resource

Once you make a successful request to use a network resource, it remains available to you continuously, until one of the following occurs:

- You (or a program you are running) terminate the request.
- The server terminates the offer to make it available.
- Your machine is reset (power off or Ctrl-Alt-Del).
- The server machine is reset (power off or Ctrl-Alt-Del).

Restating your requests to share following reset of the server is discussed later in this chapter.

Limits on Using Imposed When You Start the Network

Certain items specified at the time you start the network set limits on the network resources you can use. These are discussed further in

Chapter 13. If you need to start the network with values that differ from the defaults, see the section on changing from the default parameters in Chapter 2.

If you want to look into this further, skip to Chapter 13. Take a look at Figure 13.2: Parameters that may affect the user. Check whether one of the parameters listed there is something you should investigate further. Note that you can select different values *only* when you start the network.

If you need services from several different server computers at once, you should revise the parameter SRV. The default value is 2, but you can set it as high as 31. The parameter ASG limits the number of different devices (printers, disks, or directories) that you can use at one time. Its default value is 5, but you can set it as high as 32.

Several other parameters govern the number and size of buffers on your machine for transmitting jobs to be printed and for sending and receiving files. If you don't specify, PC Network assigns very low default values. If you can afford the space in your machine's main memory, you may make considerable improvements in performance. The effect depends on the sort of work you do. It may also depend on the values of parameters set by the server you are using. (For example, it won't help you to set aside a large buffer for transmitting jobs to a print server when the print server has only a small buffer to receive them.) It's a good idea to have the network administrator review or recommend start-up parameters so that they are consistent throughout the network.

Menu to Start or Stop Using a Network Directory or Printer

If you're not already in the menus, get to the main menu either by pressing the network-request key (Ctrl-Alt-Break) or, at the DOS prompt, by typing *NET.* Then you have to decide whether you want to use printers or to use disks or directories, since they're handled by different screens.

Accepting the Offer to Use a Network Disk or Directory

From the main menu, proceed as follows:

1. At the main menu, select *Disk or directory tasks.*
2. At *Disk or directory tasks,* select *Start or stop using a network disk or directory.*
3. At *Start or stop,* select *Start.* PC Network displays a screen on

which you can fill in details of your request; see Figure 4.1.

4. Fill in the details.

Filling In the Request

You *must* know the network name of the server computer that is offering the resource you want to use. You must also know the network name (or short name) of the resource itself, as well as the password, if any, required for access to it.

The network administrator, or the person offering the resource, should have told you the computer name, the short name, and the password. If you don't know them, the network software offers no way for you to find out.

The network name of a computer may have up to 15 characters; a short name or a password may have up to eight characters. (PC Network, like DOS, ignores capitalization, so you can intermix capitals and lowercase letters as you like.)

Tab (Not Return) to Get to the Next Field

When you press Return, PC Network assumes you're finished with the entire screen. If you mistakenly press the Return key to get to the next field, PC Network protests that you haven't filled in the other fields yet (by saying *NET104. Required field missing*).

```
                                                        IBM PC NETWORK
                  Start Using a Network Disk or Directory

Disk or Directory is on computer
     Server2________

Network name of disk or directory
     Apps____

DOS drive name on your computer for network disk or directory
     N  (A, B, C, ...)

Password for disk or directory (Optional)

     ________


     Tab - Cursor to next field
     Enter - Continue                       F1 - Help
     Esc - Previous menu                    Ctrl-Home - Return to Main Menu
```

Figure 4.1: *Menu screen to start using a network disk or directory*

Drive Names

While making your request through the menus, you *must* supply a drive name by which your computer will refer to the shared directory. The drive name is a letter of the alphabet, from A up to whatever is designated the *last drive* on your machine. The name of the last drive is stored in a file called Config.sys, which tells DOS the size of the table it must maintain to keep track of the various drives. Unless you set it up otherwise, PC Network usually sets the last drive to N. So you must pick a letter between A and N.

Note that it's legal to use a letter (such as A) that may already be the name of a real drive on your machine. If you do that, you won't be able to use the real drive A, since any reference to it will be redirected. Ordinarily, that would be an inconvenience. However, occasionally you may need to run a program over the network that has a reference to drive A built into it. In such a case you may *have* to use the name A for the shared drive, at least temporarily.

The network administrator may establish conventions so that everybody uses the same letters to refer to shared directories. These conventions make it easier to provide programs that set up pathways automatically. The conventions may also simplify human conversation between network users.

With the NET USE command, it is possible to accept an offer simply as a path, without a drive name, but there is no provision for that in the menus.

Password

The machine that has offered the resource may require you to include a password in your request to use the resource. If the operator of the server machine is following the procedure provided in the PC Network menus (she doesn't have to), the password is not written in the server's start-up program; instead, the operator sets the password manually each time she starts the network on the server machine.

When you make your request to use, you have to supply whatever password has been set from the server machine. Your screen describes the password as "optional." It's optional, all right, but you aren't the one who has the option. If the server has specified a password, you have no choice: you *must* supply the same password. (Here again, capitalization doesn't matter.)

Acknowledgment from PC Network

When you've filled in the fields, press Enter. To indicate that your offer has been made successfully, PC Network does two things:

- Writes the message *Disk or directory now available for use*
- Makes blank the fields you just filled in

Don't be disturbed that the information you wrote just vanished. That's PC Network's way of telling you it's ready for you to write another request to use a shared directory. You can decline by pressing Escape.

When there's something wrong with your request, PC Network displays an error message at the bottom of the screen. The information you supplied remains visible; you can tab back and use the Insert or Delete keys to correct what you wrote. Or you can abandon the offer by pressing Escape.

Menu to Stop Using a Network Directory

Later on, you may want to stop using a network disk or directory. Here's the route through the menus:

1. At the main menu, select *Disk or directory tasks.*
2. At *Disk or directory tasks,* select *Start or stop using a network disk or directory.*
3. At *Start or stop,* select *Stop.* PC Network displays a screen on which you can supply the needed information.
4. Fill in the drive letter you selected to refer to the network directory.

PC Network acknowledges that you have stopped using the network directory by displaying the message *Disk or directory no longer available for use.* (The wording of that message is a bit odd. The directory is still available to the network—just not accessible to you, until you again accept the offer to use it.) Then the program returns the field headed *DOS drive name* to blank and waits for you to supply the letter for another drive whose use should be ended. You can decline by pressing Escape.

Accepting the Offer to Use a Network Printer

The procedure is essentially the same as accepting the offer to use a directory. The only difference is that instead of telling PC Network what drive name you will use, you have to tell it one of the standard DOS names for a printer. The screen fills in LPT1 as a suggestion, but you can replace it with a different printer name. Here's the route from the main menu:

1. At the main menu, select *Printer tasks.*
2. At *Printer tasks,* select *Start or stop using a network printer.*
3. At *Start or stop,* select *Start.* PC Network displays a screen on which you can supply the needed information (see Figure 4.2).
4. Fill in the form.

Using a Network Printer Means You Can't Use One of the Same Name on Your Own Machine

When you use a network printer known by one of the DOS reserved names such as LPT1, you can no longer use that name to refer to a device on your own machine. Your references to that name are redirected to the network.

To recover temporarily local use of your printer, you have to request a *pause* in print redirection. See the discussion of the PAUSE command in Chapter 6.

Using Menus to Stop Using a Network Printer

The procedure is exactly parallel to the procedure for ending use of a network directory. Here's the route through the menus:

1. At the main menu, select *Printer tasks.*

```
                                                          IBM PC NETWORK
                         Start Using a Network Printer

Printer is on computer
    Server2

Network name of printer
    Fast

DOS name on your computer for network printer
    LPT1 (LPT1, LPT2, LPT3)

Password for printer (Optional)
    ______



    Tab - Cursor to next field
    Enter - Continue                      F1 - Help
    Esc - Previous menu                   Ctrl-Home - Return to Main Menu
```

Figure 4.2: *Menu screen to start using a network printer*

2. At *Printer tasks,* select *Start or stop using a network printer.*
3. At *Start or stop,* select *Stop.* PC Network displays a screen on which you can supply the needed information.
4. Fill in the network name of the printer.

PC Network acknowledges that you have stopped using the network printer by displaying the message *Network printer no longer available.* Then it returns the network-name field to blank and waits for you to enter the name of another printer you want to stop using. You can decline by pressing Escape.

NET USE: The Command to Accept or Decline Offers and Report Use

You can accept an offer to share a disk, directory, or printer by the command NET USE. The same command can also be used to terminate use once it has been started or to summarize your current use of network resources.

To use the command, you need to be at the DOS prompt. Alternatively, from within the menus, you can press F2 to get a command screen (which supplies the word *NET* for you). The parts of the NET USE command are illustrated in Figure 4.3.

Examples of NET USE

The examples that follow are matched with the examples for NET SHARE in Chapter 3, and you may want to compare them.

To accept Server2's offer to share a directory to which she has given the network name Mailfile and the password Uzbek, and to treat that network directory as your drive G, enter:

```
NET USE g: \\Server2\Mailfile Uzbek
```

To accept the same offer, but without assigning it a drive name on your machine, enter:

```
NET USE \\Server2\Mailfile Uzbek
```

To accept Server2's offer of a printer with the network name Fast, offered with no password, and to make that your LPT2, enter:

```
NET USE LPT2: \\Server2\Fast
```

You *must* provide a local name for a network printer, and it may be followed by a colon (as you can see in the preceding example).

NET USE	*drive:*	*Servername**Shortname*	*Password*	/d
	or	or		
	device:	*Path*		

drive: or *device:* — DOS name on your computer by which you refer to the network drive or printer. Optional for a directory; required for a printer. If you include a printer or drive name, it must be followed by a colon. If you omit the drive name, when you subsequently refer to this directory you will have to write its full path, including the double backslash and the name of the server machine (as you write it in this command).

Servername: — Required. The network name of the server machine that has offered the resource you want to share, preceded by a blank and two backslashes.

Shortname or *Path:* — Required; must be immediately preceded by the network name of the server computer and a backslash. This path or short name must match the name in the server's offer. If the server offered a short name, you must supply the short name; if the server offered a path, you must supply that.

Password: — Required if the server included a password in the offer to share. It may have up to eight characters.

/d — Only to indicate that you are deleting (ending) an earlier request to use.

Figure 4.3: *Syntax of NET USE*

Accepting Use of a Network Directory Offered Without a Network Name

A server may offer to share a directory solely by stating a path, with no network name. In that case, you have to write the entire path, just as the server offered it, when you accept the offer. For example, Server2 may have offered to share the directory \Perstext\Letters. When you accept that offer, you write it thus:

```
\\Server2\Perstext\Letters
```

When you accept use of that path, you still have the usual choice whether to give it a drive name on your machine. To accept the offer and treat it as your drive H, enter:

```
NET USE h: \\Server2\Perstext\Letters
```

If you elect not to assign a virtual drive name, omit the drive and colon from your NET USE statement, thus:

```
NET USE \\Server2\Perstext\Letters
```

If you elect not to assign a virtual drive, whenever you refer to a file in that directory, you'll have to write out the path to it in full. For example, to use the DOS TYPE command to display the contents of a file called Announce.124, enter:

```
TYPE \\Server2\Perstext\Letters\Announce.124
```

At present there is little you can do with paths of this type, because current releases of DOS give them little support. In the long run, such network paths may be much more widely used (see the discussion in Chapter 14).

Multiple Versions of the Same Path

It's possible (though probably unlikely) that the server has made multiple offers of the same path, but with different access rights and different passwords. In such a case, you'll get the offer (and access right) that matches the password you use.

The /d Parameter Ends Your Use of a Network Resource

The NET USE command can also terminate use of a network resource. You write the command more or less as you did when you accepted the offer, but include with it the parameter /d (for *delete*). When you include /d, the rest of the command must have only enough information to identify the directory or printer whose use you're now ending. If you accepted it with a device or drive name (for example, E or LPT2), use that (and nothing more) when you delete it. Don't include a password in a request to delete, even if you had to provide a password when you started using it.

If you started to use the directory by referring to its path (with no drive name), that's how you refer to it when you end use of it. And if it was one of a set of offers of the same path, differentiated from one another solely by their access rights, PC Network deletes them in the order in which you accepted them.

Displaying a Report on Network Resources You're Using

There are several ways to request this report. The report itself contains the same information, regardless of how you request it. (Surprisingly, there are various minor differences in format between the menu and the command versions.)

From the DOS prompt or at the command screen within the menus, the command is simply NET USE with nothing after it.

From within the menus, you select *Display devices you are using.* You can reach that from any of the following menus:

- Printer tasks
- Disk or directory tasks
- Network status tasks

Figure 4.4 shows such a report generated from within the menus. Figure 4.5 shows the same information as it is displayed by the NET USE command. The version generated directly by NET USE calls the second column *Local device* rather than *DOS name,* and lumps together *Computer name* and *Network name or path* under a single heading *Network name,* with the leading \\ in front of each computer name.

Interpreting the Use Report

In the report, each network device or directory you're using has a row to itself (or more—it's possible for a path to be so long that its entry takes more than one row.)

In Figures 4.4 and 4.5, you can see the DOS names E, M, LPT1, and LPT2. Wherever you see a DOS name (or *local name*), that's the name you assigned when you requested to use the resource. That's the name by which you refer to the resource when you make use of it and also when you stop using it. For such an entry, the name to the right (headed *Network name or path*) is the network name under which the server offered it. The network name helps you to recall how you got here, but you don't make further use of it.

Wherever the DOS name (or *local name*) is blank, you did not assign a local drive name. For such an entry, the column at the right is the path that the server offered. In Figures 4.4 and 4.5, one row describes the directory \Rcvable\Current on machine Acctsrv. When you refer to that directory, you write the entire path, preceded by the server machine's name, like this:

\\Acctsrv\Rcvable\Current

That's also how you refer to it when you stop using it (*delete* it).

Meaning of the Status Field

The first column of the reports shown in Figures 4.4 and 4.5 shows the *status* of each resource the computer is using. A blank means that no unusual circumstance has come to the attention of PC Network on your machine. In general, blank means that things are OK.

However, this report is merely a display of the last recorded information. PC Network doesn't do a new check to prepare the display. It's possible for the status column to remain blank even after the server has crashed or has withdrawn its offer to share a device you are using. The fact that a resource is affected by a pause (described later in this chapter and in Chapter 6) does *not* show in your report of network resources you're using, although it is reported in the corresponding status report run by the server.

```
                                                                  IBM PC NETWORK
                           Display Network Devices You Are Using

        DOS           Computer              Network name
Status  name          name                  or path
--------------------------------------------------------------------------------
        E:            SERVER2               \SHIKOKU
        M:            SERVER2               \APPS
                      ACCTSRV               \RCVABLE\CURRENT
        LPT1:         SERVER2               \FAST
ERROR   LPT2:         SERVER1               \LETTERQ
                                -- End of use list --





--------------------------------------------------------------------------------
-     PgUp and PgDn - Scroll list
      Enter - Redisplay list                          F1 - Help
      Ctrl-Home - Return to Main Menu                 Esc - Previous menu
```

Figure 4.4: *Network resources in use, displayed from menus*

Error Status

Any time your machine redirects a command to a network device and finds that it isn't working, PC Network reports an error. PC Network also makes a routine check of all the network devices you're using at the completion of each program or DOS command.

In Figure 4.4, the printer you call LPT2 is shown with an error. This might be because the machine called Server1 is no longer on the network or because the operator of Server1 has withdrawn the offer to share the printer called LetterQ. You won't be able to send a new print request there. However, jobs you sent to it earlier should still be in the queue stored on Server1's disk. (See the section on displaying the print queue later in this chapter.)

You should delete your request to use anything if its status is reported as *error.* Even if the erring device recovers, you'll have to make a new request to use it, and you can't do that until you've terminated your earlier use. (See the discussion of recovery from a server failure, at the end of this chapter.)

System Status

This is one you'll see only when you are a server and are sharing your printer with the network. Here's what it means. When you offer to share your printer with the network, PC Network really offers it twice: once to everybody else on the network, and once in a special offer just

```
        Local   Network
Status  device  name
------------------------------------------------------------
        E:      \\SERVER2\SHIKOKU
        M:      \\SERVER2\APPS
                \\ACCTSRV\RCVABLE\CURRENT
        LPT1:   \\SERVER2\FAST
ERROR   LPT2:   \\SERVER1\LETTERQ
End of lines; Strike a key to exit
-
```

Figure 4.5: *Network resources in use, displayed by NET USE*

for you. At the same time, PC Network automatically makes on your behalf a request to take up the special offer it just made to you. That's so you too can use your own printer as a network printer and redirect your own private output to the network print queue.

Each time you offer your printer to the network, there is automatically an additional offer to share and request to use. The extra *share/use* pair is linked by a network name formed by attaching an initial underline to the standard DOS name of the printer (for example, _LPT1 for LPT1). On your behalf, PC Network offers _LPT1. Then PC Network takes up the offer for you and assigns to _LPT1 the regular DOS name LPT1 without the underline. The effect is that LPT1 no longer refers directly to your printer but to the network printer queue on your machine. While that is in effect, you'll see LPT1 in your *use* list with *system* status.

Effects of a Pause by a Server Machine

A server machine's operator can bring about a *pause* in various activities of the server machine. That makes all the resources that the server is sharing temporarily unavailable. Pausing is the subject of Chapter 6.

If you attempt to refer to a file in a network directory whose server has paused or to submit output to a network printer whose server has paused, PC Network displays the message *NET821: Sharing temporarily paused.* The server's pause also prevents you from accepting any of the offers that the server made earlier or from deleting your use of resources on the server that has paused.

A pause in the server machine's role as server doesn't of itself stop the server from receiving messages. A pause by the server does not show in your report on the network devices you are using.

Setting Up the DOS Path So Your Computer Can Find Network Files

To make your access to network resources convenient, one additional step remains: telling your computer where to find the files it needs to execute commands; in particular, where to find commands that invoke programs stored in the network directories.

DOS provides that at any particular moment one of the drives (real or virtual) on your machine is the *default drive.* Within that, one directory is the *current directory.* Whenever you (or programs you're using) refer to a command that isn't one of DOS's *internal* (that is, built-in) commands, DOS looks for an executable file that contains the definition of the command. An executable file is one whose name ends in *.exe*, *.com*, or *.bat;* when it's looking for a command, DOS looks only at files whose names have those endings.

Whenever you mention a command but don't state a complete path to it, DOS interprets what you wrote as a path starting from the current directory of the default drive.

You can always include explicit instructions about where a file is located. But it's also possible to use the DOS command PATH to set up what in DOS jargon is called an *environment:* a list of directories in which DOS will look to find an executable file. Whenever you use what appears to be a command but DOS finds no executable file of that name in the current directory, DOS looks in the directories in your environment list. It searches the directories in the order their names appear in the list. When it finds an executable file, DOS stops looking and uses the file it has found. If it searches the entire list without finding an executable command, DOS reports *Bad command or file name.*

Public Directories That DOS Needs to Find

The IBM Installation Aid sets up on each server machine a directory called Apps and suggests that the server offer it to the network under the network name Apps. When you use Apps, ordinarily you see it as a virtual drive on your machine. IBM suggests that all the users who accept that offer give it the same agreed-on drive name. For example, by convention all users might call it drive N. What you see as drive N is divided into directories, including one called DOS, another called Network, another called Batch, and a fourth called Text (for text-processing applications). The server's directory \Apps\Batch contains files that invoke the applications stored in other directories within Apps. You need an environment that tells your machine's DOS to look for executable files in those four directories on drive N.

Private Directories That DOS Needs to Find

It's also customary for the server to set aside a private directory for each of the expected users. Within that directory, the Installation Aid creates a subdirectory called Batch. If you have programs stored in your private space on the server, that's where you should store the batch files that invoke them.

According to the Installation Aid (in a message it displays during installation), each user can give any drive name to this private directory, provided it's not the letter used for Apps. I think that this advice is mistaken. It becomes easier for the network administrator to set up automatic procedures (and hence easier for everyone) if everyone agrees to use the same letter for this also. Throughout the examples, I've assumed that everyone calls the private directory drive E.

Where DOS Should Look

Following the convention just proposed, while using the network, you (like every user) have a virtual drive N containing directories called Batch, Text, DOS, and Network, as well as directories for application programs. You (like every user) have a virtual drive E that also contains a directory called Batch. A command to tell DOS where to look might be as follows:

```
PATH \Batch;n:\Batch;n:\Text;n:\DOS;n:\Network;\
```

Here's the effect of that command. To execute a command, DOS will look for a file containing its definition in the following directories in the following order:

1. The current directory of the default drive. DOS always looks there first, regardless of what the PATH command may say.
2. The directory called Batch on the default drive. If you've made the default drive E, it will look in e:\Batch.
3. The directory called Batch on drive N.
4. The directory called Text on drive N.
5. The directory called DOS on drive N.
6. The directory called Network on drive N.
7. The root directory of the default drive, specified by the last backslash in the example above. If you've made the default drive E, it will look in E's root directory.

If a directory on the list doesn't exist, DOS doesn't complain but just goes on to the next. That means it's safe to set up an environment list that includes some directories that aren't yet accessible if you expect them to be accessible later.

Setting the Path

You could set the path by typing the command shown in the preceding section. You'd have to do it each time you start the network, or perhaps each time you take up the offer to use the server's Apps directory and your private directory on the server machine.

Alternatively, you could make the PATH command one of the lines of your file Autouser.bat, so that it is executed automatically each time you start or reset your machine.

The NETPATH Command

The Installation Aid tries to makes things easier for you by setting up a file called Netpath.bat. At the time it creates your private directory on the server machine, it routinely creates that file and stores in it a PATH command like the one shown in the preceding section. In order to include the proper drive name, it asks the person doing the installation what drive name you will be using. (Now you see why it's important for the community to agree on a drive name for the Apps directory.) Provided the instructions in Netpath remain appropriate, you can use it as a (slightly) simpler way to establish the environment you need.

First, you have to take up the offer to use Apps as drive N and your private directory as drive E. (This may have been done automatically, if you've saved your network setup while using those directories; see Chapter 2.)

Assuming that your DOS prompt shows the default drive and the current directory (for example, A:\>), the dialogue at the DOS prompt might look like this:

```
A:\> e:
E:\> Netpath
```

Conceivably, you could make things automatic by including those two commands *e:* and *Netpath* as the last two lines of your file Autouser.bat. (Because Netpath is a batch file, its name can only appear as the *last* line of another batch file. There's further discussion of alternative ways to automate your setup in Chapter 12.)

A Message from Netpath

The Installation Aid builds into Netpath.bat a message to tell you the effect you've produced by executing Netpath. During installation, the Installation Aid inserted into the text of the message the name of the server machine and the drive name you would use. Assuming the server's name was Server2 and the drive name was N, the program displays the following message:

```
You can now access applications on Server2 drive n:
```

It's an odd message. Executing Netpath isn't what gives you access to the server's applications. What Netpath does is make it OK to omit mention of drive N when you invoke applications that are located there.

Making Use of Network Files and Printers

So you've arranged to use network directories or network printers, either by having your Autoexec set things up for you automatically or by making a request with a network screen or with the command NET USE.

Question: Now what? How do you make use of the network files or printers?

Answer: Just as if they were right there on your own machine.

Using a Network Directory

The aim of this chapter so far has been to tell you how to set things up so that a drive name or a directory path on your computer refers not to something physically present on your computer, but to something that is really located on a server machine. Once you've done that, to make use of it, you refer to something on the network in the same way as you would if it were on your own computer. That's the beauty of redirection: there isn't a new set of commands. The only caution is that, since you now have more drives or directories or printers than you had before, you may have to make clear which you mean, just as you would if they were right there on your own machine.

For example, suppose you requested to use two directories on Server2. Suppose the server has set aside a private directory for you and you have made that your drive E; suppose you have made the server's Apps directory your drive N. Suppose your DOS prompt shows the current drive and default directory. A request that would display a list of files in your private directory is shown in Figure 4.6.

```
A:\> e:
E:\> dir

 Volume in drive E has no label
 Directory of  E:\

.            <DIR>      85-10-15    9.51
..           <DIR>      85-10-15    9.51
BATCH        <DIR>      85-10-15    9.51
PROFILES     <DIR>      85-10-15    9.51
NETPATH  BAT        128 85-10-15    9.18
WTEXT        <DIR>      85-10-15   11.07
LETTERS      <DIR>      85-10-27   22.41
PHONE    DIR       1055 85-09-12   16.58
APPOINT  APP       1147 85-10-15   12.07
NOTE     PAD       9560 85-11-16   22.16
NOTE     BAK       9459 85-11-16   10.20
       11 File(s)   4917504 bytes free
■
```

Figure 4.6: *Selecting a network directory and listing its contents*

A request to display the network Apps directory is shown in Figure 4.7. Since Apps contains a subdirectory for each major application, the resulting display amounts to a list of the applications available there. Within what you see as drive N, the directory called Batch contains batch files for starting the various applications. You can see a list of them by typing (after the DOS prompt here shown as E:\>) a command such as this:

E:\> dir n:\Batch

Suppose you want to use a network text editor to write a letter and store its text in your private directory on the server. You do it just as you would if the network weren't involved.

To give a specific example, make the following (quite reasonable) assumptions about how things are set up:

- The programs for PCWrite are located in the server's directory \Apps\Text, which appears to you to be your directory n:\Text.
- PCWrite can be invoked by the batch file PCW.bat, located in the server's directory \Apps\Batch, which appears to you to be your directory n:\Batch.
- As part of your normal start-up you've executed Netpath, which has told DOS that one of the places to look for a batch file is n:\Batch.

```
E:\> dir n:

 Volume in drive N has no label
 Directory of  N:\

.            <DIR>      85-07-01  15.05
..           <DIR>      85-07-01  15.05
NETWORK      <DIR>      85-10-15  10.33
DOS          <DIR>      85-07-01  15.08
BATCH        <DIR>      85-10-15  11.55
TEXT         <DIR>      85-07-01  15.08
NET          <DIR>      85-10-30  13.50
MACRO        <DIR>      85-10-30  13.51
PUBLIC   DOM <DIR>      85-10-15   8.20
IMCAP        <DIR>      85-09-20  11.19
SCOM         <DIR>      85-09-20  14.05
POCKET       <DIR>      85-09-20  16.04
NIAL         <DIR>      85-09-20  11.30
THAUMA       <DIR>      85-10-15   8.25
SMALTALK     <DIR>      85-09-20  11.51
GRAFPLUS     <DIR>      85-09-20  12.07
SAPLPCX      <DIR>      85-09-20  12.14
HDS          <DIR>      85-09-20  12.51
■      18 File(s)   4917504 bytes free
```

Figure 4.7: *Displaying the network Apps directory as drive N*

- You want to edit a new file, to be called Smith2.ltr.
- You want the new file to reside in a directory called Letters within your private directory on the server, which you refer to as drive E.

The procedure is exactly what it would be if everything involved were on your own machine. At the DOS prompt (here shown as E:\>), you first select the directory in which you will write. (That's not essential, but good practice.) Then you invoke PCWrite like this:

```
E:\> chdir Letters
E:\LETTERS> pcw Smith2.ltr
```

Using a Network Printer

If you've fixed things up so that LPT1 is a network printer, you can print just as you would if it were physically attached. A standard way of printing a file is to copy it, giving LPT1 as the destination. One way to print the contents of the file Netpath.bat, located on your (virtual) drive E, is to type:

```
COPY e:Netpath.bat LPT1
```

There is one major difference when the printer is on the network rather than on your own machine: you don't hear the immediate clatter of the printer. First, because it's located somewhere else. Second, because at the server machine, your job goes to a queue and is then processed in its turn by the server's print-queue manager.

NET PRINT Is Analogous to PRINT

If you have a printer attached to your computer and you have *not* offered to share it with the network, you can use the DOS command PRINT. As you may know, that command lets you add files to a queue and sets up a background task that manages the printer in its spare time, permitting you to keep on doing other things while it handles printing. The PRINT command also lets you see what's in the queue, add jobs to the queue, or delete jobs. Moreover, it lets you adjust the memory space used by the print manager and the relative priority of printing and foreground work. (The PRINT command is described in the DOS manual.)

NET PRINT is analogous to PRINT, but refers to a network printer. When you're a network user (and not playing the server role for a network printer), NET PRINT lets you submit requests to the network print queue. It also lets you look at the status of your jobs in the queue.

When you're a server, NET PRINT has additional powers (described in Chapter 9).

Printing a File with NET PRINT

The network command NET PRINT transmits one file to the print queue operated by a server. For example, if LPT1 is the local name you have assigned to a network printer, you can request printing of your file e:\Netpath.bat by typing:

```
NET PRINT e:\Netpath.bat LPT1
```

When LPT1 is a name for a network printer, copying a file to LPT1 and using the NET PRINT command have the same effect: a copy of the file is added to the server's network print queue. The only difference is that NET PRINT, like all the NET commands, writes the message *Command completed successfully,* whereas the DOS command COPY tells you the number of files it created while copying.

Using the Network Menus to Print a File

In the menu that deals with network printers, there's a facility to print a file. You get there as follows:

1. At the main menu, select *Printer or print queue tasks.*
2. At *Printer and print queue tasks,* select *Print a file.* This causes display of a screen in which you fill in the name of the printer and the name of the file to be printed (see Figure 4.8).
3. Fill in the blanks and press Enter.

When you press Enter, PC Network displays the message *File submitted for printing* (visible at the bottom left in Figure 4.8). It leaves the screen otherwise unchanged, with the name of the file you just printed still visible. (If you press Enter again, you'll print it again.) You may overwrite that to print another file, or press Escape to return to the previous menu.

Setting Horizontal and Vertical Spacing of a Network Print Job

The DOS command MODE affects (among other things) the form of displays on a color monitor and the horizontal and vertical spacing of a printer. The form of the command is:

```
MODE LPT1:80,6
```

The word MODE must be followed by the DOS name of a printer, then a colon, then two numbers separated by a comma. The first number selects standard or condensed printing, indicated by the number of characters that will fit into a line. The allowable values are 80 or 132. The second number is lines per inch. The allowable values are 6 or 8.

After you've assigned one of the standard DOS names (such as LPT1) to a network printer, you can execute MODE with respect to that printer. Thereafter, DOS tacks onto the front of each print file a string of control characters to indicate the mode you've selected. (However, if you execute the MODE command *before* you've requested to use the network printer, DOS understands it to refer only to your local printer.)

If you haven't executed MODE, DOS doesn't attach those control characters.

Once you've executed MODE, DOS attaches the control codes you've indicated to every print request until you use MODE again with new values or you reset the machine (by turning the power off or by pressing Ctrl-Alt-Del).

Make Sure the Network Printer Will Understand the MODE Codes

Before you use MODE for a network printer, check with the network administrator or the operator of the print server. You need to make sure that the network printer to which you're transmitting can understand the control codes that your machine sends. (This applies also to the codes generated by word processors.)

If your machine sends to the printer codes that the printer can't digest, you may ruin your print job. Worse than that, unless the print

```
                                                                IBM PC NETWORK
                                       Print a File

DOS name on your computer for a printer
    LPT1      (LPT1, LPT2, ...)

File to be printed
    \Autouser.bat_



    Tab - Cursor to next field
    Enter - Continue                             F1 - Help
    Esc - Previous menu                          Ctrl-Home - Return to Main Menu

File submitted for printing
```

Figure 4.8: *Menu screen for printing a file*

server has taken adequate precautions to reset its controls after each job, you may ruin all subsequent jobs until someone intervenes.

Every Network Print Job Has a Job Number

Each time you send a file to be printed on a network printer (by whatever means), the server machine assigns it a job number. When the server machine provides a separator page between jobs, the separator is usually set up so that it identifies each job by its job number. When you have questions about the job or want to track its progress, you'll probably need the number.

When you submit a print request, PC Network doesn't tell you what job number it has assigned. You can find out by looking at the print queue after you've submitted a job and noticing what has been added. Since you'll need to know that number, it's prudent to note it after each job you submit.

Checking Your Jobs in the Server's Print Queue

PC Network provides a report on your jobs in the print queue on a server machine. You can get the report either by way of the NET PRINT command or from the menus. Either way, the information displayed is the same. Either way, to get the report you have to know the network name of the computer that manages the print queue. The report shows only *your* jobs and omits mention of others that may be in the queue.

NET PRINT to Display a Server's Print Queue

The report is displayed when, at the DOS prompt, you type *NET PRINT* followed (on the same line) by \\ and the name of a server machine. For example, to see the queue on the machine called Server2, you type:

```
NET PRINT \\Server2
```

PC Network displays a heading and below it a report with one line for each of the jobs you submitted. The information in the report is identical to the information in the display generated from the menus, described next.

Report on a Server's Print Queue Generated from the Menus

To generate the display from within the menus, proceed as follows:

1. At the main menu, select *Printer or print queue tasks.*
2. At *Printer and print queue tasks,* select *Check print queue on another computer.*

PC Network displays a new screen headed *Check print queue on another computer* (see Figure 4.9). There's space for you to fill in the name of the server machine whose queue you want to examine. When you've filled that in, press Enter. PC Network displays as much of the queue as will fit in the previously blank area of the same screen. When the queue has more lines than fit in the space available, you can scroll with the PgUp and PgDn keys.

Interpreting the Queue Report

The rows of the report are sorted so that the numbers in the field headed Pos (for Position in queue) always appear in ascending order. When the numbers aren't consecutive, you can infer that other people have jobs in the queue.

The field headed ID is the three-digit job number that the queue manager assigned when you submitted the job. (Although job numbers have three digits and cycle from 000 to 999, the queue has room for no more than 99 jobs at a time.)

The field headed Size shows the number of bytes in each job.

The date and time are the date and time at which the server logged the jobs into its queue, according to the server's clock.

It's possible that you are using more than one network printer on the same server. The report doesn't show which printer a job was sent to.

```
                                                              IBM PC NETWORK
                   Check Print Queue on Another Computer

Computer name:  Server2

                  Pos ID  Size     Date      Time     Status
                               -- Start of Queue --
                  01  009      206 10/28/85 12:40:28 PRINTING
                  04  032    43828 10/28/85 16:12:36 WAITING
                  07  039     4801 10/28/85 17:01:14 WAITING
                               --  End of Queue  --





     PgUp and PgDn - Scroll list
     Enter - Redisplay queue                   F1 - Help
     Ctrl-Home - Return to Main Menu           Esc - Previous menu
■
```

Figure 4.9: *Menu screen for displaying user's print queue*

There May Be a Pause in Printer Operations

The operator of the server machine may arrange a pause in the activity that transfers jobs from the print queue to the printer (for example, to make adjustments to the machine or to run a job that requires local use of the printer on the server machine). A pause in that function does *not* stop PC Network from adding new requests to the queue. Presumably, a pause in printing is a temporary affair. Your report on the print queue on another machine does *not* show whether the printer is in a pause.

Interpreting the Status field

The field on the right (in Figure 4.9) reports the current status of each job. The terms that may appear there are as follows:

- *Printing:* The job has reached the top of the queue, and the queue manager has started to transfer it to the print buffer. It may actually be printing or about to start. However, if the printer isn't ready, no ink may yet have reached the paper, despite the confident message that it is printing. (The DOS command PRINT has a similar optimistic use of the word *printing.*)
- *Held:* The operator of the server machine has requested that the job be held. It will not be printed even if the printer is ready and there are no other jobs ahead of it. The print server will skip over a held job and search along the queue to the next job that isn't held. A job that is held remains so until the operator of the print queue manually releases it.
- *Waiting:* The job isn't at the top of the queue and isn't held.

There are three other terms that the person at the server machine may see but that don't appear in the report to a user. I mention them because you may hear the operator of the server machine use these terms:

- *Paused:* The printing function is in a pause (described earlier). Although the server machine can still accept new jobs to be printed, it is not at the moment transferring jobs from its temporary storage on the fixed disk to the printer.
- *Canceled:* The operator has requested cancellation, and the job is about to be interrupted and/or removed from the queue.

- *Error:* The program that manages the printer has tried to print the file, but has found it is unable to do so (perhaps because the printer isn't ready, or the file is damaged or can't be found).

Changing the Status of a Job in the Queue

Once you've submitted a job to a network printer, there's nothing more you can do about it directly. From then on, all power is in the hands of the operator of the server machine. If you need to make adjustments, the only avenue is to ask her nicely for what you want.

The operator can hold a job (delay it indefinitely), cancel it, or move it to the top of the queue. In an emergency, the operator has the power to direct the print server to start immediately on a job that's anywhere in the queue. Such a request may interrupt a job that is already printing. She does that by exercising an option called *Print Now* within the PC Network menu for managing the print queue. A job thus interrupted remains in the queue. When the print server returns to it, it ignores any portion of the job that may have been printed already and starts the job over from the beginning.

The operator does not have a command to shift a job to a different printer (although there are some maneuvers that would ultimately have that effect).

Reestablishing Use After Disconnect, Reset, or Failure

While you're using the resources of a server machine, there's a small but nonzero possibility that there will be an interruption of the link between the machines, or that either your machine or the server's will experience a failure. A communications failure might arise from a temporary disconnection of a cable or (on the broadband system) an interruption of power to the frequency translator. A machine failure might arise from an interruption of power to the machine, or a software error that paralyzes the machine until you press Ctrl-Alt-Del, or an error from which the only recovery is to turn off the power and start again.

Temporary Disconnection of the Communication Cable

The machines on the network are not in constant communication. They send messages to each other as needed. During an interval when your machine didn't ask anything of the server and the server did nothing that required a reply from your machine, the cable might be disconnected and reconnected without either machine noticing. So if you spot a disconnected communication cable at your machine, you might try putting it back. There's a chance you can continue work without interruption. Put it back before you ask your machine for a report on devices you are using, since asking for the report may call attention to the disconnection.

If your machine or the server attempt any use of the network while your machine's cable is disconnected, the first symptom you'll see may be a message such as *NET807: Network adapter hardware error* (a message that can refer to a disconnected cable as well as other more serious problems). When the server notices that your machine is not responding, it acts as if you had requested to terminate your use of the shared resource. You may see the message *NET815: Network name was deleted* followed by a general description of how this was noticed.

Following either of those conditions, your machine sets the status of the network devices you were using as *error.* Once the Error status has been set, the only way you can recover is to delete your request to use those devices and then request them anew (see You Must Delete Before You Can Reconnect, below).

When Only One Machine Fails

When your machine fails but the server does not, each server you were using treats your disappearance as if you had voluntarily discontinued use. Each server closes any files you left open and frees any interlocks on them that your programs may have set.

When a server fails, as soon as your machine attempts to interact with the server it notices that the server is not there. Your machine lists the status of all devices you were using on that server as *error.*

The Report on Devices You Are Using Shows Which Devices Have Error Status

The report on network disks, directories, or devices you are using (described earlier in this chapter) has a field for the status of each device. This field shows *error* as the status of each network device on a machine that is no longer functioning.

The internal table on which the report is based is not updated until your machine has occasion to use one of the network devices or runs the routine check scheduled at the end of each program or DOS command. There may be some brief delay between failure of the server and the posting of *error* in this display.

You Must Delete Before You Can Reconnect

Once your machine lists the status of a network device as *error,* you have no choice but to go through a recovery process that has two steps—and perhaps a wait between them. The steps are:

1. Either in the menus or by way of the NET USE command, delete each of the network disks, directories, or printers that you were using but whose status is now reported as *error.*
2. Make a new request to take up each of the server's offers of a network device you want to use.

When the error arose because the server didn't hear from your machine and signed you off, the server's original offer to share is probably still open, and you can execute step 2 at once.

When the error arose because the server really crashed, you have to delay step 2 until the server has been restarted and has again made the necessary offers to share.

Exchanging Messages

Five

PC Network provides a facility for exchanging short messages between computers. This chapter describes how to use it. There is a command for sending messages (NET SEND) and also a handy full-screen facility for preparing outgoing messages and viewing messages received. It's possible for an individual to adopt additional names under which to receive messages and to forward incoming messages to another computer.

Why Messages Are Important

Networking often requires both cooperation and sharing of information. You can't make use of resources available to you over the network unless you know what they are, where they are, and what they're called. PC Network assumes that the human users—or some leader among them—will set up procedures that permit people to share. The network itself doesn't maintain a central directory of what's available. To make good use of PC Network, users need to agree on conventions or create a shared file (perhaps even a paper memo!) to describe what's availabe. In addition, users are likely to find it convenient to send brief messages quickly and easily.

The Message Facility Is Not Electronic Mail

First, what the message facility is not: it isn't what you'd ordinarily call an electronic mail system. It's electronic, and it sends messages, but the term *electronic mail* implies something more elaborate. In particular, *electronic mail* usually implies that you can send a message whether or not the recipient is at the moment signed on to the network. PC Network has all the facilities from which to build an electronic mail system. But its message facility is more like an office intercom: handy or even indispensable for brief exchanges, but not the same thing as mail. For one thing, a message can be received only by a machine that's currently using the network.

Message Powers of the Various Configurations

This section briefly describes the message-handling options of the various network configurations (see Figure 5.1). The rest of this chapter describes them in greater detail.

Anyone Can Send, but Not All Can Receive

In all four configurations, you can send messages—either by the NET SEND command or from the message editor in the menus. Receiving is another matter. There are three different levels of support for incoming messages, depending on the configuration you're using.

You can receive messages if you're in the receiver, messenger, or server configuration. But if your machine is running the minimum redirector configuration (RDR), you can't receive messages. Someone who tries to send you a message gets the response *NET801: Computer not listening.*

Option to Save in a Log File

In any of the three configurations that can receive messages, you can have PC Network intercept the messages as they come in and append them to what is called a *log file.* While messages are being saved in a log file, PC Network emits four beeps each time a message arrives, but doesn't otherwise interrupt your work.

Network-Request Key for Instant Handling of Incoming Messages

In the messenger and server configurations only, you have the network-request key. In these configurations, PC Network provides a buffer in which it can hold incoming messages for you temporarily, without writing them to a file. Any time a message comes in, but only while you are neither diverting messages to a log nor working in the network menus, PC Network immediately signals the message's arrival by superimposing on the center of your screen a box containing the words *Message from* and the name of the sending computer. You press the network-request key (Ctrl-Alt-Break) to see the message at once, or Ctrl-Break to leave it in the buffer for inspection later in the session. Either way, PC Network restores what was on your screen previously and returns you to what you were doing.

Menu Screen to View Messages

In the messenger and server configurations only, the PC Network menus include a viewing screen on which you can display incoming messages. It handles both messages held in the incoming-message buffer and messages saved in the log file. When you press the network-request key in response to a *Message from* signal, you go directly to the view screen. Once at the view screen, you can switch back and forth to the send screen to send a reply if you wish. It's a handy arrangement!

	Redirector	Receiver	Messenger	Server
Sending				
Command to send message	Yes	Yes	Yes	Yes
Editor screen to send message	Yes	Yes	Yes	Yes
Receiving				
Log file for incoming messages	No	Yes	Yes	Yes
Buffer for incoming messages plus network-request key to signal immediate display	No	No	Yes	Yes
Screen to view buffered messages or messages saved in log file	No	No	Yes	Yes

Figure 5.1: *Message powers by network configuration*

Incoming Messages at the Receiver Configuration

As far as incoming messages are concerned, when you're in the receiver configuration (RCV), you're a poor relation. Since the receiver configuration lacks a message buffer, PC Network has no place to hold incoming messages. If you don't elect to save messages in a log file, PC Network writes them on your screen immediately upon receipt, on top of whatever was there before. I hope you have a way to refresh the screen afterwards, because in this configuration PC Network doesn't. You'd better divert messages to a log file! The receiver configuration also lacks a message-viewing screen, so it's up to you to display what's in the log file and discard old messages.

NET SEND: The Command That Sends a Message

You can send a message by using the message facility's screen editor and formatter, or (provided the message is brief) by using the NET SEND command. To use the command, you have to be at the DOS prompt or at the menus' command screen (reachable by pressing F2).

The command NET SEND must be followed (on the same line) by one word indicating the addressee and (still on the same line) the message. Blanks separate the name of the addressee from the command and the text of the message. For example, to send the message *The monthend file is ready now. Paul* to the computer named Barry, at the DOS prompt (here shown as C:\>) you type:

```
C:\> NET SEND Barry The monthend file is ready now. Paul
```

DOS doesn't care whether characters in the command and the name of the addressee are in caps or lowercase. In the text of the message itself, it preserves the characters in the message text exactly as you've typed them. The length of the message you can send with the NET SEND command is limited by the amount that DOS will let you type in a single entry: around 130 characters (including blanks). However, using the message-sending screen described below, you can write messages as long as 1600 characters. (The default maximum can be reset to 60,000 characters.)

Assuming the network can deliver the message, the NET SEND command displays a confirmation immediately below your entry: *Message sent . . . and successfully received.*

As you'll see in this chapter, *successfully received* doesn't necessarily mean that the message has been read, only that the network has confirmation that the message has reached the addressee's machine.

Appearance of the Message at the Receiver's End

Assuming that the machine from which you sent this message has the network name Server2, and that the clock on the machine called Barry gives the time as 1:30 in the afternoon, at the receiving end the message contains the following text:

```
MESSAGE FROM SERVER2 TO BARRY AT 13:30
The monthend file is ready now. Paul
```

Names to Which a Message Can Be Addressed

When you send a message, you address it either to *one* name on the network, or to *****, which means all computers now on the network and able to receive messages. (Messages to all computers are limited to 128 characters.)

When it starts the network, each computer must adopt a unique name for itself. You can always address a message to a computer by using its unique computer name. Each computer also has the option to adopt one or more *additional names* under which to receive messages. You may want to add a personal name at the computer you're using so people can address a message to you rather than to the machine.

The Message Editor/Viewer

PC Network contains a module for preparing and viewing messages. IBM doesn't seem to have a name for this module, but I'll refer to it as the *message editor/viewer,* or just editor/viewer, for short. It maintains two screens:

- The *edit* screen, or *send* screen on which you prepare and send an outgoing message.
- The *view* screen, on which you view incoming or filed messages. (When you're running PC Network in the redirector configuration, you can't use the view screen.)

While you're on either screen, pressing F4 switches you to the other. When you're writing a reply to an incoming message, this permits you to flip back and forth, looking at the message you received and working on your reply. The use of these two screens is described in more detail later in this chapter.

Entering the Message Editor/Viewer

There are two ways to enter the message editor/viewer. Which you use depends on which network configuration you're using and where you are at the time:

1. When you're already in the menus, select *Message tasks* and then either *Send messages* or *View received messages.* The only difference between these two routes is which of the two screens you see first.
2. When PC Network notifies you of an incoming message and you're not in the menus, press Ctrl-Alt-Break (the network-request key) to view the message, or Ctrl-Break to let the message wait. (You don't have to remember which key signals which action; the notice reminds you.) If you press the network-request key, it takes you immediately to the view screen of the editor/viewer.

Once at the view screen by either route, you can switch back and forth between viewing and receiving, regardless of how you started.

(The network-request key is available only in the messenger and server configurations, but those are the only configurations in which PC Network flashes a note on your screen to inform you of an incoming message.)

Exit from the Editor/Viewer

When you're finished with the editor/viewer, you press either Escape or Ctrl-Home to exit. (The program asks you to press again to confirm that you want to exit.)

When you use Escape to exit, you return to wherever you came from. If you got to the editor/viewer from the *Message tasks* menu, that's where you return. But if you got there by pressing the network-request key in response to a *Message from* notice, you return to whatever screen you were looking at then.

When you use Ctrl-Home to exit, you jump directly to the main menu. If you got to the message viewer from the *Message tasks* menu, Ctrl-Home takes you back to the main menu without going back through *Message tasks.* If you got there by pressing the network-request key in response to a *Message from* notice, this also brings you to the main menu, and from there to any of the other menus. When you eventually exit from the menus, you return to the application screen you were originally looking at.

Using the Editor/Viewer

As soon as you enter the editor/viewer, you see a screen divided into three parts. In a broad band across the center of each screen, set off by horizontal bars, is an 11-line zone that IBM has intentionally left blank. Here you write your message or the viewer displays messages you've been sent.

Sending

Figure 5.2 shows the screen on which you edit a message and send it. Across the top is the header zone in which you write the network name of your addressee. In the center is the space where you compose and edit your message. Below the message area are labels for the three or four keys that are active while you're using the editor. (The fourth, switch to the view screen, is defined only for the messenger and server configurations.)

First, the Addressee

When you reach the send screen, you start by filling in your message's destination. The program won't let you compose the body of the message until you've filled this in.

The addressee must be a name known to the network, either as the computer name of one of the PCs or as one of the additional names that may receive messages. You have to address your message either to one name or to all computers. You indicate that a message is for all computers by an asterisk in the addressee field.

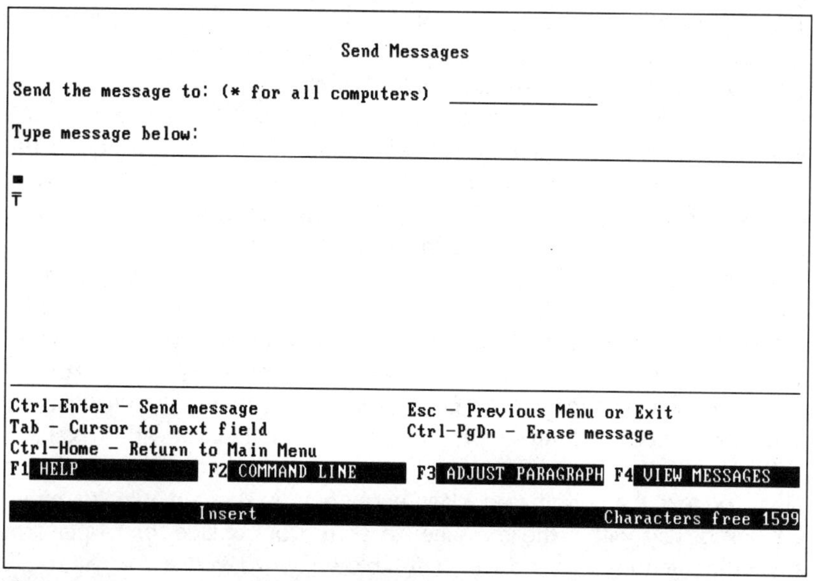

Figure 5.2: *Screen for editing messages to be sent*

When you've filled in the addressee, press Tab to take you to the message area.

Editing in the Send Screen's Message Area

You have at your disposal a simple editor. You can move the cursor around the screen by pressing the arrow keys at the right of the keyboard. Pressing Home takes you to the start of the line you're now on, and pressing End to the end of the line you're now on. The Delete key deletes the character at the cursor, and the Insert key switches you back and forth between the *insert* mode, in which new text is inserted at the cursor position while old text is pushed to the right, and the *overwrite* mode, in which new text is typed over old text and replaces it.

You can see on the screen a down-pointing triangle, which serves as an end-of-message marker. At first, it's on the second row of the screen. As you write, your message pushes the marker down.

While you're on the send screen editing a message, the Enter key acts solely to start a new line, moving the cursor to the beginning of the line thus created. Here, the Enter key does *not* send the message, although in most other contexts that's its role.

Paragraphing and Reformatting

When your typing bumps into the right edge of the screen, the editor automatically pulls the entire word you are writing onto the line below. Thus, you don't need to press Enter (Return) until you actually end a paragraph. Your lines automatically fold at the screen edge and break at a word end. However, the automatic pull-down works only when the word you are typing itself straddles the right edge of the screen. If you move the cursor back and insert additional characters earlier in the line, the line simply gets longer, so you can't see all of it on the screen at once. (Even if you transmit your message that way, your addressee receives it reformatted to fit within the width of the screen.)

As you make insertions or deletions in a paragraph, it may end up looking ragged, with some short lines and perhaps some lines wider than the screen. Pressing F3 reformats the line the cursor is on and all following lines in the same paragraph. The program has a rule of thumb to help it decide how far a paragraph extends. It reformats all lines until it comes to an empty line or a line that starts with a blank.

There's no provision in this mini-editor to copy into your message a block of text that originated elsewhere. Nor is there a way to move a block of text within the message, to search or replace, or to perform any other actions common in a full-blown word processor. After all, you're only composing telegrams.

Sending the Finished Message

When you've written what you want to say and completed any corrections, you send the message by pressing Ctrl-Enter. On the next-to-last line of your screen, you'll see a display indicating what PC Network was able to do with your message. The addressee and the message text remain on your screen unchanged (so you could send the message again, or alter the address or the text and send a variation of the one you just sent). If you want to send a quite different message, clear the message text area by pressing Ctrl-PgDn.

Switching to the View Screen

Press F4. That doesn't discard your send screen, but sets it aside while you move to the view screen. (However, the receiver configuration doesn't have a view screen for its incoming messages, and the redirector can't receive messages at all, so neither of them can use the viewer, and for them F4 does nothing.)

Exit from the Editor

Pressing Escape takes you back to wherever you came from. It discards the contents both of your send screen and of your view screen (if you had one).

Viewing

The view screen is offered only in the messenger and server configurations. You may reach the view screen directly or by switching to it from the send screen. Either way, its behavior is the same. Figure 5.3 shows a view screen.

PC Network uses the zone at the top of the screen to show the computer name of the PC from which the message was sent, the name of the addressee, and the time (on the receiver's clock) when the message was received. An incoming message that has been saved in the log file also shows the date it was received.

You can't type anything on the view screen. You do everything by pressing the function keys. Their action is summarized in the lower panel of the display and described more fully in Figure 5.4.

Saving Messages: the NET LOG Command

At the receiving end, PC Network has three ways of dealing with an incoming message. Depending on the configuration you're using and the options you elect, you may:

- See the message displayed at once, as soon as the machine receives it (added to or superimposed on the current display).
- Hear a signal and see a display indicating that a message has arrived and then decide whether to look at it now or see it later in the session.
- Hear only a beep signal to show that a message has arrived, because incoming messages are being automatically spooled to a file for later inspection.

Saving in the Log File

For all the configurations that can receive messages, PC Network gives you the option to intercept incoming messages and append them to a file. Within the menus, PC Network refers to this as *saving* messages. Curiously, the command to create a file for saving is called LOG (rather than SAVE, which doesn't exist).

Functions of the NET LOG Command

The NET LOG command can:

- Name a file or device to serve as your log, and start logging messages to it

```
MESSAGE FROM SACHIKO TO PAUL AT 13:12                              IBM PC NETWORK
                                          View Messages

 Press F3 to view waiting messages
 Press F6 to view next saved messages

 ------------------------------------------------------------------------------
 I've got the text part of the proposal ready. Do you have the budget pages?
 Could you put them in a file where I can see them and let me know where they
 are? I'll attach the budget, and then send it all to the daisy printer.

 Don't forget we need this in the mail by 4:30...                          S
 T



 ------------------------------------------------------------------------------
 Esc - Previous menu or Exit            Ctrl-Home - Return to Main Menu
 Ctrl-PgUp - Delete saved message       Ctrl-PgDn - Erase viewed message
 F1 HELP             F2 COMMAND LINE    F3 VIEW NEXT WAITING F4 SEND MESSAGE
 F5 VIEW FIRST SAVED F6 VIEW NEXT SAVED F7 SAVE MESSAGE      F8 PRINT MESSAGE
```

Figure 5.3: *Screen for viewing received messages*

- Copy an existing log file to the printer
- Stop saving further messages in the log file or resume doing so
- Report the current situation regarding logging

Starting to Save Messages in a Log File

Using the menus, you do this in the following four-step sequence. *Watch out:* The last step requires the DOS name of a file. If you were at one time saving messages and now you're resuming, PC Network will show you the name of the file you were using, and you can just assent. But if PC Network has no record of a former log file, it's going to ask you to supply a file name. So you'd better be ready with an answer before you embark on this sequence.

Key	Action
F1	Help. Describes the definitions of the other function keys.
F2	Command. This is the command screen accessible from almost all the menus. While you're in the viewer, if you need to create a log file in which to save messages, you can do so by pressing F2 and then executing NET LOG (described later in this chapter).
F3	View the earliest message in the message buffer and delete it from the buffer. (To save the message into your log file, press F7 while the message is on the screen.)
F4	Switch to the send screen, without discarding what is on the view screen.
F5	View the first of the messages in the log file.
F6	View the next message in the log file. (When you haven't yet displayed a message from the log file, start with the first.)
F7	Append the message now on the screen to the log file. (If you don't have a log file, you can create one; see the note for F2.)
F8	Copy the message now on the screen to the printer.

Figure 5.4: *Function keys while you're using the message viewer*

1. At the main menu, select *Message tasks.*
2. At *Message tasks,* select *Start or stop saving messages.*
3. At *Start or stop saving messages,* select *Start.*
4. At *Save messages in filename or DOS device,* fill in the name of the file in which you want messages saved.

For example, if you decide that you want the log file to be called Msg.log on your disk drive B, when you see the prompt, fill in the reply *b:\Msg.log.* Naming a file that doesn't yet exist causes PC Network to create it as an empty file.

Using commands, you can achieve the same result (at the DOS prompt or the command line within a menu screen) by typing:

```
NET LOG b:\Msg.log
```

In either case, the command both specifies the name of the file and starts using it to log incoming messages.

Duration of the Message Log Status

When you have executed NET LOG with the name of a file, PC Network retains the name of that file throughout the work session, whether or not you actually save anything in it. However, PC Network will carry that information over to a subsequent session only if you use the menu option to *Save your network setup* after you have executed NET LOG, or you take steps of your own to insert the NET LOG command in your file Autoexec.bat.

"Saving" to an Output Device

It's legal—but perhaps not so convenient—to specify the name not of a file but of an output device. For example, *NET LOG PRN* routes any incoming messages directly to the printer. Using CON as the name of the destination routes the messages directly to the console, where they appear at the cursor position, perhaps after or perhaps overwriting the current display. These may not be convenient choices, but they're possible and sometimes appropriate. If you attempt to use the editor/viewer to look at saved messages when they've been sent to a destination such as CON or PRN (console or printer), not surprisingly you'll find the editor/viewer can't read them for you. It protests with the message *NET278: Cannot access save file.*

Saving to a Network Device

It's also legal to name as your log file an output device or a file that isn't on your own machine, but is available to you over the network from a server machine. This is legal but possibly imprudent. If people are sending you messages because there's something you need to know, having the message spooled to a printer somewhere else may be inconvenient. Saving messages to a shared disk file isn't so inconvenient, but—like all network operations—does make you dependent on the continued availability of the server machine.

Suspending the Saving of Messages

You can tell PC Network not to divert any more messages to the log file. When you've done that, it attempts some more immediate means of delivery, described in the next section. The suspension lasts until you reverse it or the end of the session, whichever comes sooner. Unless you elect to *Save your network setup,* next time you start the network the log status reverts to whatever it was when you last saved the setup.

Telling PC Network not to save messages doesn't erase the log file, nor does it delete PC Network's record of the log file's name (stored as part of a NET LOG command in your file Autoexec.bat). You can still ask to see messages already in the file. When you later ask to resume saving messages, PC Network will again refer to its record of your log file's name.

Within the menus, you instruct PC Network no longer to save messages by the following sequence:

1. At the main menu, select *Message tasks.*
2. At *Message tasks,* select *Start or stop saving messages.*
3. At *Start or stop saving messages,* select *Stop.*

Using commands, you can achieve the same result (at the DOS prompt or the command screen) by combining the parameter *off* with the NET LOG command. This follows the DOS convention that in a command a parameter is preceded by a slash. You suspend saving to the log file by typing:

```
NET LOG /off
```

You might want to designate a log file but delay using it. For some reason PC Network won't let you name a file and suspend its use in the same command: it objects to *NET LOG b:Msg.log /off* (even though it doesn't mind *NET LOG b:Msg.log /on*). You'll have to make that two commands.

Resume Saving Messages to a Log File

Within the menus, you instruct PC Network to resume saving messages by the following sequence:

1. At the main menu, select *Message tasks.*
2. At *Message tasks,* select *Start or stop saving messages.*

3. At *Start or stop saving messages,* select *Start.*
4. PC Network shows you the prompt *Save messages in filename or DOS device* and then fills in for you as a suggestion the name of the file you were previously using to log messages. If the name is still appropriate, just press Enter. If you want to substitute the name of some other file (already existing or not), edit the name that PC Network has displayed to the name you want and press Enter.

Using commands (at the DOS prompt or the command menu screen), you resume saving to a previously declared log file by typing:

```
NET LOG /on
```

You resume saving, but to a different log file, by using NET LOG with the name of the new file (just as if you were starting a log file for the first time):

```
NET LOG b:\Newlog.msg
```

Reporting the Current Situation of Save/Log

Curiously, the menus don't provide a way for you to review whether you're currently set to save messages, and if so, to what file they'll be logged. But it's simple enough to review your save/log status with commands. At the DOS prompt or the command menu, type *NET LOG.* That causes PC Network to display a two-column table showing whether you are saving messages and the name of your log file. An example appears as Figure 5.5.

When the status is *off* and PC Network has no record of a previous log file—because, for example, you never elected to *Save your network setup* while using a log file—the field for the name of the log file is left blank.

When you're already in the menus, you can write the NET LOG command by the following sequence. (If you're already at one of the later steps in the sequence, proceed from there.)

1. At the main menu, select *Message tasks.*
2. At *Message tasks,* select *Send* or *View.*
3. At the editor/viewer, press F2 (*command screen*).
4. At the command screen, at the prompt *NET,* fill in *LOG.*

Where Incoming Messages Are Stored

PC Network has two places to store an incoming message: in the log file you have designated and in its own message buffer (which is allocated space from main memory). The buffer is available only in the messenger or server configuration.

The Incoming-Message Buffer

If you haven't arranged to divert incoming messages to a file, your machine holds them in the incoming-message buffer reserved for that purpose. The size of that buffer is controlled by the start-up parameter MBI. You can set it explicitly as part of your start-up procedure (for example, if you're trying either to save space in main memory or to allow lots of room for messages; see Chapter 13).

The default size of the incoming message buffer is 1750 bytes, which is enough to hold about ten one-line messages and their accompanying overhead. If you have a wordy correspondent who sends you a message of the maximum length (1600 characters), that'll use up the entire default buffer.

An Incoming Message That Isn't Filed and Won't Fit in Your Buffer

If somebody sends you a message at a time when you are not saving messages to a file and your incoming-message buffer has no room to hold the message, the sender gets the warning *NET035: Message sent but not received.* However (sad to say), when you're the addressee of

```
C:\> net log

 NET LOG
 Status        Name of Log File
 ------------------------------
 OFF           B:\MSG.LOG

■
```

Figure 5.5: *Report on network message log*

such an undeliverable message, your machine doesn't tell you anything, so you won't get the hint either to make some room by reading the messages already in your buffer or to make the buffer bigger next time you start the network.

Lifespan of Buffered and Logged Messages

When you use the editor/viewer, you can read messages from the buffer in the order in which they were received. As soon as you've read one message, PC Network deletes it from the message buffer. You get just one chance to see it. (However, while you have the message on the screen, you can if you wish transfer it to the file you're using for saved messages; details in a moment.)

The incoming-message buffer is strictly a temporary arrangement. If you reset the computer (Ctrl-Alt-Del) or turn off the power without reading those messages, they're gone.

Messages saved in the log file are more durable. The message editor/viewer lets you browse (in sequence) through the log file of saved messages as much as you like. It doesn't erase a message until you explicitly ask that it be erased. You erase a message from the log by bringing it up on the view screen and then pressing Ctrl-PgUp.

When you're not in the menus or are using the receiver configuration (which has no view screen), you can use any standard text editor to prune the file. To separate messages, PC Network inserts a line consisting of four asterisks. You could even use the DOS command ERASE to delete the entire file. If PC Network can't find the file to which you were saving messages, it puts messages in the incoming-message buffer.

NET NAME: Aliases for Receiving Messages

Additional names are useful as a way of distinguishing between the *person* you want to address and the *machine* at which the person is sitting. You might also want to adopt different names to match different roles you play; you could read at once messages addressed to you under one name and read at leisure those addressed to another name. Sometimes you may want to get in touch with whoever is managing the printer queue just now. Other times you may want to contact Susan, wherever she happens to be.

The issue is likely to arise when you need to send a message to someone located at a server machine. Servers tend to have names that refer to the machine, whereas users tend to have names that refer to the person regardless of which machine she's using.

Suppose that today Susan is not at her usual spot but is instead at the machine known as PrintServer1. The machine has to keep that name because that's how its various users refer to it. Susan can still receive messages intended for her by declaring that *Susan* is an additional name for the machine PrintServer1.

Like machine names, additional names must also be unique. PC Network won't let you declare an additional name if anyone else on the network is already using it. Additional names are used only for receiving and forwarding messages.

Adopting an Additional Name

Within the menus, you declare an additional name (or names) under which you'll receive messages by the following sequence.

1. At the main menu, select *Message tasks.*
2. At *Message tasks,* select *Start or stop receiving messages for another name.*
3. At *Start or stop receiving messages for another name,* select *Start.*
4. At the prompt *Start receiving messages for:* fill in a name.

The name you propose may have up to 15 characters and must be a single word (no blanks). The screen on which you enter the name won't let you write characters that are not permitted in a name. PC Network verifies that the name is not already in use on the network. Apart from that, the name can be whatever you like. Presumably, there's no sense in doing this unless you reveal the name you've adopted to someone else on the network and that person addresses a message to it.

You adopt the additional name *Susan* by typing (at the DOS prompt or in the menus' command screen):

```
NET NAME Susan
```

Enthusiasts of CB radio may have more experience in dreaming up "handles" by which they'll receive messages.

Reporting the Names You've Declared for Yourself

Within the menus, you can review your machine's computer name and the additional names you have adopted by the following sequence:

1. At the main menu, select *Message tasks.*
2. At *Message tasks,* select *Display names which can receive messages at your computer.*

PC Network displays a list of the names, starting with your machine's computer name. For each, it lists whether the name is a computer name or an additional name. The report also shows names forwarded to or from your computer. (See the discussion of forwarding later in this chapter.)

Using commands (at the DOS prompt or the command menu screen), you get the same report of names in use at your computer by typing:

```
NET NAME
```

Group Names

Although version 1.0 of PC Network does not offer *group names,* IBM has published standards for them. A group name is a name used as an additional name by several computers. It is thus exempt from the requirement that network names be unique. When several machines adopt the same group name, all receive any message addressed to the group. For example, the users of the letter-quality printer might adopt a group name to receive messages about that printer, but people who aren't interested wouldn't have to see those messages.

The group name facility seems so simple and so handy that it's likely to be included in a later release of PC Network.

Forwarding Messages

As you move temporarily from one machine to another, you may want to have messages that are addressed to you rerouted so that you receive them at a new machine. Message forwarding does that.

Suppose that your name is Susan and most of the time you use a machine known to the network as PrintServer1. You have registered *Susan* as an additional name for PrintServer1, so that machine receives messages addressed to PrintServer1 and messages addressed to Susan.

For an hour or two you expect to be working with Albert at his machine, which is called *Albert.* You'd like to have messages addressed to Susan delivered to the machine called Albert instead of to the machine called PrintServer1. However, you must leave unchanged the delivery of messages addressed to PrintServer1.

Solution: At PrintServer1, you ask to have messages for Susan forwarded to Albert. Within the menus, you can do that by the following sequence:

1. At the main menu, select *Message tasks.*
2. At *Message tasks,* select *Start or stop forwarding messages.*
3. At *Start or stop forwarding messages,* select *Start.*

4. Fill in the two fields. Figure 5.6 shows such a screen (together with PC Network's response, which doesn't show until after you've pressed Enter).

Notice that in order to forward messages, you don't have to identify the machine to which the messages should be sent. It's sufficient to identify a name on another computer. The request shown in Figure 5.6 says messages for Susan should go to the machine that receives messages for Albert.

Using commands (at the DOS prompt or the command menu screen), to get the same effect as the screen shown in Figure 5.6, type:

NET FORWARD Susan Albert

What Forwarding Really Does

When you execute a forwarding command such as *NET FORWARD Susan Albert,* what happens is this:

1. Your machine sends out a message addressed to whatever machine is now receiving messages for Albert. (It doesn't matter whether *Albert* is a computer name or an additional name.) The message requests that machine to add *Susan* to its list of additional names.
2. The machine that is receiving messages for Albert tells your

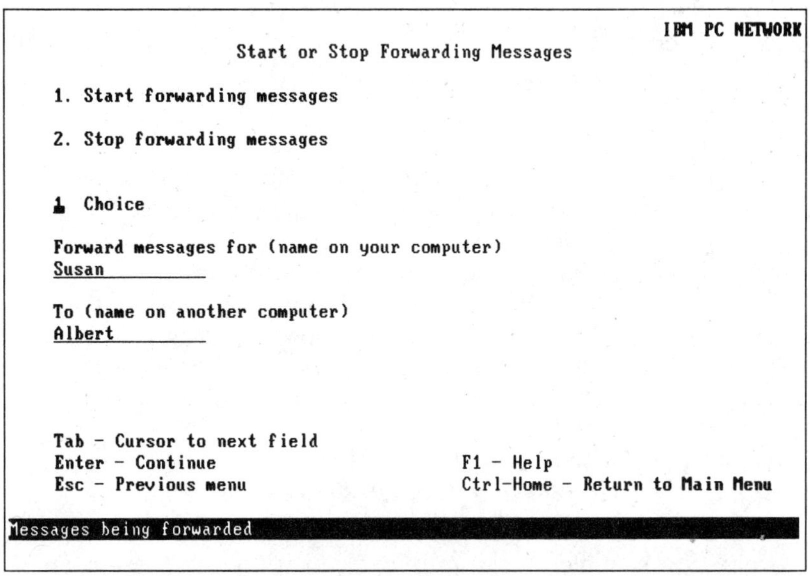

Figure 5.6: *Screen for forwarding messages*

machine whether it is able to add the name Susan. (If it lacks space in its table of additional names, it has to refuse; you get the message *Net078: Remote computer cannot receive messages for any more names.*)

3. Assuming it gets an OK from Albert's machine, your machine removes the name Susan from its active list of names to listen for.

In sum, having verified that some other machine will be listening for messages to Susan, your machine stops listening for them.

More or less the same effect would be obtained if you deleted Susan from the list of additional names at PrintServer1, and then added Susan to the list at Albert's machine. However, forwarding does a bit more than that, since the machine called PrintServer1 keeps a record of the fact that Susan was once one of its names but is for the moment forwarded to the machine called Albert; similarly, the machine called Albert keeps a record showing that the reason Susan now appears in its list of alternate names is that it was forwarded from PrintServer1.

Halt Forwarding

Forwarding requires both parties to be willing: the machine from which messages are diverted and the machine that receives them. Either side can end the arrangement. The forwarder does it by canceling the request to forward. The receiver does it by removing the forwarded name from its list of additional names.

Posthumous Forwarding

When the machine that requested forwarding goes off the network (for example, when its operator turns off the power or presses Ctrl-Alt-Del), forwarding remains in effect.

Although the process is called forwarding, a forwarded message never really goes to the machine that requested forwarding. Rather, the process works because a different machine is now accepting the message. The message—like all network communications—circulates through the network's cables until it reaches a machine that claims it.

Forwarding Is Automatically Canceled When the Receiving Machine Goes off the Network

If the machine to which messages are being forwarded goes off the network (for example, because its operator turns off the power or presses Ctrl-Alt-Del), the original addressee's machine again claims the messages. Thus, when it's no longer physically possible to deliver a message at the forwarded address, it is delivered to the original destination.

No Notification to the Sender When a Message Is Forwarded

PC Network doesn't notify you when a message you send is forwarded. Nor does it tell you when forwarding reverts to the original destination. When your message reaches a machine that claims it, you get the confirmation *successfully delivered,* but PC Network doesn't specify at what machine that was.

Forwarding Already in Effect When You Restart Your Machine

Suppose you have arranged that messages addressed to your machine are forwarded to Albert. When your machine goes off the network, Albert continues to receive messages addressed to your machine.

Then you restart PC Network on your own machine, using the same computer name as before. The network detects that messages for your computer are being received somewhere else, and asks you whether you want to cancel the forwarding or leave it in effect.

PAUSE: Suspending Network Participation

Six

PC Network provides commands that let you suspend some of its functions and later resume work. During the suspension, the network configuration you have started remains resident even though parts of it become inactive. The various tables remain resident too, so the machine retains its lists of such things as your name on the network or the names of resources you've shared or offered. When you're ready to reactivate the functions you suspended, there's no need to restate the names involved.

Suspension doesn't withdraw your offers to share or your requests to use network resources. It just temporarily disables them.

The command to suspend one or more network functions is NET PAUSE. The command to resume is NET CONTINUE. This chapter explains their use.

Reasons to Pause

The significance of a pause in your machine's participation in the network depends on the role you're playing. While you're a user, suspending is a personal matter, meaning only that you've decided to drop out for a while and return to local resources rather than those you've been using over the network. But while you're playing the server role, suspending services that you've offered to the network may have a serious effect on other people.

I have not found many occasions that require a suspension of network activities. The most common seem to be problems that arise while managing a shared printer. Other items on the list that follows are possible, but might also be handled without pausing.

- You have an old program that refers to drive A, so you've made A the name of a virtual drive on the network. But then you need to copy something from your real drive A. You suspend redirection (and thus the virtual meaning of A) long enough to copy what you need.
- You're running test jobs on a printer and want to see the output page by page (rather than as whole jobs in a queue). You suspend both the redirection of your print requests and the printing of jobs from the network queue so that the printer returns to your direct control while you make your tests.
- You need to change the ribbon on a network printer. You suspend printing from the network queue while you make the change. (On some printers, merely deselecting the printer without telling PC Network also works.)
- You wish to be free of messages while showing a program to a client. You suspend receiving messages.
- You've run out of disk space on a server machine. After arranging with those already using its directories to close any files they have open, you briefly suspend the machine's server function. That halts all network use of directories you've shared while you move or delete enough files to ease the crisis.

What Can Be Suspended

Suspension applies to broad activities, not to specific paths, devices, or names. You can name the activity (or activities) you wish to suspend when you type the NET PAUSE command, or you can select them from the network menus. The following are the activities that can be suspended. (The terms in parentheses may be used to name them in the commands NET PAUSE and NET CONTINUE.)

- Disk redirection (DRDR): your machine's use of directories on other machines
- Print redirection (PRDR): your machine's use of the network print queue
- Printing (Print or PRT): your machine's transfer of files from the network print spool to printers or to a specific printer on your machine
- Messages (Messenger or MSG; or Receiver or RCV): your machine's reception of incoming messages
- Serving (Server or SRV): your machine's processing of incoming requests from the network

(Note that the word *Print* occurs in the NET PAUSE and NET CONTINUE commands as the name of an activity that can be suspended, distinct from its use in the DOS command PRINT or the network command NET PRINT.)

Disk Redirection: DRDR

Disk redirection is the process by which DOS discovers that you have referred to a disk, directory, or file that must be accessed through the network, and relays your request to the network. Redirection deals with actions that originate with your machine and go from there to the network. Disk redirection covers everything you can request to use by the NET USE command *except* printers.

When you suspend disk redirection, all names for disk drives, paths, directories, or files revert to their local meanings: they're understood with respect to your own machine. If a name refers to something on your own machine, that's what's used. If it doesn't, DOS rejects the command, just as it would if you had never started the network, with a message such as *Invalid drive specification* or *Invalid path or file name.*

Print Redirection: PRDR

Print redirection is the process by which DOS discovers you have referred to a printer that must be accessed through the network and transmits your output to the server's printer spool. The process is exactly parallel to disk redirection. However, disk redirection and print redirection are handled separately and can be suspended or resumed independently.

When you suspend print redirection, all the standard DOS names for print devices are understood with respect to your own machine. If a name applies to a device on your machine, the output goes to that device. If not, DOS deals with the output just as it would if you had never started the network, perhaps with a message such as *Device not ready* or *Write fault error,* depending on the circumstances.

When you're playing the role of server and have shared a printer with the network, print redirection is a bit more complicated. When you stop redirecting your own output to the network print queue, your output has to go directly to the printer. But you've ceded control of your printer to the network print-queue manager. So when you suspend print redirection on a server machine, PC Network also suspends the background task that transfers jobs from the printer spool.

Printing from the Network Print Queue: Print or PRT

Network printing is a two-stage affair. First a job is transferred from the user's machine to the printer spool on the server. Then the job is transferred from the spool to the printer. When you offer to share a printer with the network, you set in motion a background task that transfers jobs from the print queue to the printer. That transfer is halted when you suspend the *print* function. The command

```
NET PAUSE Print
```

suspends all output from the network spool. You can also name a specific printer:

```
NET PAUSE Print=LPT1
```

That causes the print manager to skip over jobs for the suspended printer but continue to process jobs for other printers.

Watch out: Suspension takes effect at once. If a job affected by the suspension has started, the printer interrupts it. The job remains in the queue as if its printing had never started. When you resume printing, the job takes its turn with the other jobs in the queue and is printed again from the beginning.

The process of accepting jobs into the print queue is not affected by a suspension of the print function—except, of course, that if you suspend output while input keeps coming, the queue is going to get longer and longer.

While the print function is suspended, you can still manage the queue (for example, hold jobs, cancel jobs, move jobs to the head of the queue). Users can still inquire about the position of their jobs in the queue.

Message Reception: Messenger or MSG; Receiver or RCV

You can suspend receiving messages. While reception is suspended, someone who tries to send you a message is told *NET034: Message sent but message reception paused.*

When you suspend reception with the NET PAUSE command, you have to suspend the activity that goes with the configuration you're using. If you started the network in the server or the messenger configuration, you have to say *NET PAUSE Messenger,* whereas if you started the network in the receiver configuration, you have to say *NET PAUSE Receiver.*

The menus are more tolerant. In all the configurations that can receive messages, the menus provide a single option to *Pause receiving messages* and apply it appropriately to whichever configuration you've started.

While you've suspended reception of incoming messages, you can still use the message editor/viewer to look at the messages you've already received or to send messages. Provided you've started PC Network in the messenger or the server configuration, you can still add names to your table of message aliases or have incoming messages forwarded. Messages addressed to names you've forwarded are not affected by your suspension of reception (since your machine isn't the place they're received).

Incoming Requests to a Server: Server or SRV

When you suspend the *server* function, you halt the processing of all incoming traffic that originates on the network. That includes both requests to read and requests to write in directories shared over the network. It also includes all incoming messages and all jobs being transferred to the printer queue (including your own, redirected to the printer queue when you share a printer with the network).

This is the only suspendable activity that might have serious consequences for others on the network. It therefore has a restriction that does not apply to the others. PC Network will not permit you to suspend the server when any network user has opened a file in any of the directories you have shared with the network. If you attempt to suspend the network under those conditions, PC Network refuses, and sends you the message *NET073: Unable to pause; Files are open* (refer to Figure 6.4).

How the Suspended Functions Overlap

On a server machine, a tricky aspect of the NET PAUSE command is that some functions overlap. Suspending one may suspend others.

Figures 6.1 and 6.2 show how the various actions are related for the user and server configurations. Figure 6.1 shows the activities that a machine running one of the user configurations can use. The *messenger* and *receiver* functions are placed side by side to indicate that you pick whichever is appropriate.

Figure 6.2 shows the same relationships, but from the point of view of a server machine. Wherever one activity is shown above another, suspending the higher activity implies suspending those in the box below it also.

The essential point of Figure 6.2 is that *NET PAUSE Server* implies *NET PAUSE Messenger* (although of course the reverse isn't true).

Similarly, *NET PAUSE PRDR* implies *NET PAUSE Print* (but not the reverse). *NET PAUSE Print* implies suspension of all the shared printers, whereas suspending the individual printers has no effect on the others or on printing generally.

Timing and Duration of Suspension

The suspension produced by the NET PAUSE command lasts until you reverse it or until the end of the session, whichever comes sooner. That

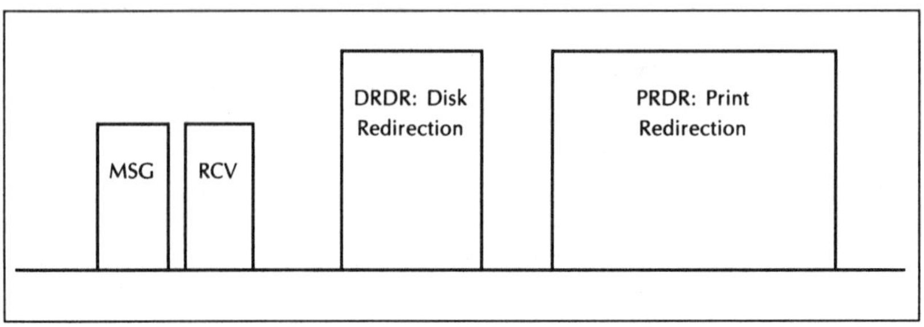

Figure 6.1: *Activities you can suspend at a user machine*

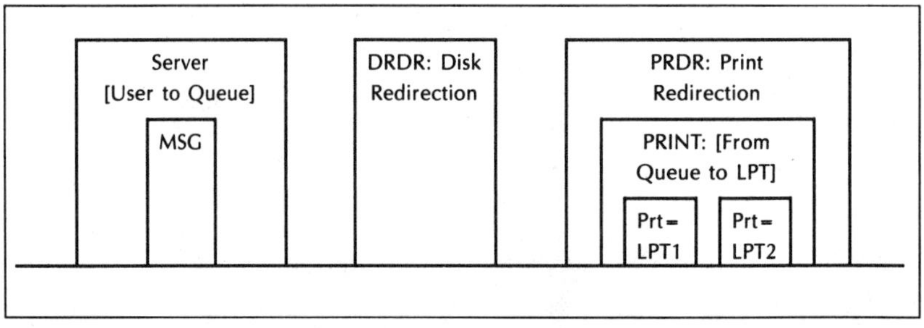

Figure 6.2: *Activities you can suspend at a server machine*

is, the next time you start the network, no suspension is carried forward from a previous session.

You can't suspend an activity until you've started it.

Watch out: Taken together, these two rather straightforward rules have a consequence that may take you by surprise. Suppose you're running a server and are having trouble with the printer. You suspend printing of the queue while you work on the problem. But it's late in the day, so you shut down your machine and resolve to fix the problem the next morning. When you next turn on your machine, the suspensions you requested the previous day are no longer in effect. There's further discussion of ways to avoid such surprises in Chapter 9 (on managing printers) and Chapter 12 (on automating operations).

Notification of Users That a Server's Function is Suspended

In general, when a user attempts to make use of a function that is suspended, PC Network generates a message indicating what the situation is. The only exception is a request to a network printer. The user who submits a job is notified if the server is suspended (because the job can't be transmitted to the print queue). But getting the job *into* the queue is only half of what's required. The user is not told whether the printer is suspended. That information isn't included even when the user subsequently displays a report on the status of the print queue on a server machine.

Resuming the Suspended Activity

The command NET CONTINUE ends the suspension produced by NET PAUSE. The activity to be continued is listed (or can be selected from a menu) in the same way as for NET PAUSE. PC Network doesn't object if you use the NET PAUSE or NET CONTINUE command to suspend an activity that is already suspended or to resume an activity that is already active.

The syntax of these two commands is summarized in Figure 6.3.

Menus to Suspend and Resume Network Functions

From the main menu, one of the choices is *Pause and continue tasks.* When you select that menu, you get a list of the functions you can suspend or resume. Figure 6.4 shows the full list as it appears at a server machine.

A machine in the redirector configuration sees only the first two choices. A machine in the receiver or the messenger configuration sees the third as well. A server sees all five. The word *devices* in choice 4 embraces disks, directories, and printers.

NET PAUSE *Function(s)*
NET CONTINUE *Function(s)*
The commands NET PAUSE or NET CONTINUE may be followed by the names of one or more of the functions valid in the configuration (each denoted by its full name or by its standard abbreviation), separated by blanks.

Function	*Configuration in which valid*
DRDR	any
PRDR	any
RCV Receiver	receiver
MSG Messenger	messenger or server
SRV Server	server
PRT Print [=LPT*n*]	server

Figure 6.3: *Syntax of NET PAUSE and NET CONTINUE*

```
                                                        IBM PC NETWORK
                        Pause and Continue Tasks

   1. Pause or continue using network disks and directories

   2. Pause or continue using network printers

   3. Pause or continue receiving messages

   4. Pause or continue sharing your devices

   5. Pause or continue printing files

   1  Choice



   Enter - Continue                          F1 - Help
   Ctrl-Home - Return to Main Menu           Esc - Previous menu
```

Figure 6.4: *Pause and continue menu for server*

When you select any choice except 5 (printing files), you get a screen asking you to select *Pause* or *Continue*. When you make that selection, the action is attempted immediately (without the request for further instructions that experience with other screens might lead you to expect). You get a message either confirming that the action has been taken or indicating why it has not (see Figure 6.5). When you select choice 5, there's an intermediate screen asking you to indicate that you mean all printers or to name one specific printer.

```
                                                          IBM PC NETWORK
                     Pause or Continue Sharing Your Devices

     1. Pause sharing your devices

     2. Continue sharing your devices


     1  Choice









     Enter - Continue                        F1 - Help
     Ctrl-Home - Return to Main Menu         Esc - Previous menu

  NET073: Unable to pause; Files are open
```

Figure 6.5: *PAUSE selected from a menu screen, and system response*

Temporary Dedicated Servers

Seven

The PERMIT command provides another way to make a disk or directory on one machine available to another machine. It is the only way a machine that lacks a fixed disk can nevertheless offer to share a directory with another machine.

PERMIT is a strange and rather awkward mechanism. Nevertheless, it can provide some useful services that are not otherwise possible in PC Network.

PERMIT from the Sharer's and the User's Viewpoints

From the user's side, it doesn't make a lot of difference whether a resource is offered by the

PERMIT command or the more conventional NET SHARE. The effect is similar (although not identical).

From the sharer's side, PERMIT is very different, involving powers that the NET SHARE command doesn't have as well as some severe limitations.

Advantages of Sharing by Way of PERMIT

First the good news. PERMIT has two special advantages.

Any machine with a network adapter can offer to share a disk or directory, not just a machine that has a fixed disk. Indeed, PERMIT is the *only* mechanism by which a machine without a fixed disk can make one of its disks or directories available to another machine. (If you do have a fixed disk, it's perfectly legal to execute PERMIT there too. However, if you have the equipment, you'll find it more convenient in most situations to use the regular NET SHARE command.)

The machine that offers the disk or directory doesn't even have to be running PC Network (but it does have to be physically connected to the network!).

Restrictions on Offers Made with PERMIT

Now the bad news. The PERMIT command imposes some restrictions that don't arise with PC Network's NET SHARE and NET USE commands.

PERMIT makes the machine that offers its disk a 100 percent dedicated server. As soon as you execute the PERMIT command to offer a disk or directory to someone else, that action completely ties up your machine. You can't do anything else until the offer is terminated. (But either side can terminate it; see Terminating the PERMIT Arrangement, later in this chapter.)

The offer extended by PERMIT can be taken up by only one other machine. You can make the offer either to a specific machine or to any machine (using * instead of a computer name). But in either case, only one machine can take it up. If you make the offer to any machine, whoever accepts it first, gets it.

You cannot type the PERMIT command from within the PC Network menus: it doesn't appear anywhere in them. Nor can you type it from the F2 command screen within the menus: there, you can only type commands that start with *NET*, since the screen provides the initial *NET* for you and won't let you erase it.

When You Might Want to Use PERMIT

Here are some circumstances that might make you want to use PERMIT:

- It's the only way (because the machine on which the disk or directory is located hasn't got a fixed disk).

- It won't take long. For example, if a co-worker needs to send a file to you or receive a file from you, the transfer won't take much time, and you can go about your business as soon as it's over.
- You have alternative communications with the person who'll be the user (since you won't be able to exchange network messages while your machine is tied up as a dedicated server).
- You're not using the machine anyway. Using PERMIT, you can in effect attach a disk drive on your machine exclusively to someone else's machine. That might make sense during a period in which you won't be using your machine anyway.
- You want to make sure that a particular machine will use your disk or directory, with no possibility of any other machine accepting the offer.

How You Make an Offer with PERMIT

The PERMIT command takes three arguments. There's also an optional parameter specifying the kind of access that you're offering (read/write, read-only, etc.). The three fields are (in this order):

- The name that the resource you're offering has on your machine (optionally preceded by a *short name* by which the user will refer to it).
- The name of the computer to which you're making the offer.
- A special name for your computer, adopted for this purpose only. The name must be different from any name already in use on the network. If you've started PC Network, it must be different from your machine's network name.
- There's also an optional parameter to indicate the type of access the other machine will have to the disk or directory you're offering. If you omit the parameter, read/write is assumed by default. The parameter starts with a slash and its order in the command doesn't matter; in the example, it's shown last.

Syntax of PERMIT

Figure 7.1 shows the syntax of the PERMIT command together with an example. The discussion that follows reviews what's in each of the fields, referring back to this example.

Identifying What's Offered

The first field identifies the disk or directory that you're offering to share. You may also assign a short name by which your user must refer to it, but that's optional. If you include a short name, the short name comes first and must be followed by an equal sign.

The resource you are offering is a directory. You identify it by writing the complete path to it, starting with a backslash. You may also specify the drive on which the directory is mounted, but only when you use a short name.

In the example, you assign the short name *Archive*. You offer to share the directory called \Catalog\Text. The directory is on your drive B; since you included a short name, you're allowed to specify the drive. When you omit the drive (for example, *Archive=\Catalog\Text*), the directory is assumed to be on your default drive.

To offer the root directory (that is, the entire disk) on the default drive, that field would appear as *Archive=*. (PERMIT also tolerates *Archive=b:* to mean all of disk B; that's the only case in which you may omit the backslash.)

When you omit the short name, you must also omit both the equal sign and the drive name. In that case, the command in Figure 7.1 would appear thus:

```
PERMIT \Catalog\Text Sachiko SecretSharer /r
```

Name from Your User's Point of View

From your user's point of view, the name of the resource you are offering is the short name (if you used one) or the path (if you didn't). Your user may assign her own virtual drive name to that, or treat it as a path (see Accepting Use of a Permitted Disk or Directory, later in this chapter).

When you execute the command shown in Figure 7.1, your user can accept that as directory Archive on machine SecretSharer. Your user may refer to the name \Catalog\Text only when you don't assign a short name.

PERMIT	**[shortname**	**=[d:]]**	**\Path**	**Offer to**	**Offer from**	**[/access]**
PERMIT	Archive	=b:	\Catalog\Text	Sachiko	SecretSharer	/r

Figure 7.1: *Syntax and example of the PERMIT command*

Identifying to Whom You're Making the Offer

In the second field of the PERMIT command, you write just one word: the name of the computer to which you make the offer. (It has to be the computer name, not one of the additional names the computer may have adopted for receiving messages.) Alternatively, if you're willing to let whoever first executes an appropriate NET USE have the resource, write just an asterisk in this field.

The computer to which you make the offer doesn't have to be already on the network when you make the offer. Your machine just waits indefinitely, listening only for a request to use its resource from a computer whose name is the one specified in the second field of PERMIT (in the example, a machine called Sachiko). Making the offer in advance is legal but perhaps imprudent: you've tied up your computer by making an offer to a not-yet-existent name.

A Special Name for Your Own Computer

In the third field, you coin a name for your own computer. You must supply a name not now in use on the network (that is, a name that at present is neither a computer name nor an additional name anywhere on the network). *Important:* The special name you provide here must not be your own computer's network name.

The person who accepts your offer must know the name you specify here. Offerer and user have to work that out between them in advance. In the example, the name is SecretSharer.

Setting the Level of Access Your User Will Have

This optional parameter, preceded by a slash, indicates what sorts of things your user will be permitted to do with files in the disk or directory to which you've offered access.

R	Read-only access
W	Write, but only to files that already exist
RW	Read/write access
WC	Write, create, and delete
RWC	Read, write, create, and delete (full access)

When you omit the access parameter, the value assumed by default is RWC. If your user attempts to open a file in a manner prohibited by this parameter, DOS sends her the message *Access denied.* (For further discussion of the meaning of the parameters, see What the Levels of Access Mean in Chapter 3.)

System's Response to the PERMIT Command

When you execute PERMIT successfully, the first response you'll see is the message *IBM PC Network Program* followed by a version number and copyright notice.

After that, if your command was acceptable to PC Network, you'll see *Permit started; Disk or directory available.* That message confirms that the offer has been made on the network. However, if there was something wrong, you'll see an error message. PC Network verifies that the new name you've claimed for your machine is indeed unique and that your description of the drive or directory you're offering is valid.

After that, nothing, until your user requests to use the device you have offered. When that happens, you'll see one more message of acknowledgment, telling you who took up your offer. For the example of Figure 7.1, that would be: *Disk or directory in use by computer name: SACHIKO.*

Accepting Use of a Permitted Disk or Directory

You make use of a disk or directory offered to you via the PERMIT command in exactly the same way as one offered by NET SHARE or by way of the corresponding PC Network menu screen (see Chapter 4).

If you choose to do this with commands, execute NET USE with appropriate arguments, as follows:

- Drive name as the resource will appear on your machine. This is optional in the NET USE command, but required in the menus. If you assign a drive name, it must be followed by a colon.
- A double backslash, followed by the special name for the computer making the offer. For the example in Figure 7.1, *\\SecretSharer.*
- A single backslash, followed by the short name (if the offer used one) or otherwise the path. For the example in Figure 7.1, *\Archive.*

To take up the offer made in Figure 7.1, and treat it as your virtual drive E, type:

```
NET USE e:  \\SecretSharer\Archive
```

If the offerer omitted the short name, you accept the path as it appeared in the offerer's command. If the offer shown in Figure 7.1 had omitted *Archive=*, to accept and use it as drive E, you'd have to type:

```
NET USE e:  \\SecretSharer\Catalog\Text
```

Watch out: In the PERMIT command executed by the offerer, the special computer name (here *SecretSharer*) comes *after* the path being offered, but in the NET USE command, the computer name comes *before* the rest of the path.

Terminating the PERMIT Arrangement

Once you've executed PERMIT to offer a directory on your machine and a user has taken up your offer, your machine remains dedicated to that user until the user terminates use of it or goes off the network. Short of forcing termination from your side, there's nothing you can do at your machine.

Message Indicating Termination by the User

When the user terminates use normally, the indication you'll receive at the offerer end is a return to the DOS prompt. When the user went off the network without a normal termination, you'll first see the message *NET468: Session ended abnormally* and then the DOS prompt.

Forced Termination by the Offerer

If you need to terminate the arrangement but your user hasn't done so, you can terminate from your side by pressing Ctrl-Break. That's Ctrl-Break, not Ctrl-Alt-Break (which is the network-request key) and not Ctrl-Alt-Del (which is system reset). Pressing Ctrl-Break returns you to the DOS prompt. Your offer is no longer in effect.

When you force termination, your (former!) user will probably get the message *NET805: Network device no longer exists.*

If you both want to restore the arrangement, you have to execute PERMIT again. From her end, the user must first *delete* her use of your directory (see below) and then make a new request to take up your new offer.

Terminating Use of a PERMIT Arrangement from the User's Side

When you're the person using a disk or directory offered by way of the PERMIT command, you terminate your use in exactly the same ways as you would when the resource was offered via NET SHARE. They are recapitulated below.

Terminate Use of a Virtual Drive

If you assigned a virtual drive name to the directory, use it in the command to terminate. For example, if you called it drive E, terminate its use by *NET USE* e: /d.

Terminate Use of a Path

If you accepted the resource as a path without a virtual drive name, you have to refer to the complete path (including the machine name) in the command to delete. For the example of Figure 7.1, that would be *NET USE* \\SecretSharer\Archive /d.

Terminate Via the Menus

Within the menus, proceed as follows:

1. At the main menu, select *Disk or directory tasks.*
2. At *Disk or directory tasks,* select *Start or stop using a network disk or directory.*
3. At *Start or Stop,* select *Stop.*
4. Fill in the name of the virtual drive and press Enter.

Managing Shared Disk Space

Eight

Directories on the fixed disks of any PC on the network may be shared with the rest of the network. This chapter tells you what you'll need to know when you're operating a server whose disk is shared with the network.

You have to start the network in the server configuration and then offer the network the directories you wish to share (see Chapter 2 on starting the network, Chapter 3 on offering to share a resource with the network). If you regularly share your disk, you'll almost certainly have the offers to share included in your Autoexec file so that the offers are made automatically when you start your machine.

When you're the operator of a machine that provides disk space to others, you thereby take on certain responsibilities to the remote users of your machine. Just how the responsibilities are balanced and distributed is an important issue for the community. The network administrator should make clear what those responsibilities are; she should make clear to users what they have to do for themselves and what they can and cannot reasonably expect from you.

The big issues are the availability of space, the recovery of data by human or hardware failure, and security. This chapter devotes some attention to each.

Allocating Space

DOS does not allocate space in advance (as some mainframe operating systems do). There is no provision in DOS to limit the size to which a particular file or directory can grow. Instead, all uses (or users) of a fixed disk draw space from a single combined pool representing the entire disk (or partition, when the disk is partitioned between DOS and another operating system).

As operator of a machine with a fixed disk, you can set up a structure of directories. But once you set the access right to even a single directory so that network users can create new files in it or can write in existing files, DOS gives you no way to limit the size to which that directory can grow. Anyone who can write at all can consume any space available on the fixed disk.

The use of a common pool has pros and cons. Since all available space is in a single pool, the amount available for temporary use is far larger than would be possible if space were partitioned in advance. Suppose eight individuals share use of a 20Mb fixed disk. Suppose 3Mb are already devoted to network administration: DOS, PC Network, and the Apps read-only directory of applications; suppose 1Mb is devoted to the printer spool. Dividing the remaining 16Mb equally among the eight users would fix them at 2Mb each. But if each user regularly stores only 1Mb, there remain 8Mb unused. Pooling makes all 8Mb temporarily available to anyone.

Sooner or later there will be contention among users. (Probably sooner. A variant of Parkinson's Law dictates that users' storage expands to fill the disks available.) You need to understand what and where the problem is; the community needs to agree on priorities regarding the use of space and conventions regarding the settlement of competing needs for space.

Develop a Space-Use Budget

If you're the network administrator, you need a plan, or at least an estimate, of the way space should be used on each server's fixed disk. If you're the operator of a server machine, you need to know how the plan affects your machine.

The plan should give you the probable normal size expected for the various directories. It should give you some rule of thumb for what you can expect as reasonable temporary fluctuations. A possible space budget is illustrated in Figure 8.1.

The leftmost column of Figure 8.1 shows the space that a directory is certain to consume for steady use. For the users' directories, you might think of that as the space each user consumes for semipermanent storage, when a project is complete.

The next column, headed Min, indicates the temporary space the user almost certainly needs in addition to the steady use (for example, as working backup of a file being edited). The rightmost column, headed Max, indicates the amount of temporary space the user may require during peak use.

Average and Worst-Case Demands for Space

The totals at the bottom of a form such as Figure 8.1 indicate your overall need. Clearly, you must have space for the steady-state storage and probably enough to cover the total of the minima. But you don't necessarily require space for the total at the right. It represents the worst case: the space you would need if every user were to want the maximum *at the same time.*

The severity of the worst case depends in part on scheduling. Can you predict *when* users will need large temporary storage? If users work independently, you may be able to treat these peaks as random events. But if your users are all driven by the same schedule, there's a real possibility they'll experience their peak loads at the same time. You need to take that into account. For example, if six users are from accounting, and accounting is known to run programs that require large temporary files at the end of every month, the amount of extra space they need collectively will be the sum of what they need individually.

When the demand of the various users is not correlated, you may serve them all with much less space than the rightmost total. Just how much margin you need may depend on the availability of space, the organization's attitude toward risk, and so on. A bank doesn't keep on hand cash to satisfy everybody who might conceivably ask for it; likewise, the server rarely needs space to meet all the possible demands at once.

Jobs That May Accumulate Files Temporarily

One highly variable quantity in your estimate is the space required by the network printer spool. That depends on the size of the jobs and the extent to which you permit them to back up in the spool before printing them. The queue-managing program permits up to 100 jobs to accumulate. The size of a job varies widely. A page of text has somewhere between 2,000 and 4,000 characters or bytes, but some formatters insert control codes that make the printer file far larger than the source text; files containing graphic images may be larger still. If the files in the spool had an average size of 80,000 bytes, 100 of them would total 8 million bytes, to come out of your total space on the fixed disk. Perhaps that's extreme. But don't forget to include the printer spool in your calculations.

Jobs That Accumulate Files Endlessly

In some roles, you never throw anything away. For example, if some of your users do the office correspondence using a word processor on the network, they may generate and save a file for every letter the business ever sends out. Moreover, some applications automatically create (but don't automatically erase) a backup copy of their working files. If there's no provision to purge those files by deleting or off-loading old

Directory	**Steady size**	**Variable: Min**	**Max**
	(thousands of bytes)		
Root directory:			
Autoexec, etc			
Network directory (server portion)	320	0	0
Spool files awaiting printer	0	100	8,000
Batch directory (for server)	3	0	0
Profiles directory (for server)			
Apps directory			
Batch (for network)	3		
Network (user portion)	320		
DOS (common to server and network)	350	0	0
Text	124		
Application1	?	0	0
Application2 (etc.)	?	0	0
User1	50	500	2,000
User2	1,000	60	1,000
User3	600	1,000	4,000
Etc.			
Totals:			

Figure 8.1: *Outline for a fixed-disk space budget*

material, the space consumed increases steadily day by day. That's not necessarily the wrong way to handle it. But when you're providing the disk on which those steadily growing files are stored, you'd better include room in your space budget for their predictable expansion.

Packing of Files on the Fixed Disk

DOS allocates space on the disk in *clusters* of consecutive *sectors.* A sector contains 512 bytes. The size of a cluster differs with the disk and with the file allocation table (FAT) that DOS uses to manage the disk. With DOS 3.10, the FAT can divide a PC/AT's 20Mb disk into clusters of 2,048 bytes. Other models of the PC or other versions of DOS require a cluster of 4,096 bytes on a PC/XT's 10Mb disk, or 8,192 bytes on a PC/AT. (Although DOS 3.10 formats the PC/AT's fixed disk into smaller clusters, I found that the dealer from whom I bought a PC/AT with DOS 3.10 had nevertheless used an earlier version of DOS to format the disk, producing clusters four times larger than necessary.)

Storing small files in large clusters can use up a lot of disk space. For example, batch files are often less than 100 bytes, but each still requires an entire cluster on the fixed disk. If you have 8,192-byte clusters, you may be using 8,192 bytes on the disk to store 100 bytes of data. To find the amount of space a file actually consumes on the fixed disk, divide the number of data bytes by the cluster size, round up to a whole number, and multiply by the cluster size. DOS doesn't perform that calculation for you, but there are programs that do. The disk utility FF from Qualitas routinely tells you not only the number of bytes a file uses for data, but also the space required to store it on the disk.

(If you aren't sure what the cluster size is, you can find it by the following: At the DOS prompt, type *dir* and note the number of free bytes. Execute *md Junk* to create a new directory. Type *dir* again, and note the reduction in free bytes. Execute *rd Junk* to remove the test directory. Cluster size is among the many items reported by Peter Norton's Norton Utilities.)

As far as DOS is concerned, the information required to describe a directory or subdirectory is a file and, like a file, requires an entire cluster on the fixed disk. Thus, each subdirectory takes up at least one cluster, quite apart from the storage required for each of the files within it.

Summarize Space Consumption by User

You need an overall view of space consumption. For that purpose, the space that a file occupies in storage is more important than the number of bytes actually used for data. However, the DOS command

DIR reports only the data bytes in a file and doesn't mention the space occupied by files or by directories, and it doesn't offer much help in summarizing the data.

Various vendors offer utilities that are helpful. I improvised a program to give me a summary by directory of the actual space on the fixed disk. The heart of this is the FF utility from Qualitas, which includes provisions to report space consumed, to organize the report by directories, to include space within subdirectories, and to add it all up. Programs containing some of those features are available from several software vendors, usually as part of a kit of DOS or file-management enhancements. You need some sort of space report program to summarize how your users are using your disk.

In my version, I give the program a list of the directories I'm interested in, together with the space budget for each. (Those are stored in a file so I don't have to type them each time.) The space budget is the amount of space I hope each user's steady storage will stay within. For each directory and subdirectory, the program looks up the space consumed by every file and directory and consolidates the figures for the tree structure of directories. The program gives me a report showing the total size of the contents of each of the directories I've asked about, and compares that with the amount allocated in my space budget. That way I can see the total situation quickly, including who's over budget and by how much. You can see a sample in Figures 8.2 and 8.3.

```
Directory Summary                                           85/11/15 15:10
Machine: Server2. Drive C:                   Free Space:  4,440,064 Bytes

                          File          Disk
              Files       Bytes         Bytes         Budget   Difference
APPS            491   4,714,280     5,644,288              0
NETWORK          22     317,132       344,064              0
BATCH            22       4,820        45,056              0

                                    6,033,408

ACCTG           122   3,187,568     3,309,568      3,006,464     -303,104  *
PAUL            145   2,136,832     2,424,832      1,998,848     -425,984  *
SACHIKO          74     663,049       770,048        999,424      229,376
DEPT8            46     444,520       491,520      1,998,848    1,507,328
BARRY            30     278,629       311,296        999,424      687,498
DAVIDK           38     345,082       393,216        999,424      606,208
LIEU             24     236,320       262,144        999,424      737,280
MERLE            18     190,996       212,992        999,424      786,432

■
```

Figure 8.2: *Sample display from a directory report program*

The report in Figure 8.2 shows the total space consumed for each of a list of directories of interest to the network administrator. The number of bytes reported for a directory is obtained by summing the number of bytes required for the storage of all its files and all its subdirectories. These are compared to the network administrator's space budget. Directories whose size can't really change are given a budget of 0 and are excluded from the calculation of difference between budgeted and actual space. The program lists those first, followed by the other directories in descending order of actual size. The asterisks flag directories that are over budget.

Following the summary, the report goes on to show an itemization of each of the directories mentioned in the main report. Within a directory, its subdirectories are listed in alphabetical order. The total report can be quite long. The first part of one is shown in Figure 8.3.

Controlling Access to Files

For each file, DOS records an *attribute* to indicate how the file may be opened. A file for which the attribute is *read-only* can be neither altered nor erased (at least until the attribute is changed).

When you offer to share a directory with the network, the offer may specify a level of access. The level set as part of a share offer applies not to a particular file but to all files within the directory being offered

```
Directory Summary                                          85/11/15 15:10

Machine: Server2. Drive C:                  Free Space:  4,440,064 Bytes

                         Directory Itemization

APPS\   491 files.   4,714,280 data bytes,  in 6,643,712 disk bytes.

                   File    Disk                              File     Disk
          Files   Bytes   Bytes                   Files     Bytes    Bytes
 BATCH       11   3,009  22,528     PUBLIC.DOM      48    318,442  348,160
 DOS         39 295,006 339,968     SAPLPC          23    481,991  512,000
 GRAFPLUS    11  65,598  81,920     SCOM             9    339,714  368,640
 HDS          3  55,516  59,392     SK               9    261,177  272,384
 IMCAP        3  72,763  75,776     SMORGAS          4     45,222   53,248
 MACRO        3 134,144 141,312     STSC            26    334,707  368,640
 NET         22 129,968 176,128     TAPESTRY        20    178,809  196,608
 NETWORK     20 317,132 344,064     TEXT            50    485,415  532,480
 NU           1  48,054  49,152     THAUMA          22     15,703   47,104
 POCKET       2 134,744 139,264     UTIL            14     11,768   28,672
                                    (more)
```

Figure 8.3: *Part of the itemization from a report on the space budget*

and its subdirectories. Access rights for network directories are discussed in Chapter 3 (on offering to share resources with the network) and Chapter 4 (on using network resources).

Directories containing programs to be used over the network are usually offered with read-only access so that network users can't alter the files in those directories.

Different Needs for Different Directories

Disk space used by other machines over the network can be roughly divided into three broad categories.

Read-Only Directories

These contain programs or reference data, and also parts of DOS and PC Network itself. For such files, it's vital to have spares on diskette or tape, but there's no need to keep making backup copies of them, because they don't change. They can be excluded from the routine backup cycle.

Private Read/Write Directories

These are the least predictable; you really don't know what people will put in them, how they'll preserve it, or when they'll want it back.

Shared Read/Write Directories

Files in these directories permit read/write access by many people, perhaps concurrently. They may be the foundation of such department-wide services as electronic mail, accounting data base, inventory, order, personnel records, and so on. Files such as these are perhaps the most challenging for network administration. Because many people may depend on them, it's important to the organization that they remain dependably available. Because many people may use them, the files are less likely to have quiet times when they're not in use.

Setting Read-Only Access for Yourself

The network access rights established by your offer to share apply only to access made via the network. Network access rights never apply to access made directly by the operator of the server machine (regardless of whether the directory is at the time offered to the network). To prevent you from inadvertently changing or deleting application files in a directory offered to the network with read-only access, the Installation Aid also sets the read-only attribute of each such file. For applications that you install yourself, you should do likewise.

You can set read-only access for everybody, including yourself, with the DOS command ATTRIB. For example, to set the read-only attribute for all files in the directory \Apps\Smorgas, the command is:

```
ATTRIB +r c:\Apps\Smorgas\*.*
```

Unfortunately, DOS doesn't offer a parameter to make this extend to files in subdirectories, so you'll have to execute it separately for each subdirectory.

If you subsequently attempt to alter or delete a file for which the read-only attribute has been set, you'll see the message *Access denied.* When you really do need to make a change or deletion, you can undo the read-only attribute by executing the ATTRIB command with −R in place of +R.

Don't Prevent Users from Changing Their Private Directories

The suggestion of the preceding section applies only to directories that are to be read-only for everybody. Much as you might think it prudent to stop yourself from inadvertently changing or deleting files in a user's private directory, that technique won't have the desired effect.

The access that network users have to files on a remote server is the access established in the offer to share *or* the access you set by the ATTRIB command, whichever is more restrictive. So even if you'd like to prevent yourself from inadvertently erasing a user's file, don't use the ATTRIB command to do it. DOS will send the message *Access denied* not just when you try to change or erase the user's file, but also when she does.

The network user can use ATTRIB with −R to reverse the effects of the ATTRIB command, just as you can. However, a network user cannot override the network access rights established by your NET SHARE command.

Backing Up Files from the Fixed Disk

A *backup copy* of a file is a duplicate record of the file as it was at a particular moment, stored apart from the original, usually in a different physical location. From the backup, it's possible to reconstruct the working file when the need arises.

The art, science, and politics of file backup and restoration merit and require several volumes to themselves. This chapter doesn't even mention all the issues, let alone solve them. It presents some observations about the nature of the problem, together with a few cautions.

Reasons for Backup

The reason you make backup copies is that you may need to restore the files. This seems obvious, but nevertheless it's easy to overlook. The needs and circumstances of the restoration phase are quite different from those of the backup. When things are working well, backup gets lots of regular exercise and restoration very little. Should the system be designed to minimize the pain of backup—or the hassle of restoration?

Types of Failure

Backup is insurance against the loss of data. Losses may arise from quite different causes, which have different needs for backup and restoration. The following lists some of the distinct circumstances of need.

Inadvertent Deletion

In my experience, much the most frequent occasion for restoring an old file arises when its owner deletes it and then realizes (somewhere between one second and several months later) that deletion was a mistake.

Some of these mistaken deletions are more or less inevitable human error. Some may even be encouraged by faith in your ability to restore mislaid files from backup. Some are made more likely by the human engineering in DOS. (When you ask to erase everything in a directory, DOS does ask *Are you sure?* but doesn't spell out the implications. Of course you're sure you want to erase *something;* the question is what. If DOS had queried *28 files totaling 623,000 bytes in directory \Paul\Book on drive E?,* I might have replied *no!* when in fact I assented.)

With inadvertent deletion, there's no real question of equipment failure. The questions for you as custodian of the fixed disk are *When was it backed up?* and *How can I restore it?* occasionally mixed with *What was it really called?* and *Did it ever really exist?*

Gradually Increasing Disk Errors

You start getting reports that some parts of some files are found to be unreadable. This may be because the disk has developed bad tracks it didn't have before or because, as DOS writes new copies of files, it has for the first time written across a track that should have been marked *bad* but wasn't. The immediate need is to restore the particular file in which the trouble was encountered. In that sense, the problem is like inadvertent erasure. However, diagnosis is also indicated to discover how many other files may be affected or whether the problem is spreading, along with preventive steps to keep the bad tracks from being written in again.

I think the important thing here is to realize that occasional failure may later become widespread. Heed the few occurrences as a warning, and take steps to provide full backup of the contents of the disk that's having trouble.

Catastrophic Disk Failure

This is the starkest form of data disaster, but comparatively rare. Despite a warning from DOS, somebody unintentionally reformats the fixed disk, thereby erasing everything on it. Or the disk drive fails so that nothing can be written or read for a considerable time (while the unit is sent for repair), perhaps forever. Or somebody steals a server PC, fixed disk and all. In these situations, you need a way to reconstruct everything that was on the disk, with no reliance at all on rescuing data from what remains.

Backup Alternatives

There are several alternative ways to provide backup protection, differing in who does them, what it takes to do them, how often they're done, and what it takes to restore data from them. Backup procedures may reflect the community's style or social philosophy: laxity or organization, caution or recklessness, paternalism or permissiveness. You may want to adopt some mix of each of the following.

Full Backup and Restoration

A *full backup* is a complete copy of everything on a fixed disk. A *full restoration* is a reconstruction of everything on the disk from the full backup.

A *full dump/restore* is a full backup, followed immediately by reformatting the fixed disk and restoring everything as it was from the backup. Quite apart from the need to make spare copies for retrieval, there may be other benefits from periodically conducting a full dump/restore of the fixed disks. Reformatting gives DOS an opportunity to generate an updated table of bad tracks. It also permits all the restored files to be written contiguously. Especially when the disk is close to full, as new files are created they are less and less likely to find contiguous space. Files that are spread in many places reduce the efficiency of the disk by requiring more time in physical motion of the head.

Incremental Backup

An *incremental* backup is one that makes duplicates only of those files that have changed since the date of a preceding backup. A series of incremental backups makes it possible to restore files as they were on a particular date in the past. The usual procedure is to make a full backup at a regular interval (for example, once a week or once a month) and incremental backups more frequently (for example, daily or weekly).

The incremental backup may be kept separate from the preceding backups or merged with them.

Incremental backups favor restoration of specific files from a specific date (for example, after inadvertent erasure). They may be more cumbersome when full restoration is required following loss of an entire disk.

Private Backup

Users who keep their working files on the fixed disk of a server machine are still free to handle their own backups and restorations. Each can treat her own directory as a disk and provide for it her own schedule of full or incremental backups.

The network administrator may want to make it perfectly clear that users have to do their own backups and restorations. Or she may want to centralize backup services as a routine part of server operations.

Even if the servers operate an extensive backup service for all network users, that doesn't prevent individual users from creating backup copies on their own machines, or even from backing up files that reside on one server into directories that reside on a second server. It seems likely that the network administrator may establish a schedule of routine backups for everybody's files, leaving individuals free to supplement that as they see fit.

Reconstructing Erased Files from the Current Disk

When you've mistakenly deleted files for which there are no backup copies, on a stand-alone machine you have some chance of reconstructing them, especially if you do so immediately, before new use has been made of the space. When DOS deletes a file, it merely marks the space the file formerly used as *available*. DOS doesn't actually erase the file. However, as new files are created, the new files may overwrite part of that space.

Certain utility programs, for example Peter Norton's Norton Utilities, make it sometimes feasible to resurrect an erased file. For a network machine acting as a server, the technical issues are exactly the same as for a stand-alone machine, but the prospects of being able to piece together an erased file are much poorer because the disk is both large and busy, so there may be less chance of catching an old file before its former space is reused by others. Also, you'd have to suspend the server while you run the resurrection program. Don't encourage users to think you can do this (but remember the possibility as a last resort in an emergency).

Programs to exhume an erased file do so by restoring the file's name in the directory and the pointer to the file's first cluster of sectors. Even when the first pointer is to a cluster that hasn't been claimed by an existing file, you still have to examine the data to verify that this is really part of the file you want.

The program consults the disk's file allocation table (FAT). During a file's official lifetime, each cluster's entry in the FAT points to the cluster containing the next piece of the file; they form a chain. The values of those pointers may still be valid. However, examining them only tells the program what once followed this segment, at some time, in some file—maybe in the one you want, maybe in some other. If you're lucky, you can verify that each segment is what you need and follows from the one before. If you're unlucky, parts of your file may have been overwritten or the chain of pointers deflected to clusters that are now irrelevant. When the file you're seeking had been saved repeatedly, the disk may be littered with parts of old versions, and it becomes difficult to detect false links or identify missing segments.

Special Equipment for Backup

As delivered from IBM, PC Network assumes that a server is an IBM PC/XT or PC/AT (probably a PC/AT, for reasons I explain in Chapter 10). File service and backup equipment is provided by the server machine and by such devices as you can attach to it. Within that framework, backup of files on the fixed disk is either to diskettes or to another fixed disk.

Other manufacturers offer specialized equipment that can be attached to the network, in particular devices intended to act as fast or high-capacity file servers. In some designs, the file server appears to PC Network as an additional PC. In others, the server is configured as a peripheral device attached to one of the existing PCs. Servers of this type may provide disks considerably larger than the 10Mb disks of the PC/XT or the 20Mb disks of the PC/AT.

In several cases, the manufacturers of these file servers provide their own software to make backups and do restorations. With some of them, the file server may run much of the time unattended, programmed in advance to initiate a backup job at a particular date or time or on a regular schedule. The file server may then make copies of all files new or updated since the last backup, or at least of those to which it can gain access. Unless the backup program can put its own pre-emptive hold on a shared file, it may be obliged to skip files in which somebody is writing. For this reason, the backup may be scheduled for a time of day (or night) when other use is unlikely.

Some systems offer what is called *streaming backup,* that is, continuous writing of a duplicate set of files on another device at the same time as writing to the working disk. This is particularly useful for protection from data lost by catastrophic equipment failure, but may do little to address the restoration of old versions from the past, which is probably better handled from an archive of former full or incremental backups.

When you evaluate a proposed mechanism for doing backup, don't forget to evaluate how it does restoration. After all, that's what backup is for.

The DOS Command to Back Up Files

The BACKUP command makes copies of a set of files and stores the copies on the disk identified by a particular drive. The command's syntax requires you to state two things: the files to be backed up and the drive on which the backup copies will be stored. Figure 8.4 summarizes the parts of the command, and following sections discuss them.

Running and Recording a Backup

Figure 8.5 shows the dialogue during the start of a backup to diskettes. In this example, for the server machine's directory called Paul, the operator backs up all files that have been modified since the last time they were backed up.

It's important to keep a record of the names of the files thus backed up. You can use the symbol > to divert the report produced by the BACKUP command to a file. You also need a record on paper, to keep with the backup diskettes. Something like this may suffice:

```
BACKUP c:\Paul\*.* a: /s/m > Backup.Rpt
TYPE Backup.Rpt
```

That does the same job as the command shown in Figure 8.5, but stores the report in the file Backup.Rpt. The date at which Backup.Rpt was created serves to record the date of the backup.

When the first diskette is full, BACKUP asks for another. It doesn't start with an overall estimate of the number required. As long as there's more left to back up, when it fills one it asks for another (see Figure 8.6).

Selecting Which Files Are Backed Up

When you name a specific file in the BACKUP command, just that file is backed up. However, you can include the wildcard characters * or ? to back up all files whose names match a particular pattern.

In addition, if you include the parameter /s, BACKUP makes copies of all the files within any subdirectories included in the files you request. To back up all files in the directory c:\Paul, as well as all files in any subdirectories it may contain, and write the backup files to drive A, type:

```
BACKUP c:\Paul\*.* a: /s
```

Selective Backup of Files Modified since Last Backup

The parameter /m indicates that you want a file to be included in the backup only if it has been modified since the last time a backup was run. (DOS records an *archive* bit for each file. Backup turns that bit off. Following modification to a file, DOS turns the archive bit on again, indicating that the file may contain something that hasn't been backed up. DOS doesn't tell you a file's *archive* status, but the Qualitas FF utility displays a letter A beside the name of each file that has been modified since the last backup.)

BACKUP *Source*:*Path* *Target*: /*Parameters*

Source — Drive name, colon, and complete path to the file(s) to be backed up. The drive name, colon, and initial \ may be omitted, in which case the current drive and default directory are understood and are included explicitly in the backup files.

Target — Drive name and colon for the device (real or virtual) where the backup file is to be stored.

Parameters — As many as appropriate of the following parameters. If you select multiple parameters, the command selects the files for which *all* are true.

- /s — Include *subdirectories* and the files within them.
- /m — Include only those files that have been *modified* since the last backup.
- /d — Include only those files whose *date* (of creation or last update) is on or after the date specified. The date is separated from the letter *d* by a colon and written in the same order (yy/mm/dd, for example) as DOS uses for displays such as DIR.
- /a — *Add* the backup files now generated to those already stored on the target device (that is, don't erase the earlier ones).

Figure 8.4: *Syntax of the BACKUP command*

Selecting Files Written No Earlier Than a Certain Date

The parameter /d:, followed by a colon and a date, indicates you want a file to be backed up only if its date of creation or last update is

```
Mon 1985-11-25 8.27.23 C:\> backup c:\Paul\*.* a: /s/m

Insert backup diskette 01 in drive A:

Warning! Files in the target drive
A:\ root directory will be erased
Strike any key when ready

*** Backing up files to drive A: ***
Diskette Number: 01

\PAUL\NOTES.SK
\PAUL\NOTES.BAK
\PAUL\WTEX0.CAP
\PAUL\NOTES.&SK
\PAUL\MSG.LOG
\PAUL\WTEXT\QCH__1.NET
\PAUL\WTEXT\FIG_4-1.CAP
\PAUL\WTEXT\FIG_3-1.CAP
\PAUL\WTEXT\FIG_3-2.CAP
\PAUL\WTEXT\FIG_3-4.CAP
\PAUL\WTEXT\FIG_3-6.CAP
\PAUL\WTEXT\FIG_3-7.CAP
■
```

Figure 8.5: *Start of a backup to diskettes*

```
\PAUL\WTEXT\FIG_3-7.CAP
\PAUL\WTEXT\FIG_4-2.CAP
\PAUL\WTEXT\FIG_3-8.CAP
\PAUL\WTEXT\QCH__4.NET
\PAUL\WTEXT\NCH__7.NET
\PAUL\WTEXT\NCH_10.NET
\PAUL\WTEXT\READINGS.NET
\PAUL\WTEXT\FIG_4-4.CAP
\PAUL\WTEXT\FIG_4-5.CAP
\PAUL\WTEXT\FIG_4-6.CAP
\PAUL\WTEXT\FIG_4-7.CAP
\PAUL\WTEXT\FIG_4-8.CAP
\PAUL\WTEXT\FIG_4-9.CAP
\PAUL\WTEXT\NCH__3.SYB
\PAUL\WTEXT\NCH__4.SYB
\PAUL\WTEXT\RULER.DEF
\PAUL\WTEXT\FIG_5-2.CAP

Insert backup diskette 02 in drive A:

Warning! Files in the target drive
A:\ root directory will be erased
Strike any key when ready■
```

Figure 8.6: *BACKUP asks for another diskette*

on or after the date you mention. Express a date in the same order (month/day/year, year/month/day, etc.). as DOS uses in a display or in its prompt for a new date. (*Note:* The examples in this book were prepared using the international order year/month/day; however, when you elect that order, a bug in DOS 3.10 requires dates for the /d: parameter of BACKUP to be written day-month-year.)

Watch out: The date that DOS records for the creation or update of a file is the date on the machine that created or updated it. If one of your users sets the time or date on her machine incorrectly and then modifies a file on the server machine, that incorrect date appears in the server's directory for that file. (On a machine that lacks an independent clock, the default date is the beginning of 1980; DOS 3.10 seems to assume January 3, others January 1.) Such files won't be selected by BACKUP with the /d: parameter set for a more recent date.

Including Hidden Files of DOS in the Backup

When you ask to back up all files in the root directory (by a full-backup command such as *BACKUP c:*.* a: /s*) and you omit the /m and /d: parameters, BACKUP includes the normally hidden DOS read-only files IBMBIO.com and IBMDOS.com. You'll need those when you restore after reformatting the hard disk.

Where the Backup Goes

The place to which the backup files are written is called the *target.* The target must be a drive name. You specify the drive letter and a colon, and that's all; you can't specify a path or directory.

When the target drive is a diskette drive on your own machine, BACKUP writes a set of files in the diskette's root directory. But when the target drive is a fixed disk, or a virtual drive really located on a fixed disk, BACKUP writes a set of files into a directory called Backup (creating that directory if it doesn't already exist).

Although BACKUP records the structure of directories and subdirectories that are being backed up, it does *not* create the same structure on the target. Instead it writes all files at the same level (and includes within each file information about the path to reach it).

BACKUP Records the Path to a File as Part of the File It Saves

BACKUP writes one short file called BackupID.@@@, and then one file for each of the files it is backing up. BackupID.@@@ includes the number of the diskette in the sequence for this backup, as well as an indication whether this is the last diskette or another follows.

The backup version of each file is slightly longer than the original. BACKUP attaches 128 extra bytes at the beginning of each file and there records the source file's name and the complete path by which the file is reached in the source directory. When you subsequently restore the backed-up file, the RESTORE command reads that name and path in order to create a file to match what is recorded there.

Watch out: When you subsequently restore a file from the backup copy, the RESTORE function will re-create the path recorded in the backup file. You can restore a file only so that, when restored, it has the same name and is reached by the same path as it had when you made the backup. You won't be able to restore with a different name or to a different directory. The operator of a server machine can't (directly) restore a file whose backup was done by a user, because users and servers see the path differently. These aren't insurmountable problems, but they are complications you should be aware of.

Choice: A New Backup or Add to an Existing One

Unless you include the parameter /a (for *add*), BACKUP erases all files in the root directory of the target diskette or in the Backup directory, as the case may be. Before it actually erases anything, BACKUP displays a warning that it's about to do so and tells you to press any key when you're ready; to call it off, press Ctrl-C or Ctrl-Break.

When you include the parameter /a, the BACKUP command adds the files it is now storing to those already stored on the target disk. It rewrites the file called BackupID.@@@, leaves all other files in the directory alone, and writes a new file for each of the files it is backing up. Note that BACKUP can write a new version of a file without disturbing an old version, even though they have the same name.

BACKUP Coins New Names for Files on the Target Disk

The BACKUP command writes one file on the target disk for each file it backs up. To make sure all the files on the backup disk have unique names, the BACKUP command coins names for them.

When the source files all have distinct names, BACKUP just uses those names. But when the names overlap (for example, earlier and later versions of the same file, or files with the same name but from different subdirectories) BACKUP provides its own little variations, usually by substituting characters such as *@01* or *@02* for the extension. The name the file had in its source environment is written inside the file, and it doesn't necessarily match the name that the backup file is assigned in the target directory.

Backup to Diskettes Can Use a Lot of Diskettes

If you're running backup to diskettes, it's wise to do some arithmetic in advance to calculate the number you'll need and to have enough formatted diskettes ready in advance. It's particularly frustrating to have chugged through 14 diskettes and then realize when DOS prompts you, saying *Insert diskette 15 in drive A,* that you have nothing left but unformatted blanks. Backing up a reasonably full 10Mb PC/XT disk on 320k diskettes takes about 25 of them; backing up a 20Mb PC/AT disk onto high-capacity diskettes takes about 17.

Keep Two Records of What's Backed Up Where

As BACKUP works, it produces a report on what it's doing. *Save that record.* Save it as a file, and save it on paper. You need the file so you can easily search through it later if the need arises. You need a paper version because your machine-readable record may be one of the things no longer available when you have to do restoration. Moreover, the printout serves as a description of the diskettes generated by backup.

When you back up to diskettes, DOS calls the first diskette 01, the next 02, and so on. It writes those numbers in the file BackupID.@@@ stored on each backup disk or library, and at the same time displays that number at the console. Write the number on the diskette.

The sequence in which BACKUP stores the various files (and hence the sequence in which they appear on the diskettes) follows some internal logic of DOS that is not apparent to the human eye. You don't want to have to insert each of an entire boxful of diskettes to find the one that contains your missing file.

Storing the Diskettes

I've found the most convenient way to keep backup diskettes apart from other diskettes but together with the printed record of what's on them is to keep both diskettes and paper in a three-ring binder. The paper listing (on $8^1/_2 \times 11$ paper) can be three-hole punched. Stationery suppliers carry plastic pockets for diskettes that fit in the $8^1/_2 \times 11$ binders.

The DOS Command to Restore Files from Backup

The RESTORE command is the inverse of BACKUP. RESTORE starts with a backup disk or diskette called the *source,* and uses the data there to re-create a list of files on the *target* drive.

You have to restore either a single file or a set of files whose names match a pattern involving the wildcards * or ?. You can't ask to restore a directory, except incidentally by asking for a file (or all files) in a particular directory. If RESTORE has to create a directory to contain the files you've asked for, it does so. But your request is always for files, not directories.

The RESTORE command's syntax requires you to state two things: the drive containing the source, and the drive name and file name of the files to be restored. Figure 8.7 summarizes the parts of the command, and the following sections discuss them.

Action of RESTORE

If the source you've asked for is a diskette drive, RESTORE asks you to insert the first diskette, but skips that step when it isn't needed.

Next, RESTORE displays a message indicating the date of the source, like this:

```
*** Files were backed up on 09/20/1985 ***
```

The program gets that date from the file BackupID.@@@, created as part of the backup process. (Apparently the display is always in mm/dd/yyyy order, regardless of the DOS date convention.)

RESTORE *Source*: *Target*:*Path* /*Parameters*

Source	Drive name and colon for the device (real or virtual) from which to take the files being restored.
Target:	Drive name (real or virtual), colon, and complete path to the file(s) to be restored. (The drive name, colon, and initial \ may be omitted, in which case the current drive and default directory are understood and must match the path explicitly written in the backup files.)
Parameters:	As many as appropriate of the following parameters.
	/s Include *subdirectories* and the files within them.
	/p *Prompt* to confirm before restoring a file when either the backup copy is marked read-only or a more recent file of the same name already exists on the target drive.

Figure 8.7: *Syntax of the RESTORE command*

When the backup was done in stages on different dates, the date displayed is the one most recently written on the first disk. Since a virtual disk appears as all one disk, for a virtual disk the date is the date of the most recent of the backups. For a set of diskettes, it's the latest date on whichever diskette you insert first—usually, the earliest diskette.

The RESTORE command displays the complete path and file name of each file it restores as it restores it.

RESTORE Recreates the Path and Name of Each Backed-Up File

For each file that it restores, the RESTORE command re-creates the name and the path as they were at the time the file was stored by the BACKUP command. At that time, BACKUP recorded in each file the file's name and the path to it. RESTORE uses the recorded path both to verify that this is the file you are looking for and to name it when it is restored. This procedure has two consequences:

- In your request to restore, you must identify the file being restored by the name and path that it had when it was backed up.
- The effect of a successful RESTORE is to create a file with the same name and path it had when backed up.

That's the only way RESTORE restores. If you want to restore a file under some other name or into some other directory, first you have to restore it the way it was. After that, you can rename it or copy it to another directory.

RESTORE Doesn't Affect Existing Files with Different Names

When you restore an entire directory of files by a command such as *RESTORE a: c:\Paul*.**, the RESTORE command searches disk A for files that fit the pattern *\Paul*.** and restores those it finds to drive C. That isn't quite the same thing as returning the entire directory to its previous state. If at the time you run RESTORE your drive C already has a directory called \Paul, RESTORE leaves untouched any files whose names differ from those it finds on drive A.

Restoring from Diskettes

When the source drive mentioned in your command is a fixed disk or a virtual drive really located on a fixed disk, RESTORE can work through the backed-up files in a single pass. But when the source is a real diskette drive, RESTORE has to work one by one through a collection of diskettes. It prefers to do them in order, and starts by asking you to insert diskette 01.

(A diskette's number in the backup sequence is recorded in the file BackupID.@@@, which BACKUP writes on each backup diskette. It's in binary; you won't be able to see it with the TYPE command.)

The standard procedure is to insert diskette 01 when prompted, then diskette 02, and so on. This continues until RESTORE finds the file you asked for, or (when you're restoring all files whose names match a pattern) until it reaches the last diskette. (Each diskette's BackupID.@@@ indicates whether it's the last diskette.)

Going Straight to the Right Diskette

If you know which diskette has the file or files you want, you can ignore RESTORE's request for the next diskette in sequence and simply give it the diskette it needs. It notices the departure from sequence and asks you to confirm (see Figure 8.8). You can do that both while looking for a single file and while searching for all that match a pattern. (Of course, it's your fault if RESTORE can't find a file because you withheld a needed diskette.)

Watch out: The BACKUP command permits a backed-up file to *span* diskettes. That is, the backup version can start on one diskette and continue on the next. In the list of backed-up files reported by BACKUP, a spanned file's name occurs on the list for every diskette that contains any part of it. However, RESTORE only looks for the beginning of a file.

```
Mon 1985-11-25  8.15.36 C:\> dir \Batch\Qlink.bat
 Volume in drive C has no label
 Directory of  C:\BATCH
File not found

Mon 1985-11-25  8.15.51 C:\> restore a: c:\Batch\Qlink.bat
Insert backup diskette 01 in drive A:
Strike any key when ready
*** Files were backed up 09/20/1985 ***

Warning! Diskette is out of sequence
Replace diskette or continue if okay
Strike any key when ready

*** Restoring files from drive A: ***
Diskette: 11
\BATCH\QLINK.BAT

Mon 1985-11-25  8.16.47 C:\> dir c:\Batch\Qlink.bat
 Volume in drive C has no label
 Directory of  C:\BATCH
QLINK    BAT      382  85-07-01  15.36

■
```

Figure 8.8: *Going straight to the disk that has the file you want*

If you start with a diskette that has some other part of the file you're seeking, RESTORE won't recognize it. Moral: When you're looking through the list of backed-up files and find the name you want at the head of the list for a diskette, check the tail of the preceding list to make sure your file didn't really start there.

**Restoring One File vs.
Restoring All Files Whose Names Match a Pattern**

When you ask for just one file, RESTORE searches the backup disk until it finds the name and path you asked for. It restores that file and stops. It displays the name of the file as it restores it, and then returns to the DOS prompt. If it searches to the end and hasn't found the file you asked for, it sends you the message *Warning! No files were found to restore.*

But when you ask to restore all files that fit a pattern, RESTORE searches the entire backup disk (or the entire set of backup diskettes). Each time it finds a file whose name fits the pattern, it restores that file and displays it. If it searches to the end and hasn't found any file whose name matches the pattern, it sends you the message *Warning! No files were found to restore.*

Those procedures sound simple enough, but lead to complications when the backup disk contains multiple versions of the same name.

**Restoring When the Backup Contains
Multiple Versions of the Same File**

It's quite possible for the backup disk to contain several versions of the same file. That can arise when you produce the backup disk in a series of incremental backups spread over a period of time, each after the first using the /a parameter to add files to those already backed up. If you back up only files that had been modified, but a user makes changes to the same file between each of your incremental backups, a version of that file might be included at each increment.

When asked to restore a file in this situation, you probably want the *most recent* backed-up version. But on occasion, your user may want a specific older version. Either way, this is a situation that RESTORE handles badly, and you have to pick your way with care.

When you use a wildcard such as * to request restoration of any files that fit a particular pattern, RESTORE reads through all the backed-up files, restoring each that fits the pattern. It works through the list in the order they were written by BACKUP. Where there are different versions of the same file, RESTORE comes to the oldest first and restores it, then overwrites that with the next version it finds, and so on. You end up with the most recent version that the backup disk contains.

But when you ask to restore a single file, RESTORE takes the first file it finds that matches the name you asked for, restores that file, and quits. In that circumstance, you get the *earliest* of the multiple versions.

There are ways of getting around this shortcoming of RESTORE. One way is to give it only the diskette that contains the one version you want. That works, but only when the different versions are on different diskettes.

Tinkering with the Backup Disk

Another technique is to alter the backup disk so RESTORE won't find the versions you don't want. On the backup disk, all the backed-up files are in the same directory (the root directory of a diskette, or the \Backup directory otherwise). Each file is stored under the first eight characters of its original name, plus an arbitrary three-character extension to make its name different from the name of any other file on the disk.

The file's complete original name, including the path that led to it (but not the drive on which it was located) are written in the 128-character prefix, along with the date at which the file being backed up was last written. When RESTORE looks for a file, it considers all the files for which the first eight characters match, and then looks inside those to check the path and extension. So one way to prevent RESTORE from finding the wrong version of a file is to rename it so that the first eight characters of its name no longer match. (Remember to rename it again, once you've completed your RESTORE. Or back up the backup disk before you start tinkering.)

You Decide What to Do with Current Files of the Same Name

When you ask to restore a file but a file of the same name already exists on the target drive, RESTORE may or may not replace the existing one with the backup version. These are the rules:

- When the backup version has a date and time *more recent* than the date of the file you now have, RESTORE always erases the current file and replaces it with the backup version.
- When the backup version has a date and time *older* than the date of the file you now have, RESTORE erases the current file and replaces it with the backup version (even though it's older) *unless* you included the parameter /p in your request to back up. When you have included /p, RESTORE asks what you want to do about each such file (see Figure 8.9).

Effect of Restoring to a Virtual Drive

A path starts from the root directory of a drive. However, what looks like a drive to a network user may look like a directory to the server machine. Suppose a diskette contains a backup file whose name and path at the time it was backed up (duly recorded inside the backup file) are *\Report\April.*

When you restore that file to the server machine's drive C, in the root directory of drive C RESTORE creates a directory called Report, and in that directory stores a file named April.

Suppose a network user has access to a directory called \Paul on the server machine, and calls it drive E. Suppose the user takes the very same backup diskette containing \Report\April and restores it to drive E. From the user's point of view, RESTORE creates a file e:\Report\April. But from your point of view at the server machine, the file thus created is called \Paul\Report\April.

At present, neither BACKUP nor RESTORE has provision for network paths starting with the double backslash.

Restoring Read-Only Files

Parameter /p causes RESTORE not only to ask about overwriting a current file with an older version, but also about overwriting a current file when the backup version is marked *read-only.* Presumably, read-only

```
Tue 1985-11-26 10.03.08 C:\> restore a: c:\DavidK\*.* /p /s

Insert backup diskette 01 in drive A:
Strike any key when ready

*** Files were backed up 11/26/1985 ***

*** Restoring files from drive A: ***
Diskette: 01
\DAVIDK\NETPATH.BAT

Warning! File \DAVIDK\PROFILES\TEXTPROF
was changed after it was backed up
Replace the file (Y/N)?
```

Figure 8.9: *RESTORE asks whether to restore an old version*

files are reference copies not subject to casual revision. You might simply skip over the restoration of a file that can't have been changed.

The Read-Only Check
When You Have Installed a New Version of DOS

Checking whether to restore a read-only file is particularly important when you're restoring files from a backup that was made earlier than your current version of DOS. If you backed up all the files in the root directory, or in the \Apps\DOS directory, your backup may include copies not only of the files you can see but also of the hidden files such as the DOS files IBMBIO.com and IBMDOS.com. When you subsequently restore, the RESTORE command routinely includes those files in the restoration.

If you now have a new version of DOS, you don't want RESTORE to overwrite your new DOS with the old. Including parameter /p causes RESTORE to ask before restoring read-only files, including the hidden DOS command files. That's when you seize the opportunity to tell it no.

Alternative Approaches to Backup and Restoration

Out of the collection of details in the foregoing sections, there emerge some general questions about how to organize backup and restoration. They're policy questions with which the network administrator and the operators of server machines have to wrestle. Put these on your agenda:

- Should backup and restoration of user directories on server machines be part of the service that the servers offer, or a private matter left to the individual users?
- How often should you run a complete backup/reformat/restore of the fixed disks of server machines?
- How often should you run a full backup (but without reformat and restore)?
- How often should you run an incremental backup (including only files that have been changed)?
- Should incremental backups be merged or saved in separate disks (or sets of diskettes)?
- Should the incremental backup include all files changed since the last full backup, or only those changed since the last incremental backup?

- Should backups you run from the server machine be divided according to the server's organization (for example: back up all of disk C) or according to the users' organization (for example: run a separate backup for each of the user directories)?
- How long should you keep old backups? How many generations of backup are needed? What should be the retention schedule for incremental backups?

I can't offer you answers to these questions. The choice between these alternatives depends on why you are doing backups, the frequency you anticipate for various kinds of restorations, and their costs and benefits. To decide these, someone has to estimate the cost of making and storing backups in various ways, and the value of the various restorations you might be able to provide.

For example, backing up only those files altered since the last incremental backup reduces the work (and perhaps storage) required to do backups, but increases the effort needed to restore a group of files (since the restoration may have to read from several different backups).

If you back up according to the organization of the server machine, you back up everything on the fixed disk, regardless of who owns it. It's a single large job. If you organize backup by user, you run a separate backup for each user directory. The choice depends in part on why you think you'll have to restore files. If restoration arises from a failure of the whole disk, backing up and restoring the disk as a whole is easiest. But if you expect restorations to arise mostly from the requests of individual users, having on hand separate backups for each user directory may make for more convenient restoration.

Security

By security, I mean whether one user's sensitive data stored in a network is safe from inspection or alteration by others. Internal security involves protection from one's colleagues on the network. External security involves protection from outsiders, or at least from people who have no normal access to any of the network machines.

These are very large topics, and this isn't the place to address them thoroughly. I content myself with a few observations about using PC Network.

Although Network Data Circulates, It's Hard to Intercept

A remarkable property of PC Network (and many other LANs) is that data is broadcast throughout the network's cables and is physically available to every machine. You might think that having everybody's information at every machine presents a security problem. Nevertheless, that doesn't seem to me where data leaks are likely to take place. Eavesdropping on the electronic signal, while technically possible, strikes me as quite demanding: something perhaps within the range of elaborate industrial espionage, but outside the range of interoffice snooping. Usually, a local-area network is so much more vulnerable to much simpler forms of intrusion that I see little need to focus attention on interception of the data signal between machines.

Access Depends on Identification

The user whose files are stored on a network server is in much the same position as the user of a time-sharing system. The server provides service to any machine that correctly requests to use the network names the server has offered and supplies the right passwords to go with them. PC Network doesn't really offer any other kind of security. (The network hardware includes a unique machine name for each machine. Using it, you could prevent access from any but particular machines. That might forfeit some of the advantages of LAN flexibility. In any event, the PC Network program doesn't make use of the hardware ID provided in the adapter card.)

Users are likely to automate start-up by putting much of what is required into an Autoexec file. The Autoexec frequently includes the network names of resources the user routinely uses, although usually not the passwords. For a machine without a hard disk, Autoexec resides on the diskette used to start the machine. For a machine with a hard disk, it probably but not necessarily resides on the hard disk; it could be on a diskette.

A start-up diskette is like a key: insert it and it gives you access, or at least partial access. If the organization takes security and privacy seriously, users have to treat start-up diskettes seriously. Users shouldn't simply leave those diskettes in drive A or in the tray beside the computer. At a hard-disk machine, access may be even simpler: merely turning the power on activates Autoexec. For machines that have keys (such as the PC/AT), the keys should be used. For machines that don't have keys, start-up should be from a diskette, and the diskette secured.

The Person Who Has Physical Custody of the Fixed Disk Can Do Anything with What's Stored There

There is no part of the fixed disk to which the operator of the machine does not have access. The operator of the fixed-disk machine can read, change, copy, or delete any data stored there. (Perhaps the operator can't decipher or interpret the data, but she certainly has access to it.)

You have to be able to trust the operators of server machines. If you put sensitive data in their care, you have to have confidence that they won't misuse it. In many ways they're running a time-sharing service; it's quite common to require that operators of large time-sharing systems be bonded. A LAN serves a smaller and more cohesive group, but ultimately the issue is the same.

You have to be able to secure the server machines. For much of the time, the server may require no intervention from the operator. The operator may either use the server machine for her own work or let the machine run unattended. If a machine is left unattended while serving the network, it's important to restrict access to it. Note that on the PC/AT you can lock the keyboard while the machine is running, and you can detach the keyboard of any PC.

Keep Physical Custody of Sensitive Data

PCs offer an approach to security that is not available to users of time-sharing terminals: you can keep your data in your desk. When you don't want to trust sensitive data to a remote server, you don't have to. You can keep it on diskettes over which you have total control.

Note that the user who retains physical custody of her own data thereby takes on the responsibility to back up and restore it. But that's something any user of the network is always free to do.

Keep Physical Control of Your Own Server

To keep physical custody of your own data, you don't have to rely on diskettes. It's also possible to partition the network so that a group of users can keep physical custody of their own server machine and its fixed disk.

For example, suppose a network serves a moderate-sized company with 25 PCs. Six of those PCs are located in the accounting department, within the premises used by the company's financial services division. The area used by financial services is separated from the rest of the company by a locked door. Accounting personnel arrange to have the server that contains their financial records physically inside their quarters. They can turn it off and lock it up when they're not using it, leaving the rest of the network quite unaffected.

Such an arrangement takes advantage of PC Network's decentralization. While in some circumstances decentralization complicates security because servers may be scattered, decentralization also permits a cluster of users to control physical access to one of the machines that serve them.

Encryption

Several vendors offer programs that encrypt data written in files. The plaintext version of your file exists only in the main memory of your machine and only while you're actually using it, while all copies ever written to a file are first encrypted. Readable versions of your data are neither stored on any disk nor transmitted over the network. The idea is that even if other people read the saved version of your data, they find only meaningless patterns of bits.

Of course, this means you have to have a program capable of decrypting the data for you. The program that does the encryption and decryption doesn't itself have to be secret. It may instead depend on a key that is different for each application. You provide the key much as you would a password at the time you use your file.

Don't Put Sensitive Data on a Disk You Share with People Who Shouldn't Read It

Even if nobody snoops or pries, there's still the risk that someone you didn't intend will end up reading your data—perhaps quite inadvertently. It happens like this: You create a file on the server machine containing your sensitive data. Then you delete the file. DOS marks it as deleted. Later, you or someone else runs a program that allocates space for a new file. DOS assigns the new file to space formerly used by your old file. Under certain not-too-farfetched circumstances, the new owner of the space may read your old data.

This arises from some loopholes in the ways DOS formerly managed files. The loopholes seem to have been closed by the *file handles,* which are now the standard method by which programs ask DOS for access to files. However, DOS continues to support programs that used the earlier *file control blocks* (FCBs). Indeed, FCBs are at present far more common. Once a program had (properly) been allocated space, some access methods using FCBs permitted the program to read from any part of its allocation, even from locations in which the program had never written. This amounts to accidental use of the technique for resurrecting erased files described earlier in the chapter.

One way to avoid such embarrassments is to use a program that overwrites your entire file with blanks before it releases the space to DOS via the ERASE command. (It has to do that, of course, for *every* copy of the file that the program may have made during your use of the file, not just to the most recent version. Notice that when you ask text processors to save, most of them create an altogether new file containing the current version and then erase the former one.) Another perhaps surer and certainly simpler technique is not to write such data on disks you share with people you wouldn't want to read it.

Managing Shared Printers

Nine

Any PC having both a fixed disk and a printer can share the printer with the network. If your machine has more than one printer, you can decide separately for each printer whether to share it or keep it as a local device. However, all printers that are shared are operated from a common queue of network print jobs. This chapter tells you what you'll need to know when you're the person operating a server with a network printer.

To share your printer, you must first start the network in the server configuration (see Chapter 2) and then offer the printer to the network (see Chapter 3). If you regularly operate your machine as a print server, you'll probably have each offer to share a printer included in your Autoexec file so that the offers are made automatically when you start your machine.

After you turn on the power to the printer, you may have to set it up. What is required depends heavily on the make and model of printer. Some may require you to determine such things as margin settings, page size, print size, line spacing, default fonts, and so on. Others may retain those settings when the power is turned off, and are therefore ready to go as soon as you turn the power on. Even with those that are ready to start at once, it may still be necessary to set the controls at the start of each job to restore settings that the preceding job may have altered. That can be done with the *separator page,* discussed later in this chapter.

If your printer needs setting up before it is ready to print, it's important to complete the initial setup *before* the network print manager starts sending jobs. Since the print manager becomes active automatically as soon as you offer to share the printer, Chapter 12 includes a procedure to warn you when it already has jobs waiting before you start it.

Organization of Printing

The work of printing is divided into three more or less autonomous phases:

- Accepting files to be printed as they come in from the network. This is handled by the *server* function of PC Network, which also handles shared disk files.
- Displaying or adjusting the queue of jobs waiting to be printed and various conditions affecting printing. This is handled by the menu screen entitled *Print queue tasks.*
- Transferring jobs from the print queue to the appropriate printer. This is handled by the *print* function of PC Network, which I here refer to as the *print-manager program* or just the *print manager.*

You Too Are a Network User When Your Printer Is Shared with the Network

A printer can serve only one master at a time: your machine or the network. While your printer is shared with the network, you too must use it as a network printer. When (for example) you make your LPT1 a network printer, PC Network automatically redirects your own use of the name LPT1 so that jobs you send to LPT1 go to the network print queue, just as if they were sent over the network. (Details of the automatic offer are described in Chapter 3.)

Once you have started the network in the server configuration, you can no longer use the DOS command PRINT for any purpose—not even for a printer that you have withheld from the network. If you try, you'll get the message *Cannot use PRINT - Use NET PRINT.* That's true whether or not you've offered to share a printer, and whether or not you've used *NET PAUSE* to suspend print redirection. Once you've started the server, PC Network's print-manager program is the sole mechanism for running the printer as a background job.

One Printer Local, Another Shared with the Network

When you have more than one printer, you can share them all with the network, or share some and retain local control of others. Unlike the PRINT command, NET PRINT requires that you include explicitly the name of the printer on which a job is to be printed, after the name of the file. When you name a local printer (that is, one not included in an offer to share), NET PRINT sends the job to the local printer immediately. But when you name a printer you've offered to share, your job goes to the network print queue.

Several Printers on the Same Machine

It's quite possible to attach several printers to the same machine. If you have such a configuration, you can choose to share any number of your printers with the network. The network treats each printer as a separate network device. You can suspend or resume printing of the various network printers independently.

There is only one printer spool and only one print queue, regardless of the number of printers shared with the network. When network print jobs are received at your machine, they all go to the same spool and are recorded in the same queue. Each job's entry in the print-queue file \Network\PQ.spl records the printer for which the job is destined. When the job comes to the top of the queue, the print manager sends it to the appropriate printer.

You can tell from the foregoing that it is possible to operate several network printers on the same machine, but PC Network isn't optimized for multiple shared printers. As long as one printer is busy, the print manager won't send out another job, even though the printer to which the next job is destined is idle. You can overlap the operations of multiple printers only to the extent that the printers themselves contain large buffers.

The Print Queue and the Printer Spool

When a network user's request to print a file is redirected to the network printer on your machine, here's what happens. (Remember that for this purpose you too are a network user.)

PC Network renames the file to be printed and stores it in the \Network directory. The file is given a name in the form *PQ000.spl.* As files arrive, each is given a number one higher than the file before. When the numbers reach *PQ999.spl,* they recycle. Collectively, the set of files with names in that form is called the *printer spool.*

At the same time the file is stored in the spool, a record of it is entered into the *print queue.* The queue is a table with room for 99 print jobs. The table is stored in the file *\Network\PQ.spl.* The bulk of that file is a 99-row table containing a brief description of each of 99 possible print jobs.

Each row of the table includes the *job number* of the job it describes. The job number is the three digits in the name assigned to the file when it was stored in the spool. Each row also records the name of the machine that submitted the job, the size of the file in bytes, the date and time the job was received (according to the server's clock), the printer on which the job is to be printed, and the job's current status (waiting, printing, held, etc.). (Most of this is in binary machine language, so it doesn't help you to display the file with the TYPE command.)

To indicate their positions in the queue, each record includes a pointer to the row of the table containing the jobs that precede and follow it. From that linked list, the display menus construct a report showing the jobs in the order they will be printed.

How Jobs Get into the Queue

The network software adds jobs to the queue automatically. Jobs are transferred to the spool and listed in the queue without any action or intervention on your part and with no outward sign.

The process of accepting jobs for printing is among the activities suspended when you suspend the server by the command *NET PAUSE Server* (see Chapter 6). During such a pause, a user who tries to submit a print job gets the message *NET821: Sharing temporarily paused.* PC Network won't let you suspend the server while any user has a file open on your shared disk, including a file opened by the network to transfer a job to the printer spool. Thus, your request to suspend can't interrupt a transfer that has already started.

The process of accepting jobs to be printed halts when there's no more space on your fixed disk to store an incoming job or when all 99 rows of the queue table are filled by pending jobs. Under those conditions, a person who tries to submit a print job gets the message *NET813: Not enough space for print file* or *NET812: Print queue full,* as appropriate.

Recovery from any of these conditions is automatic. That is, when the condition that caused the halt has been cleared up, the network again accepts requests for printing without your having to tell it to do so.

Start-Up Parameters That Affect the Flow of Jobs into the Spool

Start-up parameters and their tuning are discussed in Chapter 13. Here I simply list those that may affect the operation of the printer.

- TSI: The balance between network data transfers (including transfers from the user to the printer spool) and work local to your machine (including transfers from the spool to the printer).
- REQ and RQB: The number and size of the independent buffers your machine uses to transfer files to and from the network, including files arriving for the printer spool.

How Jobs Get from the Queue to the Printer

As soon as you make the offer to share a printer with the network, PC Network activates the print manager. It runs as a background job, making use of the program \Network\PSPrint.exe, but you are never involved directly in invoking it and so you never use that name. The print-manager program periodically turns your machine's attention to checking the print queue. As needed, it transfers a block of text from one of the spool files to the printer's buffer. Usually this takes so little of the computer's time that it can keep the printer continuously busy and still devote most of its attention to whatever you are doing in the foreground.

When the print-manager program notices a job in the queue, it sets about transferring the job to the printer. Provided the printer is connected and enabled (or *selected* or *on line,* depending on the manufacturer's jargon), the print manager starts the printer. All this happens with no intervention on your part. (In fact, it may even happen before you're ready; see the section on premature start of printing, later in this chapter.)

When there is no backlog of jobs to be printed, a job starts appearing on the printer within seconds of being submitted. When several jobs are submitted at about the same time, they probably arrive faster than the printer can print them and accumulate in the queue.

There's a great deal of difference between the speeds at which various printers can print, and even wider variation in the rate at which users submit jobs. In most situations, the limiting factor is the speed of the printer itself, rather than of the print manager. If 99 jobs are waiting in the queue, users will be unable to submit more until some of the waiting jobs leave the queue (by being either printed or canceled).

**Start-Up Parameters
That Affect the Flow of Jobs from Spool to Printer**

The following parameters govern the transfer of jobs from the spool to the printer:

- PRB: The size of the buffer used for transferring data from a file in the printer spool to the printer.
- PRP: Relative priority of the print manager versus tasks initiated from the keyboard of the server machine.

The Print-Queue-Manager Screen

Within the menus, one screen lets you both display and alter the print queue. As operator of the server machine on which the print queue is located, you are the only person who can alter the queue. Once a print request reaches the server machine, the remote user who submitted it has no further control over it. For this reason, when users want to hurry along or cancel jobs they've submitted, you're likely to hear from them.

Curiously, there are no commands to manipulate or display the print queue directly; you do it all through the menus. The route is as follows:

1. At the main menu, select *Print queue tasks.*
2. At *Print queue tasks,* select *Check or change the print queue on your computer* (see Figure 9.1).

PC Network displays a screen on which you can see the print queue and select an option regarding individual jobs within it. The screen has room to show only a dozen queue entries at a time, but when there are more, you can use the PgUp and PgDn keys (on the numeric keypad) to scroll the display so you can see other jobs in the queue.

Meaning of Terms in the Status Field

Printing: The print manager has begun the task of transmitting the spool file to the printer. (Perhaps the job is printing. However, the print manager doesn't know one way or the other. This message can't tell you whether anything has reached the paper yet.)

Held: You earlier told the print manager to hold this job. A job that has been held retains its place in the queue but remains ineligible to be printed until you release it.

Waiting: The job is not held, but has not yet reached the top of the queue. A job that is waiting cannot be processed while another job is still listed as *printing*.

Printer error: The print-manager program attempted to print the file but was unable to do so (usually because the printer was not ready or because of some other malfunction of the printer). The help screen offers some odd advice about this condition; see Recovery from Printer Errors later in this chapter.

Print file error: The print manager attempted to print the file (and perhaps did print the separator page that precedes the job itself, showing its job number). However, the print manager was unable to find the file itself. This usually arises because for some reason you erased or renamed the file after it was logged into the queue. Possibly it can arise from a failure after an incoming job has been assigned a position in the queue but before the file itself has been received from the user—but that's such a split-second thing that I haven't been able to verify it.

Canceled: This is a transitory report: a job has been interrupted or you have asked to cancel it, but the print-manager program has not yet disposed of it. Usually a job reported as *canceled* is being removed from the queue and vanishes when you next display the queue.

```
                                                                IBM PC NETWORK
                          Check or Change the Print Queue

1. Update queue    ID  User Name        Size     Device   Status
                                 -- Start of Queue --
2. Hold            011 SERVER2         56154 LPT1      HELD
                   012 SERVER2           100 LPT1      HELD
3. Release         030 LIEU            64182 LPT2      PRINTING
                   031 PAUL             3174 LPT2      WAITING
4. Cancel          032 SACHIKO         15922 LPT2      WAITING
                   033 PAUL              400 LPT1      WAITING
5. Print next      034 LIEU             9102 LPT1      WAITING
                   035 BARRY           80187 LPT1      WAITING
6. Print now       036 SACHIKO          6540 LPT1      WAITING
                   037 DAVID            3332 LPT1      WAITING
                   038 SERVER1          1230 LPT1      WAITING
1  Choice          039 SACHIKO               LPT1      SPOOLING
                                  -- End of Queue --

     ↑ and ↓ - Select file                    PgUp and PgDn - Scroll List
     Enter - Change queue                     F1 - Help
     Ctrl-Home - Return to Main Menu          Esc - Previous menu
```

Figure 9.1: *Display of a server machine's print queue*

However, a job whose printing has been interrupted by a rush job shows *canceled* for a moment but then returns to *waiting.*

Paused: All the jobs destined to a printer whose printing has been suspended (by the NET PAUSE command) are described as *paused.* The status *paused* supersedes the report of the job's individual status, so you can't see whether it is also *held* or merely *waiting.* Personally, I think this a mistake in the design of the report. Naturally, you'd like to know the status of the printer, but the printer's status should be reported independently of the status of the individual jobs. Curiously, remote users never see the message *paused;* when they inquire about their jobs in the queue, they continue to see the job's own status, with no indication of the status of the printer.

Changing the Print Queue

The menu that shows you the present status of the queue also offers you six possible actions (see leftmost column in Figure 9.1). Action 1, Update queue, simply generates a new display that takes into account changes since the last display was generated. Each of the other actions applies to *one* of the jobs in the queue. These five actions are described in the sections that follow.

On your screen, one of the jobs in the print queue is shown highlighted (in reverse video or a contrasting color). When you select one of the actions labeled 2 to 6 from among those listed on the left side of the screen, the action you select applies to the one job that is highlighted. The up and down arrows move the highlighting to the job you want. The arrows also scroll the display.

Hold a Job

When you *hold* a waiting job, it remains in the queue and continues to progress toward the top of the queue. However, when the job reaches the top of the queue, the print manager does not print it, but instead turns to the next job that is not held.

It's sometimes possible to hold a job whose printing has already started. That interrupts printing, but keeps the job in the queue; later, you can release it and the print manager will print it again from the beginning. However, sometimes when you signal *hold,* PC Network replies *Net217: Cannot change status of file at this time,* probably because printing is already too far along.

Release a Held Job, or Recover from a Print File Error

After you've held a job, the print manager does not consider it eligible to be printed until you *release* it. If the job you release is at the top of the queue, the print manager starts to print it. If the job isn't yet at the top of the queue, signaling *release* converts its status from *held* to *waiting*.

Release is also supposed to be useful in recovering from certain printer errors, but I've had little success with it and found other steps preferable; see Recovery from Printer Errors in the last part of this chapter.

Cancel a Job

You can *cancel* a job that is held or waiting, and you may be able to cancel a job that has started printing. Canceling deletes the job from the queue, erases its file in the spool, and abandons any part of it already printed.

Print Next to Change the Sequence of Jobs

The action *print next* takes the selected job from wherever it happens to be in the queue and places it next in line to be printed. If there is no active job at the top of the queue, the job you selected moves to first place; otherwise, the selected job moves to second place.

Signaling *print next* for a job whose status is *held* does not remove the hold. If you really want the job to be printed next, you have to signal *release* as well.

Print next is the only mechanism for reordering the queue. There's no way to say "print this third." However, you can produce any order you like by working through the desired sequence from last to first. For example, suppose the jobs in the queue are numbered 71 to 80, but you'd like to print 73 first, then 77, then 75. With printing paused and everything held (so nothing starts before you're ready) move 75 (your lowest priority) to the top of the queue first, then move 77 ahead of it, and finally move 73 to the top.

Print Now to Supplant What's Already Printing

The action *print now* is strong medicine. It cancels whatever is now printing so that printing the selected job can begin at once.

The job thus rudely interrupted remains in the queue. Its printing starts again from the beginning, when its turn comes. Unless you move other jobs as well, the interrupted job comes next after the one that interrupted it.

Pauses to Make Adjustments to the Printer

Printers being mechanical devices, there are times they need adjustment. Ribbons need replacement, paper needs replenishing, margins must be set, top of form calibrated, fonts loaded, and so on. It's wise to take care of as many of those as you can before you start the network printer. But inevitably, it will at times be necessary to suspend the flow to make adjustments.

PC Network provides a command *NET PAUSE Print.* (See Chapter 6 for general discussion of the NET PAUSE command.) For printer adjustments, *NET PAUSE Print* may be appropriate or it may be overkill. To achieve the temporary suspension you need, it may be sufficient or even preferable simply to deselect the printer (take it off line) by the appropriate setting of the printer's own switches, without any network command. This alternative is discussed further below.

The NET PAUSE Print Command

You can use the NET PAUSE command either to suspend the work of all network printers on your machine or to suspend the work of one particular network printer. To suspend all your network printers, the command is:

```
NET PAUSE Print
```

To suspend one printer (for example, LPT1), the command is:

```
NET PAUSE Print=LPT1
```

Notice that this suspends printing: that is, the transfer of jobs from the spool to the printer. It doesn't stop new jobs from being added to the printer spool.

Menu to Suspend Printing

The same choice is available in the menus: you can suspend all network printers or a specific network printer. The route is:

1. At the main menu, select *Pause and continue tasks.*
2. At *Pause and continue tasks,* select *Pause or continue printing files.* PC Network shows you a menu of four options. Select the one that's appropriate (see Figure 9.2).
3. If you asked to suspend a particular printer, fill in its DOS name (LPT1, etc.).

Effect of NET PAUSE Print on Jobs in Progress

Executing NET PAUSE Print or the corresponding menu option causes the print-manager program to interrupt a job in progress. Any output already printed is abandoned. The job remains in the print queue. When you resume printing (with the command NET CONTINUE) the job will start again from the beginning.

Because a considerable number of characters may already have been sent to the printer's buffers, the printer probably won't halt instantly when you execute NET PAUSE Print. It will probably print somewhere between a few lines and a few pages before it exhausts its buffers.

At the end of the printed output, the last thing visible is a message appended by the print manager: *File canceled by operator.* After that, the print-manager program sends a form feed and the alarm signal, which may cause the printer to beep or display a warning light.

A More Modest Suspension

As you can see from the foregoing, NET PAUSE Print may be more than you need. What you'd really like is a way to say *Hold at the end of the next complete page.* On some printers, tripping the switch that detects the end of the paper will do that.

Depending on the printer, for many small adjustments it may be neater, more effective, and more immediate simply to press the button on the printer labeled *Deselect* or *Off line.* That may cause the printer to stop instantly, or perhaps after printing what's already in the buffer. If you can make your adjustment without turning the printer's power off, go ahead and make it. When you've finished, press *Select* or perhaps *On line.* Printing continues exactly where it left off. In fact, as far as the print-manager program is concerned, the job has never been interrupted.

```
                                                          IBM PC NETWORK
                    Pause or Continue Printing Files

1. Pause printing on all printers

2. Continue printing on all printers

3. Pause printing on a printer

4. Continue printing on a printer

1 Choice




Enter - Continue                          F1 - Help
Ctrl-Home - Return to Main Menu           Esc - Previous menu
```

Figure 9.2: *Menu to suspend or resume one printer or all*

For some adjustments, such as changing a ribbon, you probably need to turn off the power to the printer, which may also reset some of its controls. Turning the power off will almost certainly cause PC Network to list a *Printer error* for your job. But don't give up yet; the print manager recovers very well from those. When you turn on the printer's power again (and if necessary press *Select* or *On line*), there's a fair chance that the print manager will return the job's status to *printing* and continue work on it with nothing either lost or duplicated.

If the job fails to resume where it should, you can still signal *hold* (so that you can restart the interrupted job from the beginning) or fall back on NET PAUSE Print. However, in my experience it has rarely been necessary to use NET PAUSE Print to make small adjustments to the printer.

Recovering Temporary Private Use of a Network Printer

On occasion, you may need temporarily to regain direct control of a printer you've shared with the network. To do that, you need to suspend both the printing of network jobs and the redirection of your own output to the network print queue. The command NET PAUSE PRDR is what you want (followed, optionally, by the DOS name of a particular printer).

As the name implies, PRDR suspends redirection to the printer spool. Not only does a command such as *COPY file LPT1* now go directly to the printer without passing through the print queue, but so also does a request such as *NET PRINT file LPT1*.

At the same time that NET PAUSE PRDR suspends redirection, it also suspends printing from the spool (see Chapter 6).

The Separator Page

At the beginning of each job, the print manager ordinarily prints a *separator page*. The separator serves two quite different functions. The first is to mark the beginning of each job and identify it. The second is to reset printer controls that may have been affected by the preceding job, so that a setting elected by one job doesn't propagate into the next. Both of these strike me as not merely useful, but essential. There are not many conditions under which I'd run without a separator page.

Menu to Control Use of a Separator Page

PC Network has a standard separator page that it uses by default. You have the option to instruct the print-manager program not to include a separator page or to use a different one. You can specify independently for each printer whether to print a separator, and if so the name of the file that describes the separator. The route through the menus is as follows:

1. At the main menu, select *Print queue tasks.*
2. At *Print queue tasks,* select *Start or stop printing a separator page.*
3. At *Start or stop,* select *Start.* PC Network shows you a screen in which it asks for the name of the file containing the separator file and fills in a suggested answer (see Figure 9.3).

The NET SEPARATOR Command

This command lets you specify a separator to be used, stops using a separator, or reports what separators are now being used. The word *separator* may be spelled out in full or abbreviated to *sep.*

You identify the printer by its DOS name (LPT1, for example). Following that, you write the name of the file containing directions for the separator. (If the file doesn't exist, you'll see the message *Net352: File not found.*) Here's a possible command:

NET SEPARATOR LPT2 c:\Apps\Text\PQLPT2.sep

If you omit the drive name or the complete path, PC Network assumes the default drive and current directory at the time you

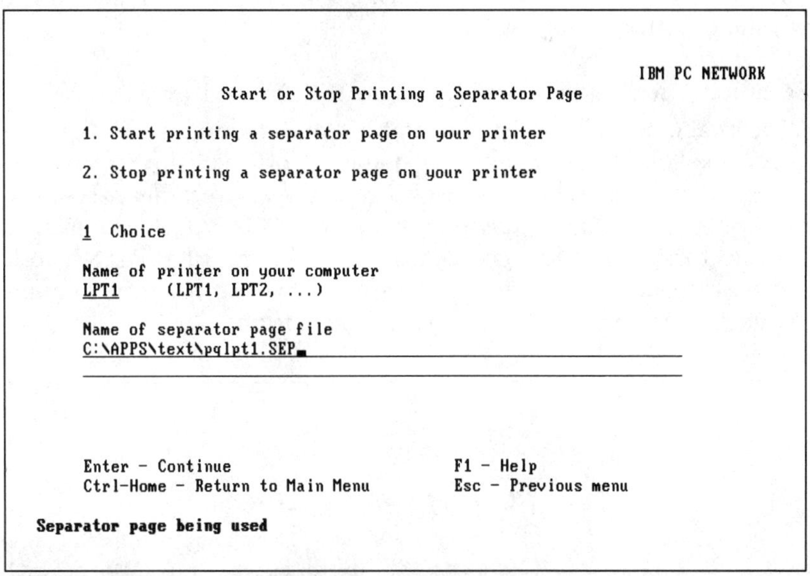

Figure 9.3: *Menu screen to specify a separator page*

executed the command. You can omit the name of the separator file, in which case PC Network uses *c:\Network\PQ.sep.*

The NET SEPARATOR command is always specific to one printer. Although PC Network doesn't always insist that the printer be shared with the network before you specify its separator file, it's safer to proceed in that order.

Ending Use of a Separator File

Termination requires NET SEPARATOR followed by the device name and the parameter /d (for *delete*). You can terminate the assignment of a separator file to a printer even when the printer isn't being shared. An example of a command to delete use of a separator file is:

```
NET SEPARATOR LPT2 /d
```

Inquiring about Separator Files

The command NET SEPARATOR with nothing following it gives you a report on the separators in use by all printers on your machine for which separator pages have been specified (whether or not the printers are now shared with the network); see Figure 9.4.

Watch out: Since the command NET SEPARATOR with nothing after it generates a report on separator files in use by any printer, you might think that NET SEPARATOR LPT1 would give you a report on the separator file used by LPT1. Wrong. Instead, it assigns to LPT1 the default separator \Network\PQ.sep.

Separator Specifications Are Stored on Disk Immediately

Facts about the use of separators are recorded in the file \Network\PQ.spl (along with the queue of print jobs). PC Network updates that file as soon as you change the specs regarding separator files (whether via the menus or via the NET SEPARATOR command). Because those items are recorded immediately in a file, PC Network can recall them at subsequent work sessions; they do not need and are not affected by the option *Save your network setup.*

Device	Separator File
LPT1	C:\APPS\TEXT\PQLPT1.SEP
LPT2	C:\APPS\TEXT\PQLPT2.SEP

Figure 9.4: *Report on separator files in use*

The Separators Provided by IBM

PC Network comes with a ready-made separator page in the file \Network\PQ.sep. As supplied, it is appropriate to the IBM Color Printer.

The codes in the file instruct the print-manager to reset several printer settings to normal defaults, in case the previous job has altered them. Then they generate a block-letter display to print *IBM PC NETWORK* on each job. Lower down on the page, they display the name of the machine that submitted the job in narrow block letters (because the names can have up to 15 characters), and below that the job number in wide block letters (see Figure 9.5).

If you're using a printer other than the IBM Color Printer, you need to edit the separator file to delete instructions that don't apply. You may also need to add others. Any text editor can do the job. Chapter 10 of the PC Network *User's Guide* contains a complete listing of the IBM default separator file. With the listing, the *User's Guide* provides a line-by-line explanation of how the codes in that file produce the separator page and which lines to delete to adapt the file to other IBM printers.

While you're making technical adjustments to the separator file, you could also edit its text to suit your organization's needs or taste. About the only thing I would add is some text indicating the name of the printer, which might be important if your network has more than one printer.

Separators for Non-IBM Printers

If your printer doesn't recognize the codes generated by the separator file that IBM supplies, you'll need to construct a separator of your own. This is essential. At best, inappropriate codes will print as junk on your separator sheet. At worst, they may send your printer quite berserk. (An IBM separator mistakenly sent to my Toshiba printer caused it to set its right margin next to its left margin, forcing a new line after every character of output.)

As a skeleton upon which you can build your own separator file, IBM distributes a bare-bones separator in the file \Network\PQ.OEM. A listing of it, with my added comments, appears in Figure 9.6.

Codes in the Separator File

Different printers are likely to need different separators. To build your own separator, you have to write a program in the language used for that purpose by the print manager. The separator file is a string of text, divided into lines in the usual way. The division into lines is for the convenience of the programmer, but note that a new line in the separator

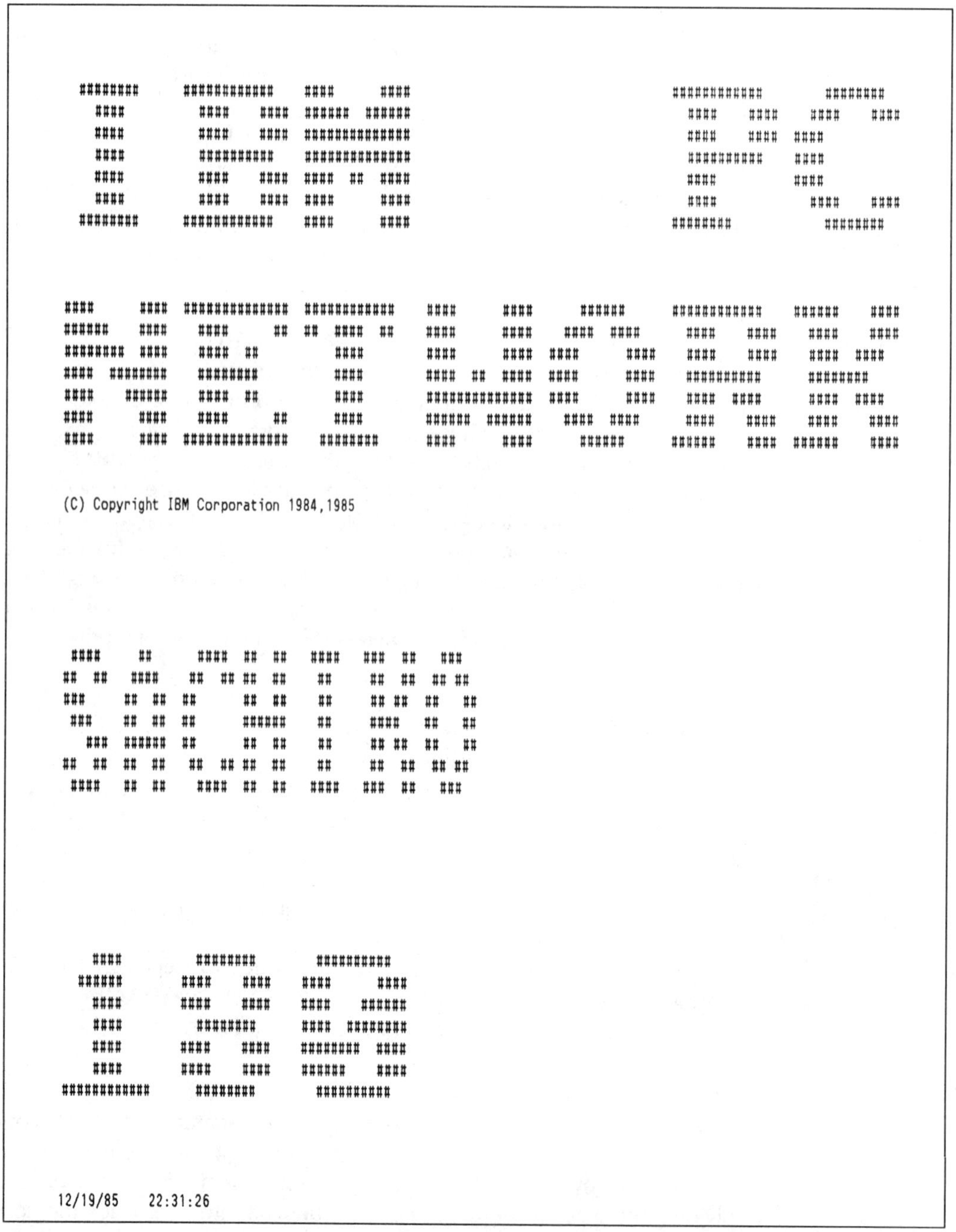

Figure 9.5: *Separator page generated by instructions in the default file \Network\PQ.sep*

file does *not* automatically become a new line in the finished separator page. Instead, the end of a line must be explicitly marked by a code (described in a moment).

Each code consists of an *escape character* followed by one or more characters. The escape character can be any ordinary character except blank. Whichever character occurs first in the separator file thereby becomes the escape character. In Figure 9.6 the first character (and hence the escape character) is @. The various codes are as follows:

@0	Numeral zero means end of line (described as <Cr>, for carriage return, in my comments to Figure 9.6). Each end of line must be shown explicitly.
@*n*	Skip *n* lines (where *n* indicates a numeral other than 0). A convenient way to indicate a vertical gap.
@B	Start block letters. The print manager replaces each ordinary character by a block of characters nine lines high (including two blank lines at the bottom) to form the shape of the character. The effect is to produce letters that are very large (although crude) without the use of special printer codes or graphics.
@S	Start single width. @B must precede. Sets the width of each block character to eight columns (the last of which is blank). When you start block characters, single width is assumed by default, so this code is necessary only to return to single width after you've used double width.
@M	Start double width. @B must precede. Sets the width of each block to 16 columns (the last two of which are blank).
@U	End block characters.
@L	Print the text that follows. All the characters that follow @L are printed, up to but not including the next escape character.
@F	Must be followed by the name of a file. Inserts the characters found in the named file as if they had been part of the separator file.
@I	Print the three numerals of the job number. The print-manager program obtains these from the job's entry in the queue.

@N	Print the 15 characters of the name of the machine that submitted the job. The print-manager program obtains these from the job's entry in the queue.
@D	Print the eight characters that represent the current date.
@T	Print the eight characters that represent the current time.
@H*nn*	Include one character, here defined by its two-character hexadecimal code. Used for sending a control character to the printer (see next section).
@E	Eject page. Sends a form-feed character. It is essential to send a form-feed as the last character of the separator page so that each job will start at the top of a fresh page.

Date and Time in the Separator Page

As you can see, the separator codes include codes for the date and the time. The print-queue file \Network\PQ.spl includes the date and time at which each job was submitted. PC Network displays the date and time of submission as part of its response to a user's inquiry about the print queue. Oddly, when you put @D and @T in the separator file, you get not the date and time of submission but the date and time of printing. I suspect a misunderstanding somewhere in the IBM programming team. At present, there's no way to get the separator page to divulge the submission date and time.

@@LIBM PC NETWORK@0	Make @ Escape. Print "IBM <tab> PC Network".	<Cr>
@4	Skip 4 lines.	
@B@M@I@0	Start block letters; start double-wide; print job no;	<Cr>
@U@4	End block letters. Skip 4 lines.	
@N@0	Print name of computer that submitted job.	<Cr>
@4	Skip 4 lines.	
@D@L @T@0	Print date now; Print "<tab> "; Print time now.	<Cr>
@E	Eject page (form feed).	
	End of file.	

Figure 9.6: *IBM's bare-bones file \Network\PQ.OEM, with comments added*

Control Characters to Set Up the Printer

In your separator file, it is prudent to include codes to return to normal all those printer controls that might be reset in the course of the previous job, in case the next job relies on the default values rather than setting its own. (A user can include any characters whatever in a job sent to the printer.) Depending on the printer, there may be quite a long list of options to reset. Control codes often require characters that are not normally printable. You can either identify the control characters by their hexadecimal codes (preceding each hexadecimal pair by @H) or insert the control characters themselves in the zone following @L (indicating the control character by pressing the Alt key and typing the character's decimal value on the numeric keypad).

Putting a Substitute Separator File into Use

To make use of a substitute separator file, you need only tell PC Network where it is, using the NET SEPARATOR command. Alternatively, if you have only one printer, you can rename files so that your substitute file takes on the default name \Network\PQ.sep.

Recovery from Printer Errors

PC Network's print manager recovers quite gracefully from error conditions. This section mentions several possible problems and approaches to recovering from them.

Reset or Failure of the Server Machine

You may get into a jam from which there's no escape but pressing Ctrl-Alt-Del or turning the power off to reset your computer. Or there may be a power failure that stops the server while it's sending work to the printer. Although these occurrences are inconvenient, they rarely result in any loss of print jobs.

The print-manager program removes a job from the queue and erases its file in the spool only after it has completed transmission of the job to the printer. If the computer is reset at any time before that final erasure, the file will still be there when you next start PC Network and so will its entry in the print queue, just as if printing had never started. The interrupted job can be started from the beginning.

The principal inconvenience is that when you restart PC Network, the print-manager program may resume work before you're ready for it. That issue is discussed next.

Premature Start of Printing Following a Crash or Following a Halt While Suspended

Whenever your machine offers to share a printer (for instance, when it executes NET SHARE as part of your Autoexec file), the print-manager program immediately starts printing any jobs that remain in the queue and were either *printing* or *waiting*—that is, were not marked *held*—when the preceding session ended. Those waiting jobs may have been affected by a *pause* that was then in effect. However, a pause does not carry over into a new session. Any jobs listed as *paused* at the previous session now revert to their earlier status, either *held* or *waiting.* Those that are now listed as *waiting* are immediately eligible for printing.

To avoid being caught unprepared, you should place commands needed to set up the printer ahead of commands to start the network in your file Autoexec.bat (see Chapter 2). Chapter 12 suggests a batch file that checks for the presence of pending print jobs before you start the network. (You might suppose that you could include NET PAUSE Print in the batch file to suspend printing before you offer to share the printer. Sorry; PC Network only permits you to suspend an activity after you've started it.)

If the printer has already started before you're ready, an improvised correction is to turn off the printer. That forces a *printer error* for the file at the top of the queue, considered next.

Recovery from Printer Error for a Specific File

After certain errors, the print manager gives up trying to print a file and lists its status as either *printer error* or *print file error.* If you then signal *hold,* the print-manager program ends the current attempt to print that job, but keeps it in the queue. You can signal *release* when you're really ready. (However, before you *hold* the job at the top of the queue, hold any that follow it, or they'll try to start too.)

The help message for the print queue screen advises that after *printer error* you should signal *release.* Perhaps the message assumes you have already signaled *hold* and have done something to correct the error, although it doesn't say that. In my experience, signalling *release* following *printer error* (as suggested in the help screen and in the *User's Guide*) doesn't help but yields the message *NET216: Cannot release a printing file.*

On the other hand, the print manager seems to recover spontaneously from printer errors caused by disconnected equipment, restarting at once when the equipment is connected, ready or not.

Recovery from Print File Error

The status *print file error* (distinct from *printer error*) is reported when the print-manager program is unable to read or find the file it is supposed to print. It is possible to recover, but the procedure isn't neat.

Following a print file error caused by a missing file, I have restored the missing file and then signaled *release.* On each occasion, the job's status has changed from *error* to *waiting.* In fact everything was waiting, but I don't know for what. I suspect a bug. When I cancel the job that has experienced the error, after that job disappears the job following it (also shown as *waiting*) reaches the top of the queue but cannot start.

I have found one way to get the print manager printing again: wait until the next occasion to start the network (or force one by resetting the computer with Ctrl-Alt-Del). That isn't exactly convenient, but it does the trick. When PC Network is again started, the print manager resumes its normal processing of jobs listed as *waiting,* and without losing print jobs.

Recovery from Damage to the Print Queue

In some circumstances, the print-queue file \Network\PQ.spl may become internally inconsistent or inconsistent with the files in fact in the spool. I've never experienced this, and I don't know how it can happen. The word from IBM technical people is that it is possible. If it happens to you, you'll see the message *NET058: Print queue not correct.*

Along with the description of that message in the PC Network *User's Guide,* you'll find a rather severe remedy. The manual suggests you delete all the files in the spool and copy a fresh print-queue file \Network\PQ.spl from the installation diskette.

To avoid throwing away the jobs now in the queue, I would amend that advice as follows:

1. If you can, display the print queue and note who submitted which jobs.
2. Delete \Network\PQ.spl. (This will cause an error for anyone who tries to submit a job while the print queue is deleted, but that person can resubmit the job.)
3. Rename all other files remaining in the spool, by a command such as *RENAME \Network*.spl *.old.*
4. Copy a fresh \Network\PQ.spl. There's one that should be in its virgin state in \Apps\Network\PQ.spl, or there's always the installation diskette.

5. Copy each of the renamed spool files to your network printer. (In case the files contain some control codes that DOS will otherwise mistake for an end-of-file, use COPY with the parameter /b, which indicates a binary file rather than one confined to standard ASCII characters.) Since your printer is shared with the network, copying the unprinted files to the printer will put them back in the queue. You'll have lost the information about who submitted them, but if you were able to get a display of the damaged queue, you should be able to match them up. And you won't have lost the jobs entirely.
6. Delete the renamed files.

Part II

Planning, Installing, and Maintaining PC Network

Planning the Network

Ten

The first part of this book describes the work of people who use and operate PC Network. The second part focuses on planning the network, setting up its hardware, and installing its software.

Although planning and installation logically come first, starting with operations was deliberate. The parts of the book you'll consult frequently are up front. Indeed, if for you the network is a fait accompli, something you use but did not build, you have little need to read further.

But if you are indeed planning for a network that has not yet been installed, whose plans are still fluid, the following chapters will tell you how to begin. I hope that on the way here you've looked at what's involved in operating the network. While you're setting up the tools people will use, it helps to have in mind the sorts of things they'll be doing when they use what you are planning.

The aim of this chapter is to give you a basis for reviewing some key questions: How many machines? Located where? With what memory? With what printers? With what fixed disks? Serving how many people? Doing what tasks? Located where? With what skills? Organized how?

Before Anything Is Installed

As you plan the installation of a network, start with the work you need computers to perform and the way you want the network to contribute to the various tasks. Analyzing your work to allocate functions to computers is a vast and fascinating topic well beyond the scope of this book. Here I can only assume that you know more or less what you'd like to achieve, and move on to the steps you need to go through to set it up.

The Cast of Machines and People

Before you start buying PCs or connecting cables, you'll need a list of the machines you want to put on the network and the configuration of each.

Machines are used by people. For each machine you expect to connect to the network, you should list the human role that goes with it. Just as machines have different roles in a network, so do the people who use them. Indeed, networking creates some human roles for which your organization may not yet have provided. So the list you need is not just a list of machines, but a list of roles, with both the machines and the people that you expect to fill those roles.

Servers and Users

In PC Network, the major distinction—both for people and for machines—is between the roles of servers and users. PC Network has a rather egalitarian style, in which almost anybody can in some situations be in a serving role, and the roles of users and servers often overlap. In setting up the network, the key questions for planning are:

- How many many users will there be (both people and machines)?
- How many servers will there be (both people and machines)?

It isn't possible to state precise rules for deciding those questions, but in what follows I present some issues that bear on them and some rules of thumb that may be helpful in estimating a plausible setup for your network.

Linking Existing Machines versus Installing New Ones

If you're planning a network from scratch, you have a little more freedom in deciding the mix of machines you'll purchase. Conversely, if you're linking the machines you already have, features of the existing machines may constrain what you can do. But it may not make a great deal of difference, provided you arrange in one way or another that all machines meet the minimum requirement for playing the role of user, and you have sufficient machines capable of playing the role of server.

Typically, an organization sets up a network when some of its members already have some PCs operating in stand-alone fashion, plan to get more, and realize it would be useful to create a network that can connect both the existing machines and the new ones. So installation of a network often requires both linking existing machines and writing specs for the acquisition of some new ones.

Starting Small and Growing

A major advantage of PC Network is that you can start small and add gradually. The number of users can increase as the need arises, and so can the number of servers. Costs are more or less linear; the only cost that's fixed for an entire network is the *translator* (required for the broadband version, which uses just one translator regardless of the number of computers).

As you increase the number of users of the network, you will also need to expand the number of server machines and the number of people experienced in working with servers.

Centralized versus Distributed Servers

If you're talking about only a small number of machines—say, half a dozen—a single server can probably handle everybody. Even then, there are times when you'd probably find it convenient for other machines temporarily to take on the role of server.

As your network grows beyond a handful of machines, PC Network both permits and requires decentralized serving. In this regard PC Network differs strikingly from a time-sharing system with a single host computer surrounded by a cluster of terminals. It also differs from those local-area networks that depend on a single large central server for the entire network of PCs.

A machine playing the role of server is ordinarily limited to serving no more than 25 other machines at the same time. So it is necessary to have more than one server if the total number of machines exceeds 26. It's almost certainly desirable to increase the number of servers before that. (The 25-machine limit comes from the maximum value of the start-up parameter RDR, derived in turn from the capacity of the adapter card. A specialized server such as the Sytek 6110 apparently permits this limit to be doubled by installing two adapter cards in the same machine.)

The Various Roles of Machines

You need to estimate the number of machines in the following categories. For each, you need both the physical configuration you want for each machine and the skill level and approximate work description of the person or people using it.

1. *Users:*
   a. Heavily reliant on one or more servers for disk space
   b. Heavily or totally reliant on one or more servers for printing
   c. Limited use (occasional use of shared disk space or printing)
   d. Rare ad hoc use to transfer a file
2. *Servers:*
   a. Widely used by others for disk storage
   b. Widely used by others for printing
   c. Limited use by others (probably for shared disk storage by a limited group)
   d. Rare ad hoc use by others to transfer a file

Memory Requirements of User Machines

A user machine needs enough main memory to run the largest of the applications it will use and to keep resident the particular user configuration of the PC Network software (and any other programs that remain resident). The memory requirements of the various user configurations are considerable. They are summarized in Figure 10.1. The heading *Consumes* indicates the space required (in bytes) for the programs and their buffers and tables, but not such open-ended items as files used to store messages or printer jobs. The heading Requires indicates (in bytes) the smallest memory size on which it is reasonable to run the configuration, according to IBM. (To leave room for additional files that PC Network may create and for the user's application programs, the amount required is larger than the space actually consumed by the network software.)

Powers of the Three User Configurations

The various configurations in which you can start PC Network are described in greater detail in Chapter 2. This section reviews the alternatives with a view to deciding how much memory each user machine will need.

The three user configurations (messenger, receiver, and redirector) differ considerably in memory requirements. However, they have exactly the same powers to use network directories and printers. They differ only in ancillary services—what you might call frill services. But the frills are probably important to satisfactory use of the network. These ancillary services are in two areas: network request and messages.

Network request refers to the ability, while running an application program, to press a particular combination of keys (Ctrl-Alt-Break) to suspend whatever you're doing and jump immediately into the network menus. You might do that to make some adjustment to the way you're using the network, or to send or receive a message, or anything else. When you've finished with the menus, you return to exactly where you were before. The network-request key is convenient, but it's available only in the messenger configuration (and also the server). If you don't run the messenger configuration, you can use a network function only by finishing what you are doing, returning to the DOS prompt, and there writing a network command or entering the PC Network menus by writing *NET.*

	Messenger	**Receiver**	**Redirector**
Requires:* (Minimum)	256k	192k	128k
Consumes: (assuming default values of other parameters)	138.3k	47.4k	28k
Available: (on minimum machine)	119,126	150,528	104,704

*k stands for kilobytes—2^{10}(=1024) bytes—the standard unit for describing memory units.

Figure 10.1: *Space requirements of the three user configurations*

Messages are a handy way to communicate with other people who are active on the network at the same time you are. Every configuration can *send* messages. However, *redirector* (which has the lowest memory requirements) can't receive messages, and *receiver* can't forward messages to another machine or adopt more than one name under which to receive messages.

In an office where most of the network users are within sight of each other or can readily talk over an intercom or local phone, messages may not be terribly important. But where people are more spread out, or the server machines (especially print servers) are located elsewhere (for example, to isolate their noise or the commotion of people tearing and stacking printouts), messages become more significant. Messages between users and the people who operate their servers may be fairly common and useful. Messages also give users the means to address a broadcast message to all computers.

My guess is that IBM designed PC Network with the assumption that the normal user runs in the messenger configuration. The other two configurations were probably added to accommodate systems with relatively small amounts of main memory.

If you're hesitating on this question, my advice is to get more memory. Get enough so your users can run the full messenger configuration. Memory is getting cheaper and cheaper; future applications are likely to consume more; you'll get more out of the network if your hardware has enough memory to run it properly. Notice that in Figure 10.1 the required memory is IBM's *minimum* to run that configuration. More than the minimum is highly desirable.

Disk Requirements of User Machines

Each machine needs a floppy-disk drive. For one thing, it needs something from which to boot up and start the network. Once redirection is set up, a user machine can refer to a server machine for the remainder of DOS and the PC Network software.

(The network adapter permits a machine with *no* disk drive to operate on the network. If you have set a jumper on the adapter card, when you turn on the power the PC automatically identifies itself to the network by a unique 16-character ID recorded in the adapter's read-only memory and then sends a request to load DOS from a server machine operating on the network under the name IBMServer. However, this facility is not supported by the PC Network software and would require a specially written application program to take advantage of it.)

A floppy-disk drive is also useful to permit the machine to load programs not available in the libraries of the server machines. At a user machine, a floppy drive is also useful when you want to make a copy of data to be sent somewhere not on the network.

For data that (for whatever reason) you don't want to trust to anyone but yourself, it's essential to have your own way of writing it, independent of the server. That way you can keep a private backup copy of data you regard as vital, independent of the backup procedures of the server.

For all these reasons, a user machine must have at least one floppy-disk drive. On the other hand, a user machine rarely requires more than one. If the user can exploit disk space on a server, most applications that would otherwise require a second drive can be copied to a virtual drive physically located on a server's fixed disk. (Exception: DOS *diskcopy* requires two drives of the same format on the same machine.)

Of course, if you happen to have them, additional drives (whether floppy or fixed) don't disqualify a machine from playing the role of user. There may be situations in which a machine makes heavy use of its own private fixed disk, but nevertheless obtains other programs from the network or sends its output to a network printer.

Printer Requirements of Users

Printer output that is easily handled by a queue (especially output that can be printed on fanfold paper) is easily handled by a print server. For a lot of routine work, a user doesn't need a separate printer.

Printing more specialized output may depend on the devices available. It may be possible to direct office correspondence to a print server, provided it can handle letterhead appropriately or has provision for envelopes. It's also possible to connect a device such as a plotter as a sort of printer, and to handle its work through a queue on a server machine.

Where there is sufficient volume or the work itself requires the operator's personal supervision, you may want to handle printing locally. Here again, having a local printer in no way disqualifies a user from also making use of network printers for jobs they can handle.

Display Monitors for Both User and Server Machines

Any machine that ever displays a network screen—which is to say, just about any machine—requires an 80-column display.

If you happen to have a color monitor, the network menus and message editor/viewer make minor use of color to distinguish fields, but otherwise color is superfluous. Hence, the decision to use a color display should be based on the needs of the applications, not on the network software itself. For applications involving text, standard monochrome monitors have noticeably better resolution than standard color monitors (basing each character on a 9×14 dot matrix rather than on the 8×8 matrix used for color).

Services Offered by Server Machines

Any regularly used server must have a fixed disk. Beyond that, serving roles can be broadly divided into two types: directory service and printer service. The same machine can play both roles.

A server that makes space on its fixed disk available to other users does so by offering to share *directories*. The directory may be only part of the fixed disk of the machine that makes the offer, but it usually appears to the user as a root directory.

Capacity of a Server

A server machine's ability to serve a group of users depends mostly on the amount of available space in its fixed disk, the speed with which data can be transferred to and from the fixed disk, and to some extent on the amount of main memory available.

Space

The server's fixed disk must have space both for read-only storage made available to all users and for private space controlled by individuals. Although the public read-only directories may be quite large, a single copy is available to all the server's users. Conversely, although the private directories may be individually small, there may be many of them, so the total space they consume may be considerable.

DOS does not directly regulate the size of files or directories. The server may periodically have to review the free space available and the amount consumed by user directories (see Chapter 8).

Speed

The transfer rates to the fixed disk of the IBM PC/AT machine is significantly faster than that of the PC/XT. (The difference originates in the size of the data bus more than in the disk itself.) This means there is a distinct performance advantage in using PC/ATs as file servers.

Time Required to Transfer Data through the Network

When you're a user, data transfer is typically between main memory and disk memory—wherever that is. The relevant comparison is the speed with which the transfer is completed when done locally (using your own machine's disk drive) versus the speed with which it's completed through the network (using the hard disk of a server machine).

When the network and the server are not busy, it may be *faster* to transfer data to or from a network disk than from your own local diskette. That's possible because transmission time through the network is only a small part of the total, and your local diskette drive is probably a great deal slower than the server's fixed disk. For example, to transfer a text file of 50,000 bytes (from the time you press Enter until the transfer is completed) takes about five seconds when executed locally, but between three and four seconds from the fixed disk of a remote PC/AT server. Only about a quarter second of that is the actual transmission time on the network. (Whether the physical link is broadband or token ring makes only a small difference to effective throughput; see Appendix B.) Network delays arise mostly because either the network or the server is busy at the time your request comes through, and so there is a delay until the hardware starts to carry out the request.

Memory Required for Printing

Printing is a multistage operation; it requires space both in main memory and on the fixed disk.

When a user requests to have a file printed on a network printer, the flow of data is from the user's machine to a set of buffers in the main memory of the server. All data arriving at the server (including print requests and also file transfers) pass through the same set of buffers. Space for those buffers is set by default at 16k of main memory, but may be set as high as 48k (see Chapter 13).

From there, the data to be printed go to a file on the server's fixed disk. A background task on the print server manages the queue of jobs to be printed. The background task transfers the file from the server's disk to the printer, passing through the print buffer in main memory. The print buffer is by default given 0.5k, but may be given as much as 16k.

Printing thus involves two buffers in the server's main memory. Larger buffers reduce the work the server must do to transfer information, and thus improve the speed with which it can handle incoming requests for printing, other network requests, or its own foreground work. These affect the speed with which a user's request to print is accepted, even though they have little or no effect on the speed with which the printer produces pages of output.

Printing also involves substantial storage on the server's fixed disk. The server requires space to store all the jobs waiting to be printed (up to 99 of them; see Chapter 9).

Should Several Printers Share a Server?

It's possible to attach several printers to the same PC. It's common to have printers with quite different characteristics, for example a fast printer for drafts and program listings, and a slower high-resolution printer for correspondence. The same server can make a separate offer to share each of them. Users can then treat them as different printers.

Each server maintains a single combined queue for all its print jobs, regardless of the printer to which each job is destined. When a job comes to the top of the queue, the server sends it to the printer that the user requested. The practical effect is that only one printer is working at a time, apart from small overlaps produced by the printers' own internal buffering.

If the individual printing jobs are large, and you have work to keep all the printers busy much of the time, you'll get more use of the printers by connecting them to different servers. But if you don't need to keep the printers simultaneously busy, it is straightforward to attach them to the same server. Managing a queue that mixes jobs for different printers may require somewhat more intervention from the operator of the server machine (see Chapter 9).

Estimating the Number of Server Machines Needed

As part of their training program when PC Network was first introduced, developers at the Entry Systems Division of IBM constructed a model for estimating the number of user machines that a server could handle satisfactorily, given various assumptions about the load. Their criterion of satisfactory performance was a 90 percent probability that when a network user's machine makes a network request, the server can act on it at once. Because the PC/AT has faster access times and transfer rates than the PC/XT, they defined *at once* differently for the two machines. For the PC/XT, the criterion was no network activity *in progress* when the request is received. For the PC/AT, the criterion was no network activity *queued* (although the machine might still be working on its previous request).

Obviously, the load on the network depends on what the users do. The IBM group undertook to construct a reasonable mix of activities for a hypothetical standard workload (see Figure 10.2).

The numbers in Figure 10.2 seem a reasonable description of a user who is not just staring out the window, but who is also not pounding relentlessly on the network or churning away in a program that repeats many data transfers automatically. Its developers included in the model a load factor, multiplying the standard load by 1, 2, 3, 4, 5, 6, and 7. The model's estimates of the number of users that a server can handle satisfactorily are shown in Figure 10.3. The upper band shows the probable number of users for the PC/AT, and the lower band for the PC/XT.

Although it is difficult to predict the combined effects of the work by members of a particular group, the model does suggest some probable upper and lower limits. From it, I deduce the following rules of thumb:

- A PC/XT can handle a small group (6 to 12 users) only if the users' workloads are at the plausible but moderate range described by a load factor of 1. As the load factor reaches 3, a PC/XT server can't maintain the target performance for more than about four users. This may be entirely reasonable for a small working group within a network, but is clearly unsatisfactory for a server that is to be used more widely.
- According to the model, a PC/AT could handle 30 users easily at load factor 1. (However, the PC Network software and hardware doesn't permit more than 25 different users at the same time.) At load factor 3, a PC/AT should still be able to handle 18 to 22 users. The PC/AT is clearly the machine of choice for widely used network services.
- What the users choose to do—or how their work is

Activity	Kilobytes of data transferred	Times per hour
Load a program	64	6
Load data (spreadsheet)	2	3
Save data (spreadsheet)	2	2
Load data (text file)	12	3
Save data (text file)	12	2
Send a message	0.5	4
Receive a message	0.5	4
Quality print request	4	2

Source: IBM Corporation, Entry Systems Division, proceedings of Independent Developers' Training Seminar on PC Network, Table 2F-133, 1984. Quoted by permission.

Figure 10.2: *Hypothetical mix of activities of a single network user*

organized—can have a major impact on network performance. Putting it crudely: a few hogs on the network could make a major difference in the number of users who can be satisfactorily served.

Several vendors offer specialized fileservers with much greater disk capacity than the 20-megabytes common on the IBM PC/AT. These larger disks may reduce the squeeze on network directories. But the limitations on the number of users that a server can support come not from the *size* of the disk but from the *rate* to which the machine can make transfers between disk and main memory and between main memory and the network adapter. If those rates are no better, greater disk capacity is of limited benefit.

Avoiding Needless Net-Hogs

It may really pay to examine the way an application is structured. For example, a program that treats a small part of a very large file might be written so that it repeatedly reads and writes back the entire file, when

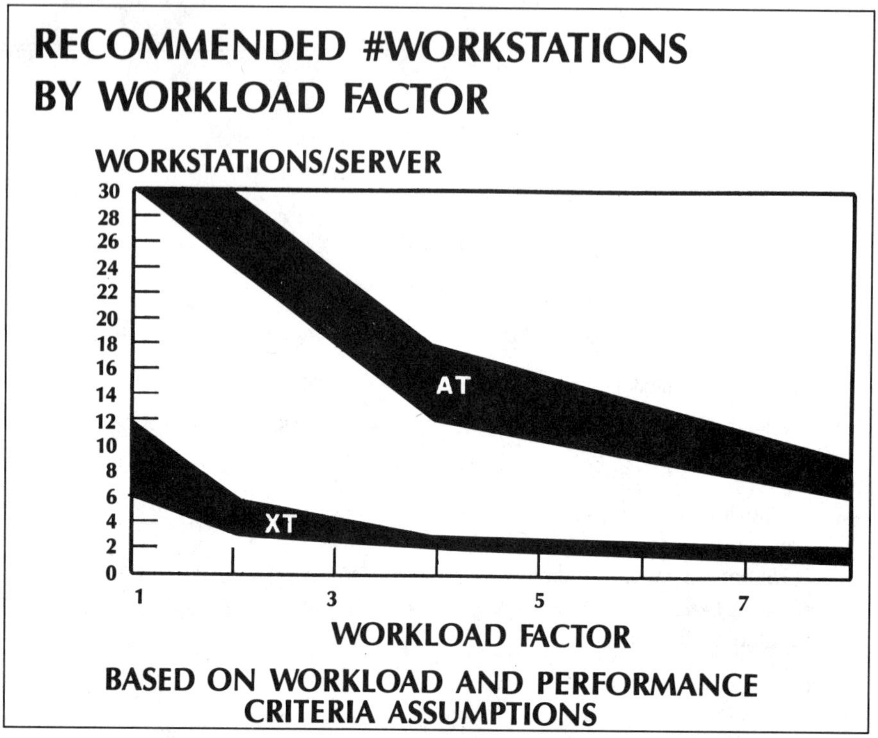

Figure 10.3: *Number of users supported to criterion of 90 percent ready, by workload factor and type of server (chart courtesy of IBM Corporation)*

the same effect could be achieved by reading and writing only the relevant segments, or rewriting only at certain milestones, and so on. Similarly, a program that permits many PCs to post orders against an inventory data base may be written so that each PC reads the entire data base, or so that only one of them does so, while the other PCs merely pass transactions to the one that maintains the data base. These different approaches to organizing the same task could have major consequences for the volume of data that the server must import and export and hence the number of users that it can serve.

Ratio of PCs to Users

It is common for an organization at first to share a PC among several users and gradually to increase the availability of PCs. (PCs are pretty cheap compared to people.) It is little or no burden to the network to keep a PC connected while it is idle. As PCs become more numerous—approaching one on every desk—the demand on the network from any one PC is likely to decline. It's important to remember that the network is not serving machines, but serving people-at-machines. Is it more cost-effective for the organization to pay for machines that are idle while waiting for people or to pay people who are idle while waiting for machines?

A Service-by-User Matrix to Allocate Services in Advance

When you're planning a network for the first time, it's very useful to prepare on a large sheet of chart paper (or in a computer spreadsheet) a table showing each user and each network resource to be offered. The following describes one possible way to organize and use such a chart.

The chart has rows and columns. A cluster of adjacent columns represents a particular user machine. Include a cluster for each machine in the network, including the server machines (since any server may also be a user). Within each cluster, individual columns represent different human users of the machine (if it has more than one). Separating the different human users is important only when they use the machine in different ways; if the same role is played by several people in rotation, you can combine them as a single column. You may have some users attached to no particular machine; don't forget to include them, in a group of columns of their own.

Figure 10.4 shows part of a possible set of column headings. As you can see, it has a column for each human user, grouped by the machine to which the user is regularly assigned.

Similarly, each row of the chart shows a shareable resource of a server PC, clustered by the machine on which the resource might be located. You are preparing this chart before committing the machines—perhaps even before buying them. So the machines listed in the clusters may be hypothetical rather than actual. You're preparing a plan for how you think you would distribute work if you had those servers, or perhaps how you can distribute work to reduce the number of servers.

Each row refers to a resource: a printer or disk directory shared over the network. (You may want to look at the discussion of network directories in Chapter 11 for more details on the likely arrangement of directories offered over the network.) Figure 10.5 shows part of a possible set of row headings.

Distributing the Load before Installing the Network

To show that a particular user makes use of a particular resource, you put a mark at the intersection of the appropriate row and column. (Or you may want to indicate the volume of use.) Then you compute the subtotal of users for each server machine. This pushes you to make explicit who's going to use what service and on what machine. It also permits you to iterate, shifting whom you assign where. (No doubt, someday someone will produce a program to optimize this for you.) This exercise has two objectives:

- To end up with an estimate of the number of server machines you'll need.
- To prepare you in advance to state a specific allocation of services. You'll need that to answer questions from the Installation Aid program when you install PC Network on the server machines. (What you answer then isn't permanently binding, but it's nice to have thought about it before the installation program asks.)

You make a trial allocation of services to servers first, to see whether your estimate of the number of servers is plausible and whether the

Machine 1			**Machine 2**			**Machine 3**	**No fixed machine**		
Pers 1	Pers 2	SUBTOT	Pers 3	Pers 4	SUBTOT	Pers 5	Pers 6	Pers 7	. . . etc

Figure 10.4: *Column headings for the service-by-user matrix*

work can be reasonably divided between them. After you've distributed the various printer services and the public and private network directories to the various servers, the subtotals for each machine should fit within the maxima imposed by various system tables. For example, no server can serve more than 25 different users at one time. You may also want to distribute users among the servers so as to maintain some balance in the total size of the shared directories on the various machines.

It is useful to go through this exercise before you make a final commitment to the number of machines that will take part in the network, and in any event before you attempt to install the PC Network software

Server1	APPS public directory	__________
	User1 private directory	__________
	User2 private directory	__________
	User3 private directory	__________
	Daisywheel printer and its spool	__________
	SERVER SUBTOTAL:::::::::::::	__________
Server2	Network printer 1	__________
	Department 1 group directory	__________
	User4 private directory	__________
	User5 private directory	__________
	User6 private directory	__________
	SERVER SUBTOTAL:::::::::::::	__________
Server3	APPS public directory	__________
	Department 2 group directory	__________
	User7 private directory	__________
	User8 private directory	__________
	User9 private directory	__________
	SERVER SUBTOTAL:::::::::::::	__________

Figure 10.5: *Row headings for the service-by-user matrix*

on the server machines. When you are ready to install (described in the next chapter), the Installation Aid program will ask you to specify what resources each server will regularly share, and the names of the users for whom it will create private user directories. It's essential to have the answers ready before you get there.

Depending on the number of users, it may be necessary to provide duplicate copies of the applications library, one on each of several servers, and assign some users to one server and some to another.

Balancing the Load in the Light of Experience

If you're the system administrator, you should keep old copies of this chart and also maintain a current version. As new users or machines are added to the network, you'll be able to see how to distribute services to them.

When one part of the network experiences performance problems, indicating perhaps that it is more heavily loaded than other parts, the charts will serve as a guide for redistributing the load so as to balance it more effectively.

Human Roles and Skills

For each machine on the network, there is a human operator or user—perhaps several of them. Successful use of a network depends in part on matching machine functions with appropriate human ones and arranging (by selection or training) that the various human participants are ready, comfortable, and productive in the roles they'll play on the network.

Cast of Human Roles

Like the machines, the humans are broadly divided into users and servers. The levels of specialized skills demanded of them vary considerably. The following lists some of the likely roles for a network and estimates the proportion of users who can play them.

Network Administrator

The network depends on cooperation between its machines, their programs, and ultimately on the people who use the programs and machines. In particular, the community must establish conventions about who will use what resources, how the server machines will offer them, and how the user machines will take up those offers. To coordinate all this, it is highly desirable (if not absolutely essential) to have a single ultimate authority and coordinator who keeps track of public conventions and is the final arbiter of contentions about resources. This person doesn't need to be a regular network user and doesn't need to be involved in running the servers.

Network Programming Expert

The network needs one person available occasionally—perhaps on a consulting basis from elsewhere or perhaps from among its regular users—who is highly familiar with DOS, programming the PC, and use of the network. This person may be involved in tuning the network to set parameters, writing procedures for particular applications, or advising on the structure of directories. On occasion, network users may discover or suspect they've discovered a bug, and it's useful to have someone who has the experience to solve it or to verify and document it so it can be reported and fixed.

Network Guru

For every six to ten regular users, it's useful to have an experienced user to whom the others can turn for suggestions, troubleshooting, advice, or tutorial sessions. These persons should be familiar with DOS and with operating the server machines, but they don't need to be programmers except in the sense that writing batch files is a sort of programming. Being able to answer questions for others may take no more than 10 percent of their time, but it's an explicit and recognized part of their duties.

Server Operator

These persons are responsible for the operation of the server machines. Their duties include seeing that server machines are available when needed and responding to messages from users. For print servers, there's a fair amount of managing the printer queue and physically feeding paper, checking ribbons, stacking output, and so on (see Chapter 9). For directory servers, there is the important responsibility of maintaining backup files and, on occasion, restoring them.

Experienced User

Some users of the network are likely to have considerable experience operating their own PCs. As network users, they require little instruction or supervision, since the additional skills needed for the network are much like what they've already been doing.

Application Users

Possibly as many as two-thirds of the users of a network have no special knowledge of programming or networking, but are already proficient at using one or more applications. If they come to a machine that is already set up, they use the application effectively, but they depend on someone else to provide the initial setup. In the event of a failure or problem, they need to call on help from an experienced user, server operator, or guru, but in the regular course of things they can work well without assistance.

Issues Regarding Staffing and Training

In planning a computer network installation largely for users (rather than for programmers, software developers, technicians, etc.), a few questions arise repeatedly and bear some brief discussion.

Can People with No Special Training Really Use It?

Yes—but. Like any computer application, PC Network requires familiarity with the keyboard (which is quite a bit more complicated than the keyboard of a typewriter). It also uses a fair amount of jargon. These are minor issues for the novice who has an experienced user nearby for advice, but can be quite daunting for the novice left alone to face so many novelties at once.

PC Network's menu screens are really useful for the inexperienced, even if occasionally they break an operation into irritatingly small steps. However, there remain places within the menus at which familiarity with DOS terminology for drives, printers, and directories is absolutely essential. The terminology is not really difficult, but it is essential to realize that users will encounter it and need to use it. Most users can easily learn the basics in a half day of orientation; their questions are easily answered when an experienced user is readily accessible.

One of the three diskettes distributed with the PC Network software is a pleasant, rather cute little demonstration of some network screens and concepts, at an elementary level. If requested, the Installation Aid program will install it in a server's applications library under the name \Apps\Net. It may be useful to show this demonstration to novices who are about to use the network. It's a pity that it doesn't include material on the tree structure of directories, which is important to understand and might have been readily illustrated in some of the animated screens.

At times PC Network emits inscrutable messages, reporting things that may have gone wrong, some of which are quite outside the user's control. For some of these, the "suggested action" steps in the PC Network *User's Guide* are equally inscrutable. Here again, most of these can be taken in stride when there is an experienced person to ask, but may be disconcerting or disruptive to an inexperienced individual left alone with a machine.

Who Should Sit at the Server? Doing What?

The practical question for both disk-space servers and print servers is this: how much local work (in addition to their work as servers) should you try to get those machines to do? Who—if anyone—should be asked to sit there?

There isn't a fixed answer to that. My own suggestion is this: It's highly desirable to have a print server attended. There are too many things that can go wrong physically with an unattended printer. It also takes human intervention to do such things as cancel jobs submitted by mistake, alter the priority of jobs for someone who has an urgent need, and so on. There's some advantage in having a disk-space server attended, too.

On the other hand, when the server machine is busy, its response to foreground jobs may deteriorate. So it's better to plan to use the servers for tasks that are not file-access or computation intensive. Probably many keyboard-intensive tasks of a semiclerical or secretarial nature would fit that description; so would many stages of programming.

When a network is new and the staff has little experience with it, it seems highly desirable to keep server machines staffed with people who can respond to questions over the network, detect abnormal conditions, and improvise action as needed. That suggests that at first, server machines need relatively sophisticated staff. On the other hand, you have to allow for the fact that server machines may have a slow or erratic response to the foreground work. This suggests that you shouldn't assign important rush jobs to a server machine or tie up people whose time is precious.

Responsibility and Security at the Server

Server machines are essential to the work of all the people who use them. This means you have to take special care that the server doesn't fail because of ill-considered actions of the person sitting at it. A server isn't the place for programmers to do debugging. Nor is it the place for the inexperienced trainee who may—inadvertently—do something silly.

The person who sits at a server machine has the power—if she chooses to use it—to do anything at all to files in that machine. You have to be able to trust that person. (That's why the machine room of a large time-sharing service is usually locked, and the people who work there are frequently bonded.) A seat at the console of a server machine is no place for the immature, irresponsible, or disgruntled. It's wise to lock up a server's keyboard while its operator is away from it.

From these considerations, a picture emerges of the human staff that goes with the role of server. The server should probably be attended most of the time, and staffed by a trustworthy, sensible person, experienced with the network, who can give half an eye to the network or messages regarding it, and is otherwise engaged in nonurgent work that is probably keyboard-intensive rather than file- or processor-intensive (such as text entry or data entry).

Assigning Names to Servers and Users

In the conversation of people who use a network, there's a tendency to use names to refer both to colleagues and to their machines. Sometimes you really want to identify the person who knows something, has something, can do something. On other occasions, you need to identify a particular piece of hardware, if only to explain where someone is sitting or which box needs the attention of a repair person.

The network encourages confusion because machines must adopt names, and the names are often the names of people. Strictly speaking, PC Network uses a name to identify a *work session.* A work session is a particular occasion when a particular person is working at a particular piece of hardware. Does it make better sense to chose a network name that matches the occasion, the person, or the machine? When there is a strict one-to-one correspondence between people and machines—each machine has exactly one user, and each user has exactly one machine—the machine can have the same name as its user, and no one is confused. But in most offices, people trade off and move around, so the correspondence between people-names and machine-names isn't consistent.

Generally, the decision whether to match the network name to the person or to the machine depends on the role that the work session will play on the network. The principles are:

- A machine acting as server needs a name that identifies the machine

- A machine acting as user needs a name that identifies the person at the keyboard

When you offer resources to others (use of a printer or space on a fixed disk), what you are offering is something physically attached to a particular device. The people who are going to use your fixed disk over the network don't really care who's at the keyboard of your machine, but they do care about having access to the appropriate device.

Quite the reverse is true when you're a user. If you don't have a fixed disk of your own, you must rely entirely on diskettes (which you can carry with you anywhere) or on your access to the fixed disks over the network. Either way, it doesn't matter which machine you sit at. But it does matter that the disk file allocated to you is available to you, and not just to whoever happens to sit at a particular place.

For that reason, the servers are likely to have institutional names that reflect their roles in the organization or simply identify the server's hardware. By contrast, the users have personal names, independent of machinery.

Installing the Network

Eleven

The product called PC Network includes both hardware and software. This chapter discusses the hardware first, then installation of the software.

There are two versions of PC Network: token ring and broadband. (The concepts underlying these alternate systems are reviewed in Appendix B.) The procedures to install them are quite similar. This chapter contains two alternative sections on installing the cabling—one for the token-ring system, followed by a slightly different one for the broadband system; skip the one that doesn't apply.

Installing the Network Adapter Card

There's one adapter card for the token-ring network and a different adapter for the broadband network. But the installation procedure is the same. The only tool required is a small screwdriver. IBM supplies clear installation instructions with the card.

Setting Nonstandard Adapter Address and Interrupt Level

Each card comes preset with the address the PC must use to refer to the adapter's memory and the interrupt level that the adapter will recognize in instructions from the PC. Each also provides a way for you to select settings different from those supplied by default. It is rarely necessary to make any change when you have just one network adapter in a machine. However, if you have two adapters in the same machine, it's essential to give them different settings so the PC can tell them apart. (You would have two adapters in a machine that serves as a LAN-to-LAN bridge, one connected to each LAN; some manufacturers' specialized servers increase the number of concurrent users by installing a second network adapter.) The different settings are also necessary to resolve possible conflicts between the network adapter and some other specialized adapter you may have installed.

To make changes, on the token-ring adapter you select options by setting switches, whereas on the broadband card you select options by moving jumper blocks on pins. The respective *Installation Instructions* supplied with the cards give clear instructions. Before you install the adapter card, check whether you need to make any changes.

Inserting the Adapter Card

The adapter card fits into a vacant long slot in the chassis of the PC. To install it, you have to turn off the power to the PC, remove the cover, and remove the strip of metal that covers the opening for an unused slot. (On the PC/AT, opposite the metal strip you just removed, there's a slot into which the other end of the card fits. Other models of the PC may lack that slot, so IBM includes with the card a plastic card-support, which you install first to form a slot that will receive the new card.)

Carefully lower the card into the matching slots and press it into place. Secure it with the screw that formerly held the metal cover of the slot.

When you have installed the adapter, all that shows at the outside is the connector, ready to receive the network cable. On the token-ring version, it's a D9 connector (like the one on the graphics adapter that connects the monitor, but of opposite gender). On the broadband version, it's a threaded coaxial tap for an F-connector. That's where you attach the network cable.

Replace the cover of the machine. Put the metal slot cover where you'll be able to find it one day when it's needed again. One final item: IBM also gives you a decal that says *PC Network* to affix to the front of the PC.

Accompanying Software

The diskette accompanying the token-ring version contains the adapter handler program Tokreui.com. As part of the installation, you need to copy it to the disk from which you will start the system, and include it in Autoexec.bat.

The broadband version does not need or use the adapter-handler program.

Diagnostics

The diskette accompanying the adapter contains a diagnostic program for the adapter. You should run it before connecting the adapter to the network to verify that installation is correct. After that, it's intended for use only when you suspect something's wrong.

Cabling the Token-Ring System

In the token-ring version of PC Network, PCs are connected in such a way that the electrical path between them forms a ring, from which comes part of the system's name. (For more discussion of the underlying idea of the token ring, see Appendix B.) However, the ring structure is not at all apparent from the outside. Each PC is connected to a box called the IBM 8228 *multistation access unit.* Since many PCs plug into the same box, the system is wired in a *star* pattern.

The Multistation Access Unit

The multistation access unit (or access unit, for short) is a metal box about 18 inches long, 4 inches high, and 6 inches deep (see Figure 11.1). In a row along the front, it has ten data connectors. The eight in the middle are for connecting PCs to the network. The two connectors at the ends are for patch cables used to connect one access unit to another.

The job of the access unit is to maintain the continuity of the ring so that each PC can pass the signal to the next PC throughout the network.

When you plug a PC's cable into a data connector on the access unit, that PC and its cables are able to join the ring, becoming one of the *lobes* of the ring. When you disconnect a PC (for example, by turning it off or unplugging its cable), the access unit drops that lobe out of the ring and connects the remaining PCs without it.

Figure 11.1: *Multistation access unit for token-ring (photograph courtesy of IBM Corporation)*

Location of the Access Unit

The multistation access unit is a center from which cables to the various PCs radiate. When there are more than eight PCs, several access units can be wired together, in effect forming one large access unit. Some access units may be located at a distance from the others to form an additional center. Under some conditions, there may be several such centers.

The access unit uses no external power and has no other connectors, cables, or switches besides the ten data connectors mentioned earlier. The front panel extends wider than the body to facilitate mounting in an equipment rack or wiring closet. However, it is not essential to mount it. If you don't already have a wiring closet and you have only one or two access units, the access units can just as well sit on the floor or on a shelf or table.

The IBM Cabling Systems

The token ring is part of IBM's general wiring scheme for office buildings, called the *IBM cabling system.* Announced in 1982 and elaborated in documents published in 1984, it envisions the installation of cables during construction of a building. Wiring closets bring the many cables together in looms or patchboards analogous to those already widely used for telephone systems. The wiring closet has racks on which you mount equipment such as the access units. From each wiring closet, cables fan out through the walls to faceplates mounted in the various offices.

In a building already wired that way, installing the hardware consists of mounting the access units in a convenient closet and plugging in the data connectors for the rooms your network will serve. It's marvelously simple—provided the wiring closet and the wiring are already in place.

Since the IBM wiring system was announced only a few years ago and the token-ring version of PC Network is the first IBM product to make use of it, it's quite likely you don't have the IBM wiring system already installed. In what follows, I outline what you need to do to connect the PCs without benefit of built-in wiring.

Types of Cable for the Token-Ring Network

The token ring can use either of two types of wiring: *data-grade* wiring (which is what the IBM wiring system is mainly concerned with), and *voice-grade* wiring (the sort of wiring ordinarily used for telephones). Under some conditions, the token-ring system can be run on voice-grade wiring. If you already have sufficient installed capacity of telephone wiring, you *may* be able to use it to connect PCs on the network.

In its proposals for a wiring system, IBM distinguished several types of cables. The types commonly referred to include the following:

- *Type 1.* Two twisted pairs, each 22 gauge, shielded. (Also available in a version with an additional exterior sheath for outdoor use.)
- *Type 2.* Same as type 1, but also has four pairs of telephone wire between the metallic shield and the plastic cover.
- *Type 3.* Telephone-type cable with two or more twisted pairs, each 24 gauge.
- *Type 5.* Fiber-optics conductors (not yet in use).
- *Type 6.* Like type 1, but 26 gauge, used only in short runs such as patch cables within a wiring closet.
- *Type 8.* Like type 1, but with the conductors arranged in the cable so that it is relatively flat and can more easily run under a carpet.

For installing the token-ring network, type 1 is optimum. (Type 2 works just as well, but the network doesn't make use of the additional telephone pairs.) Type 1 is what IBM sells as cabling for the token-ring network. Under some conditions, type-3 cable can be used instead of type 1, but it reduces the number of PCs that can be connected and the distance over which the network can operate.

Appearance of Data-Grade Cable

The type-1 cables that IBM sells for the network, to run from each PC to the access unit and from one access unit to another, each contain four solid-copper conductors in white plastic insulation, arranged as two pairs, each pair twisted in a spiral and wrapped in a thin plastic sheath. Both the metal conductors and the insulation are substantially heavier-gauge than those normally found in telephone cables. The pair of pairs is enclosed in a braided metallic shield, and the entire cable is enclosed in a black plastic tube. The whole thing is about as thick as your pinkie and fairly pliable. IBM sells the cable both in precut lengths with connectors already installed, and in bulk from which you can cut your own lengths and attach connectors yourself.

Voice-Grade Wiring

The token-ring system can be installed on voice-grade wiring for all or part of the link between the access unit and a PC. However, you still need data-grade cable to run between one access unit and another. Voice-grade wiring is lighter-gauge wire and lacks shielding, and so is less bulky and more flexible than the data-grade cable.

The principal advantage of voice-grade wiring is that it is widely used in telephone systems, so a building's data wiring can be integrated with its telephone wiring. It may then be possible to handle some of the tasks of routing a network access unit to an office's wiring faceplate not by moving patch cables in a wiring closet but by requesting the building's telephone switching equipment to make the appropriate connections.

Connectors and Cables for the Token Ring

The token-ring system uses plastic-bodied *data connectors* of a form and design introduced as part of the IBM wiring system (see Figure 11.2). They're genderless: two identical connectors fit together with no need for the complementary shapes of the usual plug and jack. Each is shaped rather like a hand with thumb and fingers held to form two parallel planes; two connectors of the same shape slide together much as two people might join their right hands. Electrical contact is made not by a pin fitting into a socket, but by flat metal tabs that slide past each other and touch.

Each connector has two plastic locking tabs that engage the corresponding tabs on the other connector and prevent the two connectors from pulling apart. To plug a cable into a connector on the access unit, you lightly squeeze the hinged plastic plates that form the sides of the connector's body. That opens the jaws of the interlocking tabs and lets them slide together. When you let go, they lock.

Connection to the PC's Adapter Card

The token-ring adapter card has a D9 connector (so called because it has 9 pins and is wider on one side than the other, like a letter D; see Figure 11.3). To connect the adapter card, IBM sells an eight-foot data-grade cable having a D9 connector at one end and a data connector at the other. To prevent accidental disconnection, fasten the D9 connector to the adapter card with the two small screws mounted in the sides of the connector.

The other end of the adapter cable leads to the multistation access unit. If the access unit is within the cable's reach, you can plug the

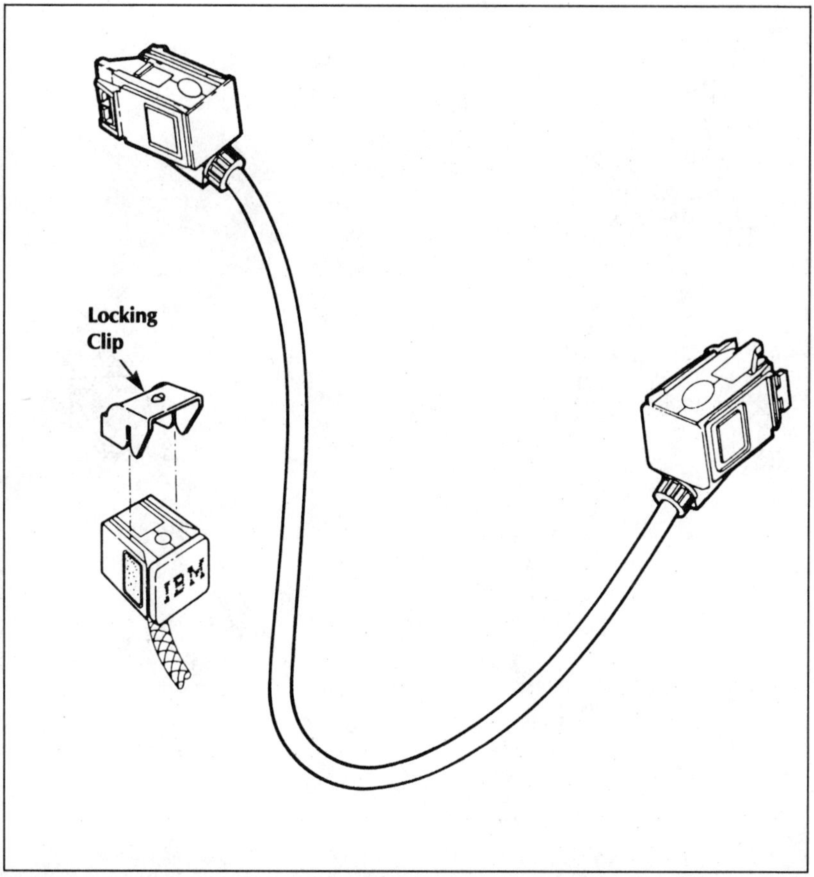

Figure 11.2: *Data connectors, cable, and locking clip used for the token-ring network (drawings courtesy of IBM Corporation)*

adapter cable directly to it. If you have a data-connector faceplate near the PC, you can plug the adapter cable to it.

Locking Data Connectors in Place

A data connector can be locked in place (for example, where it plugs to the access unit or to another cable) by a technique different from the screws that fasten the D9 connector. Supplied with the data connector is a locking clip made of cream-colored plastic. It looks as though it might be a piece from a three-dimensional jigsaw puzzle. The clip fits over the top of the connector in such a way that the two lobes that form the sides of the clip drop into the slots at each side of the connector and prevent an accidental squeeze from releasing the connector's interlocking tabs (see Figure 11.2).

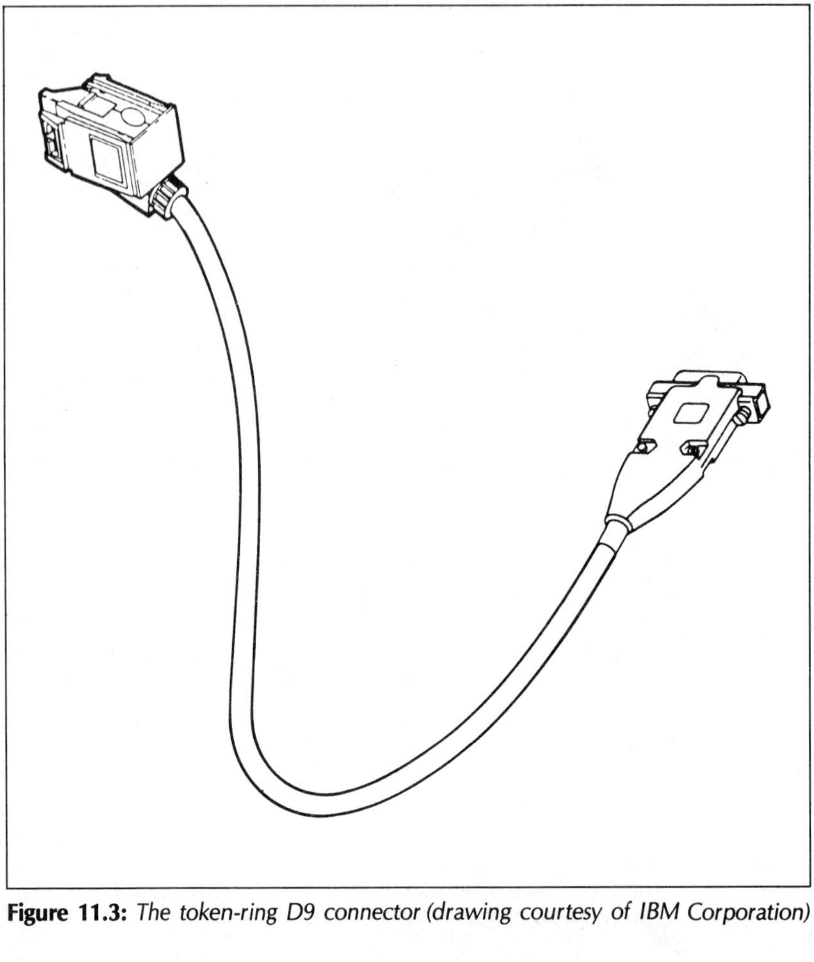

Figure 11.3: *The token-ring D9 connector (drawing courtesy of IBM Corporation)*

Telephone-type Cable from the Adapter Card

In a building wired with voice-grade cables, the cable from a wiring closet may terminate in a faceplate fitted not with a data connector but with a telephone-type six-pin modular jack. In that case, instead of connecting the adapter with a D9-to-data-connector cable, you need to use a D9-to-modular cable. Because the voice-grade cable is not shielded, to meet FCC regulations limiting the amount of electrical signal radiated from it, the D9 connector requires a built-in low-pass filter (see Figure 11.4). IBM doesn't make those, but they're available from other vendors (see the checklist of components later in this chapter).

Extension Cables

A type-1 *patch cable* has a data connector at each end. Because the connectors are genderless, a patch cable can connect to another patch cable or can be used to link one access unit to another. A patch cable of appropriate length serves as an extension to bridge the gap between the end of the network adapter cable and the multistation access unit. (When your office is wired with data-grade cables and a data-connector faceplate, in effect you have such an extension built into the wall.) Data-grade patch cables with data connectors at both ends come in lengths of 8, 30, 75, and 150 feet.

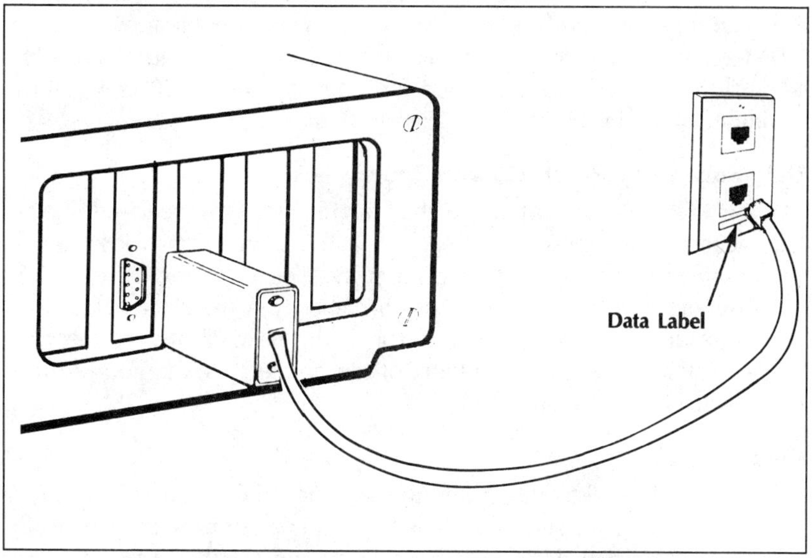

Figure 11.4: *Connecting the PC's token-ring network adapter by way of voice-grade cable with a low-pass filter (drawing courtesy of IBM Corporation)*

Faceplates

For built-in data-grade wiring, IBM supplies one type of faceplate that can be surface-mounted and another that can be flush-mounted in a wall. (It also makes one with an accompanying modular jack for type-2 cable.) The faceplate accommodates a single data connector recessed in a plastic molding, much as data connectors are mounted on the multistation access unit. Inside the wall, data-grade cable leads from the faceplate to a wiring closet, where the cable usually terminates in a data connector. To make the faceplate usable, you have to plug its data connector at the wiring closet to a multistation access unit, probably by using a patch cable having a data connector at each end.

Where the building uses telephone-type wiring, the faceplate has a six-pin modular jack rather than a data connector. At the wiring closet, the cable from the faceplate terminates at a telephone-style connection block. Since the access unit has data connectors, the link from the connection block to the 8228 multistation access unit is made by a jumper cable having color-coded wire leads at one end and a data connector at the other. IBM doesn't make those, but says they're available from vendors.

Area Served by Token-Ring Cables

IBM describes both a recommended and a maximum length of cable between the PC and its access unit (see IBM pamphlet 59X-7205, 1985). The recommended limit is about 330 feet, with a maximum of about 1000 feet. When the link is by voice-grade cables, the figures are considerably lower: the recommended limit falls to about 150 feet, with a maximum of about 330 feet (see Figure 11.6).

A Network Using Several Access Units

When the network has more than eight PCs, you need additional 8228 access units. You can put several in the same wiring closet (or in the same room, if you don't have them installed in wiring closets).

To connect access units, run a patch cable from the *ring-out* connector of one unit to the *ring-in* connector of the next. Those are the connectors at the two ends of the bank of ten connectors, marked RO and RI respectively (see Figure 11.5).

More than One Hub

To span a great distance among the network's PCs, you may need to locate access units in several distant places. The connection is basically the same as when they're all together: you run a cable from the ring-out connector of an access unit at one location to the ring-in connector of an access unit located somewhere else.

How many such scattered clusters you can have and how far apart they can be placed depend strongly on the type of cabling you're using to link the individual PCs. When the PCs are connected by data-grade cables, IBM stipulates that clusters of access units should be no more than about 650 feet apart and there should be no more than 12 such clusters. But when the PCs are linked by voice-grade cable, IBM sets a maximum of two clusters no more than 400 feet apart. The distances between access unit and PC and between clusters of access units are summarized in Figure 11.6.

Regardless of the cabling used for the PCs, the link from access unit to access unit must always be data-grade cable.

In planning these distances, notice that a location at which no PC is working has nothing to relay the signal. The signal sent from the last position at one cluster must continue unaided around the ring until it reaches a working PC that receives the signal and repeats it for the next PC. If there is a risk that a cluster will have no working PC, the effective span is the distance to the first cluster where a PC is sure to be working.

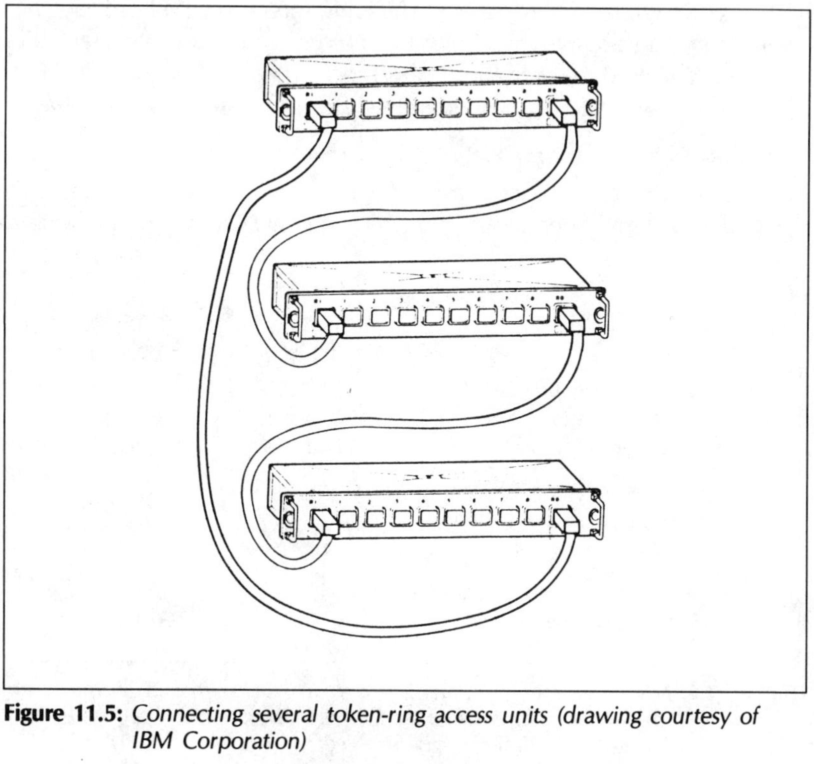

Figure 11.5: *Connecting several token-ring access units (drawing courtesy of IBM Corporation)*

Redundant Loop from Last to First Unit

IBM recommends that you run a cable from ring-out of the last access unit to the ring-in of the first one. This connection is not logically necessary. A single cable running from ring-out of one unit to ring-in of the next is sufficient to create a ring that passes through all the units. Connecting the last back to the first provides a redundant path that may provide an alternate route in the event of a failure in the ring (see Figure 11.5).

Laying the Network Cables

If you don't have built-in data-grade wiring, you may nevertheless want to consider building in the cables that you lay for the network. It is possible to purchase the racks, cabinets, conduits, connectors, boxes, faceplates and so on, so that, when you've installed them, each PC connects to the network by plugging to a convenient faceplate.

Alternatively, the network may work just as well if you simply lay cable neatly out of the way without attempting a permanent or built-in installation. The data cables don't carry more than minute amounts of current, and thus don't present hazards of fire or shock.

The voice-grade cables, lacking shielding, are susceptible to electrical noise from fluorescent lamps, electric motors, and many other electrical devices. The IBM publication *Token-Ring Network Twisted-Pair Media Guide* discusses sources of interference and safe distances from them.

Running Cables through Walls, Floor, or Ceiling

In an office, it's fairly common to run cables along the floor at the base of a wall or under desks. If your cables must pass through walls or

	Data Grade	Voice Grade
PC to access unit		
Recommended limit	330 feet	150 feet
Maximum	1000 feet	330 feet
Number of separate clusters of access units (wiring closets)	12	2
Access-unit cluster to next access-unit cluster	650 feet	400 feet

Figure 11.6: *Maximum and recommended distances between PCs on the token ring—distances published by IBM are in meters and are here expressed in round numbers of feet*

between the floors of a building, the local fire or building codes may require enclosing them in conduit. The cables are not themselves able to cause fire, but the plastic insulation can burn in a fire or act as a wick that carries fire from one room to another. Some jurisdictions, therefore, require them to be enclosed. The requirements of local governments vary widely and it's impossible to give more guidance here than to say: better check this out in your own area.

Labeling the Cables and Connectors

Each data connector and faceplate has an inset for a data label to help keep track of it. At each access unit, IBM provides a chart on which you record the location and device to which each connector on the access unit leads. The sequence of these determines the *ring sequence* of the PCs on the network, which is essential information in diagnosing a fault.

Although it is essential to know where on the ring a PC is located when you're trying to pinpoint trouble, in most other respects a PC's location on the network is immaterial. You're always free to connect any PC to any available connector. That's because on the network each PC identifies itself; the connectors simply insert a PC into the ring. All data flows through all the network's operative lobes. Assigning PCs to an access unit, or to a particular cluster of access units, has no significance except that PCs should be distributed to minimize the likelihood that a remote location is left with no operating PCs at all.

Checklist of Physical Components of the Token-Ring Version

One per cluster of eight PCs:

- IBM 8228 multistation access unit.
- Patch cable, eight feet, data-grade, with data connectors at both ends (part 8642551). Also available in lengths of 30, 75, and 150 feet. Type 6, eight feet (part 4716743).

One per PC:

- Network interface card (part 6339100). Comes with a diskette containing the adapter diagnostic program, ring diagnostic program, and token-ring interface handler, program Tokreui.com.
- A D9-to-token-ring data-grade connector cable (part 6339088), or the equivalent D9-to-modular connector, using voice-grade cable with low-pass filter (ONAN Power/Electronics part 3-50174).
- Copy of the current release of DOS (at least 3.10).

- Copy of the IBM PC Network program (part 6024195).
- Copy of the IBM Token-Ring NETBIOS program (part 6467037).

Components likely to be useful in installation of cable:

- Data connectors (part 8310574), sold in lots of 25.
- Faceplate for data connector: flush mount (part 8310572) or surface mount (part 4760486).
- Distribution panel, capacity 64 data connectors (part 8642520); wiring concentrator, capacity 9 data connectors (part 6091077).
- Jumper cable, eight feet, with horseshoe terminals to data connector (part 8310554), or color-coded wires to data connector (Brand Rex part BR 1100-29-1).

Cabling the Broadband System

In the broadband version of PC Network, the center of the network is the *frequency translator.* The PCs communicate with each other by sending signals on one cable TV channel and receiving signals on a second channel. The job of the frequency translator is to listen for signals sent by any of the PCs on their sending channel and rebroadcast the signals on their receiving channel. (For more discussion of broadband communication in PC Network, see Appendix B.)

The frequency translator is contained in a metal box just a little larger than this book (see Figure 11.7). It requires a low-voltage power supply, provided by a small transformer that comes with it and remains permanently plugged into an ordinary AC power outlet. The translator has a small indicator lamp to show that it's running. You never turn the translator off; it doesn't have an on/off switch.

The various PCs are linked by coaxial cable of the same type widely used for cable TV. A single cable starts at the frequency translator and then fans out through a series of two-way and eight-way signal splitters until a single coaxial cable reaches each PC.

Running from the translator is a single five-foot coaxial cable (black, type RG-6). This cable carries all signals coming into and going out of the translator. From the translator, the cable leads to a two-way splitter. One branch of the two-way splitter is connected by a one-foot beige cable to an eight-way splitter. From each of its eight taps, a coaxial cable runs to the adapter card of a PC; each cable may be from 10 to 200 feet long. The eight-way splitter is thus the hub of a cluster of up to eight PCs within a 200-foot radius (see Figure 11.8).

In a small network, with all PCs linked to the same eight-way splitter, the other branch of the two-way splitter remains unused and has a terminator cap. Since the cables between the translator and the eight-way splitter are quite short, the eight-way splitter is close to the frequency translator.

Multiple Clusters

When the network has more than eight PCs or when some PCs are too remote from one another to participate in the same cluster, you need additional clusters connected to additional eight-way splitters. (To avoid crowding, you may want an extra cluster even when you have fewer than eight PCs.)

To connect more than one cluster, you need a *base expander.* It connects by a beige one-foot cable to the other branch of the two-way splitter near the frequency translator; a network can have at most one base expander.

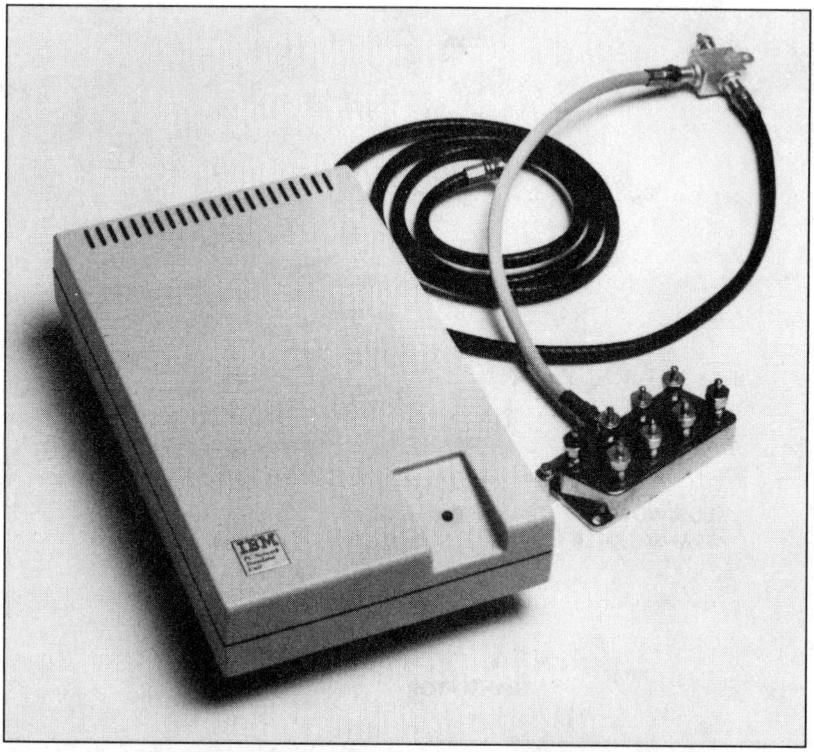

Figure 11.7: *View of the broadband system's frequency translator, and an eight-way splitter (photograph courtesy of IBM Corporation)*

A base expander looks rather like an eight-way splitter. It too has one cable coming in at the side and eight screw-threaded taps on top. From each of those taps, you can install a cable leading to an eight-way splitter to which, in turn, eight PCs can be attached. That gives the network its maximum capacity of 72 PCs: 64 connected through the base expander, plus the 8 connected by the first eight-way splitter, which doesn't go through the expander (see Figure 11.9).

Watch out: Although the base expander *looks* like the eight-way splitter at the hub of a cluster of PCs, you should not attach a PC directly to it because the signal strength will be wrong. However, the kit includes a 30-decibel attenuator through which it's possible to connect a PC directly while testing the layout.

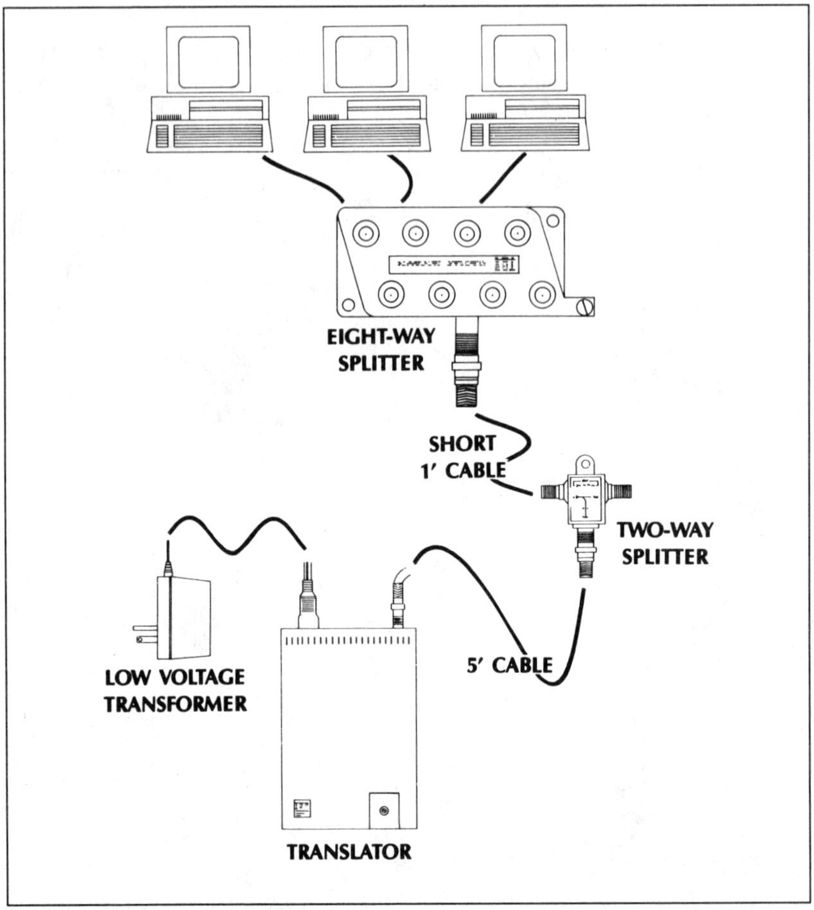

Figure 11.8: *Diagram showing connections from the broadband frequency translator to the two-way splitter and a single eight-way splitter*

Expansion Kits

For each cluster connected through the base expander, you need an *expansion kit.* The kit contains the eight-way splitter that will be the hub of a new cluster, and a length of cable to connect it to the base expander. There are three kits, called the short-, medium-, and long-distance kits. They vary in the length of the cable between the base expander and the new eight-way splitter. Each provides the appropriate attenuators and tilt compensators to equalize the signal at the point where the PCs connect.

The short-distance kit includes a 1-foot cable. (With this one, you aren't going anywhere, just providing more connections in the same vicinity as the frequency translator). The medium-distance kit has 400 feet of cable, and the long-distance has 800 feet. Those are the only distances for which the kits are calibrated.

Since the greatest distance allowed between a cluster and the base expander is 800 feet, and since each PC must be within 200 feet of the center of its cluster, that makes a 1000-foot maximum distance from the translator. This range permits a considerable spread among offices in a single building but rarely to more than one building. Figure 11.9 shows the pattern of connections in a network with a base expander to connect several clusters of PCs.

Connecting the PCs to Their Eight-Way Splitter

Each PC on the network is connected to an eight-way splitter. A coaxial cable runs from the threaded tap on the PC's network adapter card to one of the threaded taps on an eight-way splitter. The eight-way splitter is a metal box about four inches long and two inches wide, with one cable coming in at the side and eight threaded taps on the top in two rows of four. They're standard cable-TV F-connectors, the same size as on the adapter card (so the cable is the same at either end). You can see an eight-way splitter in Figure 11.7.

Although each eight-way splitter can connect eight PCs, it's a good idea at first to connect only four or five PCs to it. Then there will be vacant slots to which you can connect extra PCs as you expand or move the present ones around.

Connecting the PCs

Supplied with each network adapter is a ten-foot cable. If that's sufficient, you can use it to connect the PC directly from its adapter card to one of the sockets of the eight-way connector.

When the ten-foot cable that comes with the adapter isn't enough to reach the eight-way splitter, you may use up to 200 feet of IBM coaxial

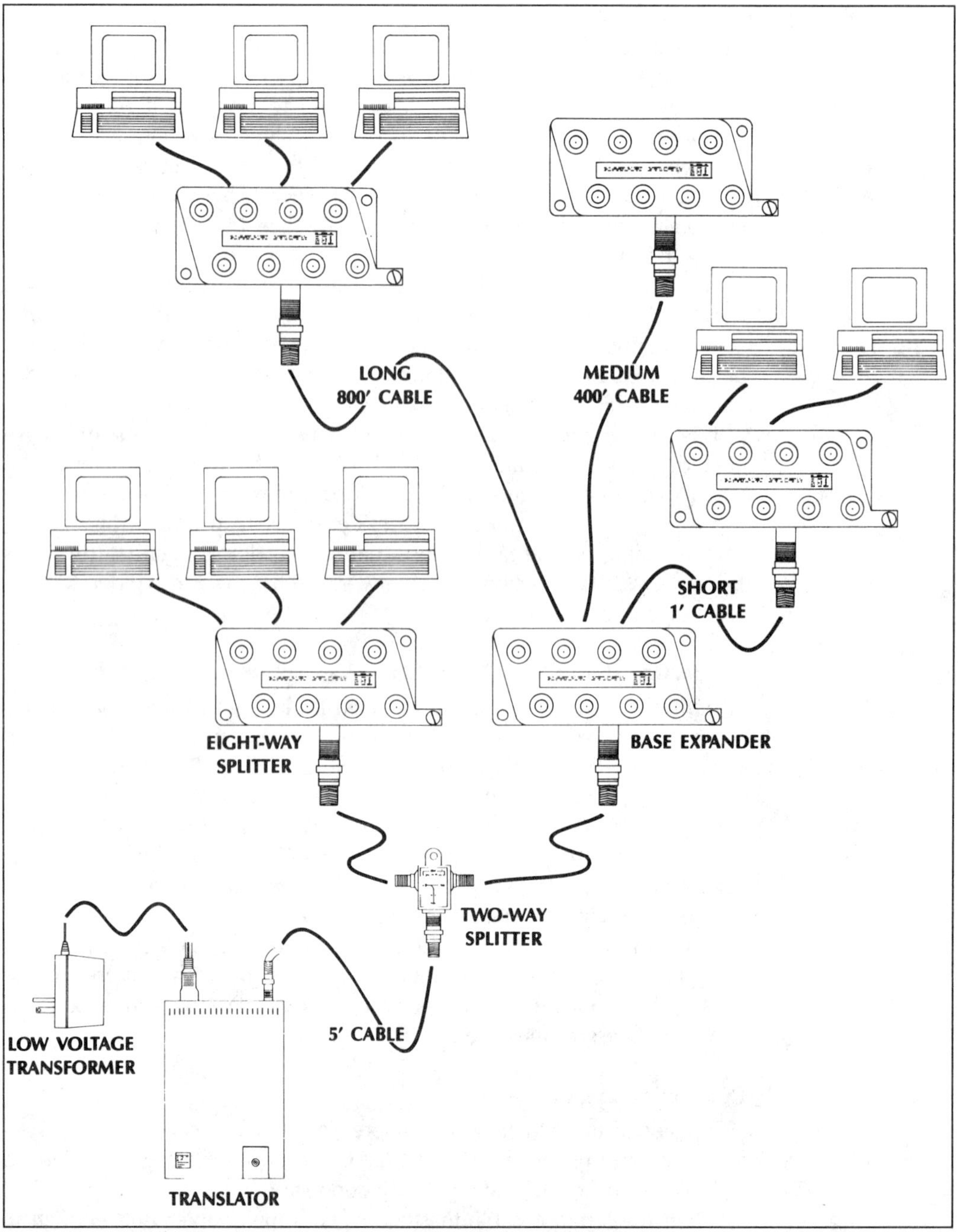

Figure 11.9: *Connections in the broadband version of PC Network, including a base expander and multiple clusters of PCs*

cable (type RG-11; it has a white PVC cover). It comes in lengths of 25, 50, 100, and 200 feet. The lengths are premeasured and come with appropriate attenuators and tilt compensators to adjust the signal strength. It's important not to cut the cables. Where you need a longer length than the cables at hand, you may plug together a few of the ready-made cables to give you the length you need.

Terminator Caps for the Coaxial Connectors

Each tap on a two-way or eight-way splitter comes with a terminator cap. The terminator cap looks a little like the onion dome of an Eastern Orthodox church. It's threaded and screws onto the tap. When you connect a cable, you unscrew the terminator cap and screw the cable connector there instead.

And what do you do with the terminator cap? Since it's small, shiny, and not in use, you put it somewhere. Trouble is, it's going to be needed again—weeks or months later, when you've forgotten where you put it. Sad to say, in designing these beautifully nickeled splitter boxes, IBM didn't include a place to hold or fasten the terminator caps while they're not in use. Here's an early opportunity for the network administrator to make an executive decision: invent a home for them, and see they're kept.

When you subsequently disconnect the cable, you need to replace the terminator cap. The terminator cap provides a measured impedance. When the tap has neither cable nor terminator attached to it, the radio signal in the cable is reflected at the open tap. The reflected signal arrives somewhere else on the network slightly later than a signal that traveled directly. The very slight difference in timing creates multipath interference (which in TV pictures is responsible for ghosts).

Laying the Network Cables

The coaxial cables used by the broadband system are about as thick as your pinkie and moderately stiff. They don't carry more than minute amounts of current, but they do carry radio-frequency signals. Ordinarily, the RF signals are contained by the shielding of the cable, but they can leak if the outer metallic shield of the cable is damaged. You should avoid kinking or sharp corners.

At the PC's network adapter card and at the various splitters, the connectors screw together. IBM supplies you with two identical wrenches that fit the connectors. You probably don't need them to tighten the connectors; finger-tight will do. But sometimes a wrench is handy when you have to undo a connector that someone has tightened enthusiastically.

Running Cables through Walls, Floor, or Ceiling

In an office, it's fairly common to run cables along the floor at the base of a wall or under desks. If your cables must pass through walls or between the floors of a building, the local fire or building codes may require enclosing them in conduit. The cables are not themselves able to cause fire, but the polyurethane dielectric inside the cables and the PVC cover around them can burn in a fire or act as a wick that carries fire from one room to another. Some jurisdictions, therefore, require them to be enclosed. The requirements of local governments vary widely, and it's impossible to give more guidance here than to say: better check this out in your own area.

Labeling the Cables and Connectors

For each eight-way splitter, IBM provides a set of tags so that you can label the cables, and a chart so you can record which goes where. This is useful if you have to move the cable or trace a fault in it. However, it doesn't matter to which tap you connect a PC. You're always free to connect any PC to any available tap. That's because on the network each PC identifies itself; the connectors simply link a PC to the common bus, which is the same throughout the network. As far as the network is concerned, all points on the network are equal. It makes no difference which machine is on which tap or on which cluster. Assigning PCs to clusters is solely a matter of your convenience in running the cables.

Checklist of Physical Components of the Broadband Version

One per network:

- Frequency translator (part 5178001). Included with it: a low-voltage transformer for its power supply, a wrench to help tighten the cable connectors, a two-way splitter, and an eight-way splitter. (You always get a two-way splitter, but you use its second branch only to connect the base expander, if you have one.)
- Base expander (part 6450230). You connect this to the frequency translator and use it to connect up to eight expansion kits; you don't need it if you have a total of eight or fewer PCs and all are within 200 feet of their eight-way connector. The kit includes a 30-decibel attenuator, which permits a PC to be connected temporarily to one of the taps intended for an expansion kit.

One per additional cluster of PCs:

- Expansion kit: short-distance (1 foot; part 6450231), medium-distance (400 feet; part 6450232), or long-distance (800 feet; part 6450233). Each kit includes the cable with the necessary tilt attenuators, and an eight-way splitter for connecting up to eight PCs.

One per PC:

- Network interface card (part 6450213). The interface card provides the physical connection between a PC and the network and the computing power to manage the interface. IBM calls this card the IBM PC Network Adapter.
- Copy of the current release of DOS (at least 3.10).
- Copy of the IBM program PC Network (part 6024195).

Installing the PC Network Software

Once the network adapters and cables are in pláce, you can install the PC Network software. In principle, you could install the software first. However, you wouldn't be able to test it. If the network adapter isn't there, the software immediately detects that fact. It is possible (but dull) to run the software with only one machine on the network.

When you purchase the PC Network software, you get a manual entitled PC Network *User's Guide* and three diskettes, labeled:

- IBM PC Network Program
- IBM PC Network Program Installation Aid
- Exploring the IBM PC Network

(The PC Network *Technical Reference* is a separate—and expensive—purchase. It is concerned mostly with NETBIOS and the PC Network hardware. It's essential for people doing custom installations or developing software that will exploit the network directly, but it contains little for the user of PC Network.)

Installing for a Server versus Installing for a User Machine

The *User's Guide* gives one set of instructions for installing on a floppy disk and a different set for installing on a fixed disk. The instructions assume that if you have a fixed disk, you will configure it as a server—noblesse oblige, perhaps. (If you really wanted to, you could install a user configuration on a fixed-disk machine and keep the disk all to yourself.)

The procedure for installing the server configuration on a fixed disk uses the Installation Aid. If you're not installing as a server, you don't need the Installation Aid.

Procedure for Installing for a User Machine

The objective is to create a diskette containing a minimum amount of DOS (so you can boot from it) and as much as you'll need of the network software. The procedure is as follows:

1. Start DOS 3.10 in the usual way.
2. Format a new diskette, using *FORMAT b:/s* to copy the DOS kernel to the new diskette. In a moment, you will use the PC Network diskette to copy part of itself onto this newly formatted diskette, which you will generally use in future both to start DOS and to start PC Network.
3. Put the PC Network diskette in the default drive. At the DOS prompt, type something like this (substituting the appropriate parameters as noted below):

```
install b: ds
```

In the example, B is the drive on which you put the newly formatted diskette that is about to receive the PC Network software. If you use a different drive, substitute accordingly.

In the example, DS means you are using a double-sided 320k diskette. If you are using a high-capacity (1.2Mb) diskette (often installed in the PC/AT), write HC instead of DS. You can't install PC Network on a single-sided diskette.

The program called Install copies parts of the PC Network diskette onto your new diskette. If you had an Autoexec.bat on your DOS diskette, Install copies it (unchanged) onto your new PC Network diskette. Install also creates a new file Config.sys containing the specs:

```
lastdrive = n
fcbs = 16,8
```

(Or, if you already had a file Config.sys, it appends those two lines to the file you had.) *Lastdrive* sets the size of the table DOS uses to maintain information about directories. The table has an entry for each drive from A to the letter of the alphabet indicated here.

Some (but not all) application programs use a file control block (FCB) to create, open, read, write, or delete files. The values accompanying *fcbs* set the size of the table DOS uses to keep track of them and determine whether some of those may be closed in the event you attempt to use more FCBs than the table provides. The details are explained in the DOS 3.10 reference manual. PC Network increases the values that DOS would otherwise assume by default, permitting a greater number of files to be open concurrently.

What's on the Diskette Thus Produced

Regardless of whether you specified DS or HC, the diskette contains the DOS processor Command.com, but does not contain the files that define the external (non-resident) DOS commands. While you're on the network, it's assumed that you'll be able to use the DOS files stored on a server machine or fall back on a regular DOS diskette. (You couldn't fit all of DOS as well as PC Network on a double-sided diskette, anyway.) Your diskette has the files necessary to run the network in any of the three user configurations.

The effect of specifying DS or HC shows up in the way the files are stored. On a double-sided diskette, all files are in the root directory. On a high-capacity diskette (which has a lot more storage space), the Install program creates a directory called Network and puts all the network files in it.

You're Not Yet Ready to Start the Network Automatically

Eventually, the aim is to have a diskette that automatically starts the network for you. It has to know who you are, what network configuration you run, and what network devices you want to use.

At this point, you have a diskette containing the network software needed to be a user, but your diskette is not yet set up for a personal automatic start. To do that, you have to start the network menus, establish the various options you want, and at that point opt to *Save your network setup.* Then PC Network will create for you an automatic-start file Autoexec.bat, based on a snapshot of what you're doing then. That procedure is described further in this chapter, following the description of the Installation Aid, in a section on getting each user ready. Use of the auto-start facility is discussed in Chapter 2, on starting and restarting the network. The general strategy for automatic starting is described later in this chapter; see the section on PC Network's strategy for automatic start-up.

Installing for a Server Machine

Installation on a fixed-disk machine that will be a network server is more of a production than installing on a user's diskette. For this, you need the Installation Aid supplied on one of the three PC Network diskettes.

Before you start the Installation Aid, be aware that it does considerably more than just copy the program to your fixed disk. It also:

- Creates a directory called Network, into which it copies the PC Network programs.
- Creates a directory called Apps, intended to be read by network users. Into Apps, it copies (as needed or as you request) DOS, the PC Network programs, and application programs, each in its own subdirectory.
- Creates, for each of the applications it installs, two versions of a batch file to start the application. One is for use by the server machine itself and the other for network users.
- Creates a separate private directory for each name on a list of users that it asks you to supply. Each directory contains a batch file to help the user set up paths so the user's machine can find applications on the server.

This Might Be a Good Time to Reformat the Fixed Disk

If you're just beginning to set up a machine that will share directories on the network, you will be setting up several new directories and perhaps installing a lot of programs. This might be a good time to sort out what's on the disk already, discard what you won't need, save what you do need, and start with a clean slate.

Before you use the DOS command BACKUP to save material that's now on the disk, look ahead to the directory structure that the Installation Aid will create (described in the last part of this chapter). For example, when the Installation Aid creates a directory for each of the other users, you may want it to create one for you too. However, if you anticipate changing the directories in which your present files are stored, restoring them is easier if you change their directories *before* you execute BACKUP and reformat the disk. (Backup and restoration procedures are discussed in Chapter 8.)

Note: Formatting the fixed disk of a PC/AT under DOS 3.10 builds a file allocation table (FAT) that makes more efficient use of storage than the file allocation table built by DOS 2. The size of a cluster, the minimum unit of file allocation, is reduced from 8k to 2k. I found this an unexpected benefit of reformatting the disk with DOS 3.10. (To change the cluster size, as a preliminary step to formatting the fixed disk, you must execute FDISK to delete and then reinstate the DOS partition.)

Do Your Homework Before You Start the Installation Aid

As it proceeds, the Installation Aid asks you several questions for which it's nice to have your answers ready:

- The network name that your computer will use as a server. (The Installation Aid doesn't do much with this information, but squirrels it away and then quotes the name when it writes messages to the users telling them how to use your server.)
- The names of users. It needs a distinct name for each of the private directories so it can create them.
- Whether you want to install DOS and PC Network. (If this is your initial installation, you almost certainly want to install both. Later on, you may run the Installation Aid again just to add a new user or a new application, and then you might not want to reinstall DOS and PC Network.) When you elect to install either of these, be ready with the appropriate diskette from which to read them. If you install DOS, you'll need the diskette of DOS supplementary programs as well.
- The names of IBM application programs that you want the Installation Aid to install. You select the ones you want from a menu screen listing the programs that the Installation Aid knows how to install. You can preview the list by consulting the booklet *Installation Aid Quick Reference* (part 6138935) tucked into the back of the PC Network *User's Guide.* Have ready the diskettes containing the programs you are requesting so you can insert them when the program asks for them.
- Whether to print a list of the applications and users it installed. Since you'll probably have to pass this information to others, it's useful to request the printout (so have a printer ready).

Starting the Installation Aid

To start the Installation Aid, proceed as follows. First, if you aren't already running the latest version of DOS (PC Network requires at least 3.10), put the new DOS diskette in drive A and press Ctrl-Alt-Del to restart the machine under the control of the new version of DOS.

Then, put the Installation Aid diskette in drive A. If the DOS prompt doesn't already say A, select drive A. At the DOS prompt, type G (for go). That causes DOS to execute the program G from the Installation Aid diskette. Program G shows you a screen with an IBM logo. The Installation Aid has started. When you press Enter, it proceeds with menus.

The Installation Aid's main menu is shown in Figure 11.10. For the first installation, you should work through each of its options in order.

Note that installing DOS and installing PC Network itself are both covered by choice 1, *Install your IBM applications.* Thus, you need to select choice 1 when you first install PC Network, even if you have no application programs to install.

When you ask the Installation Aid to install a program listed in the menu, it prompts you to insert the appropriate diskette. Although it doesn't say so, what the Installation Aid does then is as follows. For each application, it creates a separate subdirectory within your fixed-disk directory c:\Apps, and copies there whatever it finds on the application diskette. If the diskette has subdirectories, it copies them too, and makes them subdirectories of the application's directory. It also creates two forms of a batch file for invoking the application and stores one in the directory c:\Batch (for the server) and one in the directory c:\Apps\Batch (for network users).

You can use the Installation Aid only to install applications listed in its menu. The procedure for installing an application that isn't in the menu is described later in this chapter.

After each installation (of DOS, PC Network, or an application program), the Installation Aid returns to the menu of possible applications to ask if you care to install another. When you decline (by pressing Escape), it returns to its main menu.

Naming Network Users for Your Applications

When you select choice 2, the Installation Aid asks you to fill in names on the screen shown in Figure 11.11.

```
                          MAIN MENU

      Choose one of the following:

      1.  Install your IBM applications

      2.  Name the network users who can use your applications

      3.  Display information about your installed applications

      4.  Display how network users can use your applications

  ■
```

Figure 11.10: *Main menu of the Installation Aid*

The prompt and example don't make clear what is wanted or why. In fact, they mislead. The Installation Aid wants to create a private directory for each person who will be a user of your machine (and to whom you want to give private disk space). It will try to use the names you supply as the names of directories within the root directory of your fixed disk. That has nothing to do with whether or not your users make use of the public applications on your machine.

It's misleading to call this a "network name." The name you attach to this directory will show up in your display of the directories on your disk. But a user won't see that. When a user asks to use this directory, she'll have to know a name by which to ask for it. She'll have to know its *network name* or *short name*, a synonym that you set each time you offer to share this directory and that is unrelated to what you fill in here. (The process of offering is discussed in Chapter 3.)

The thing to remember here is this: the names the Installation Aid is requesting here are for your convenience in naming directories; they are not the names the users will see (unless you deliberately make the short names match the actual directory names).

As you supply each name, the Installation Aid displays a message to confirm that it has created a directory with that name. The confirmation is nice to have, but it comes with the misleading message *XXX will be able to use applications,* which is true but irrelevant, since using public applications on the server doesn't depend on having a private directory there.

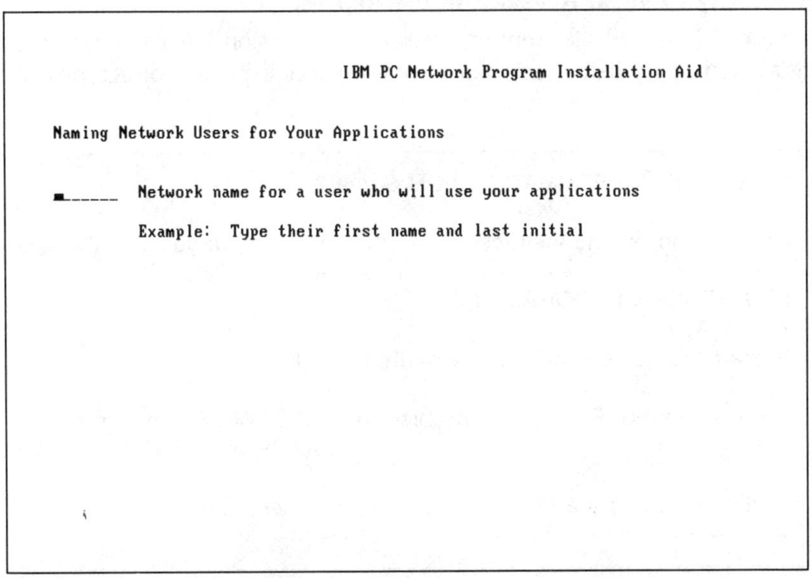

Figure 11.11: *Supplying names for user directories on the server*

Displaying a Report on the Installation

After the Installation Aid has installed DOS, PC Network, and whatever applications you've asked for, you can generate reports summarizing what it has done. One is a report to the server on the applications just installed. The other is a report concerning each of the private directories it created in response to the list of names you supplied.

You get the server's report by selecting the option *Display information about your installed applications.* You can choose a display on your screen or at the printer. It's useful to have it printed; save the printout in a binder for the network administrator. Figure 11.12 shows a server's report on the installation of PC Network.

When you select the option *Display how network users can use your applications,* the Installation Aid generates a report for the server and one for each of the directory names you entered during the installation.

The report addressed to the server points out that you still need to offer the directories you've installed to the people who will use them. The report tells you where to look in the *User's Guide* for instructions on making directories available to users. (In this book, that information is in Chapter 3.) Figure 11.13 shows a sample report to a server.

Following the description of the applications, the report continues with a segment (still addressed to the server) describing each of the private directories. Figure 11.14 shows an example.

A Security Problem Revealed in the Reports

Figure 11.14 illustrates (unfortunately) the confusion introduced by the Installation Aid when it asks for names to install private directories. It

```
APPLICATION INFORMATION FOR Server2

Read and follow the instructions on this sheet before you use the applications.
----            ----            ----            ----            ----
PC NETWORK PROGRAM (1.00)

To start the PC Network Program, enter: NET

The PC Network Program is installed in: C:\NETWORK (for the Server computer)
                                        C:\APPS\NETWORK (for Remote computers)

Continue reading the PC Network Program User's Guide.
----            ----            ----            ----            ----
```

Figure 11.12: *Installation Aid report on installation of PC Network on a server machine*

asks for just one name per user. (In the example, the name supplied was Sachiko.) In generating its report, the Installation Aid uses the same name, Sachiko, for three different purposes:

- DOS name for a directory on the server's fixed disk
- Short name (also called network name) under which the server is presumed to offer to share this directory
- Computer name the user is presumed to adopt when starting the network

The same confusion shows up in the report that the Installation Aid generates and suggests that you give to the user. Figure 11.15 shows such a report.

```
PLEASE GIVE THIS INFORMATION TO: Server2
Follow these instructions to share your directories with the network

IF YOU'RE USING MENUS, DO THESE STEPS:

1. You should be following the instructions in the PC Network Program
   manual. You should already have:
     a. Read Chapter 1.
     b. Read and followed the instructions in Chapter 2.
     c. Read Chapter 3.

   You should be in Chapter 4 and have started the PC Network Program
   on your computer. You should be following the instructions for
   "Setting Up the PC Network Program for Your Computer."

2. You need to start sharing your applications directory so that
   other users on the network can use your applications. Use this
   information to complete the menus:

   DOS name for directory: C:\APPS
   Network Name of disk or directory: APPS
   Password: (leave this blank)
   Other users can: (choose 1)

3. You also need to start sharing the private directories for each of
   the other users. Use this information to complete the menus,
   then continue with the instructions in Chapter 4.
```

Figure 11.13: *Installation Aid report giving general instructions to the operator of a server machine*

Somebody at IBM may have thought that using the same word for all three purposes would make life simpler. Unfortunately, it confuses three things that should be kept distinct. It is quite unnecessary, and probably bad practice, to use the same name for DOS name, user machine name, and short name in an offer to share. It's also a serious privacy violation.

The name the user adopts for her computer is likely to be widely known to everyone on the network because she'll send and probably receive messages under that name. It is false simplicity to employ a widely circulated name as the real DOS name for her private directory. It's even more unwise to use that same name as the network name that the server offers. If that were known to be the general procedure, anybody on the network would know how to gain access to anybody else's private directory. Security would then be entirely dependent on passwords, which are cumbersome and shouldn't be the sole mechanism of privacy control.

A Solution for the Network Administrator

Fortunately, although the Installation Aid generates these reports, they're just pieces of paper. The Installation Aid doesn't itself carry out what the report suggests. So you—as network administrator—can avoid the problem by the following steps:

Step 1. Create your own private roster of the people who use the network. For each person, in addition to such handy things as full name, phone extension, and so on, write down the following:

- Computer name under which the person will use the network.

```
Share information for remote user named: SACHIKO

    DOS name for directory:  C:\SACHIKO

    Network name for your directory: SACHIKO

    Password for directory (Optional): your-choice

NOTE: If you provide a password on this screen, you must also tell
the corresponding remote user the password.

    Enter the number 5 to choose READ/WRITE/CREATE/DELETE
```

Figure 11.14: *Installation Aid report providing instructions to the operator of a server machine regarding directories installed for individual users*

- Additional names under which the person will receive network messages (optional).
- DOS name for the person's private directory. (This is the name you gave the Installation Aid.)
- Network name under which this resource will be offered by the server. The server and the user must both know this

```
PLEASE GIVE THIS INFORMATION TO: SACHIKO
Follow these instructions to start using applications from Server2:
1. You should be following the instructions in the PC Network Program
   User's Guide manual. You should already have:
     a. Read Chapter 1.
     b. Read and followed the instructions in Chapter 2.
     c. Read Chapter 3.
   You should be in Chapter 4 and have started the PC Network Program
   on your computer. You should be following the instructions for
   "Setting Up the PC Network Program for Your Computer."

2. The applications on Server2 are installed in a directory named APPS.
   You need to start using the APPS directory so that you can use
   the applications. Use the following information to complete
   the menus:

   Disk or directory is on computer: Server2
   Network Name of disk or directory: APPS
   DOS drive name on your computer for disk or directory: N

3. Server2 also has installed a private directory for you. You need to
   start using the private directory so that you can use the
   applications from Server2. Use the following information to complete
   the menus:

   Disk or directory is on computer: Server2
   Network Name of disk or directory: SACHIKO
   DOS drive name on your computer for disk or directory: _
     (You choose the letter, from E to N, but don't use N)
   Password: _____________(if the directory has a password, Server2
                           must tell you what it is)

4. Continue with the instructions in Chapter 4.
```

Figure 11.15: *Installation Aid report to an individual user. Note: The drive name N in this report is something the Installation Aid reproduces from your answer to a question during installation. It reflects a convention for the user community, but need not be observed to use the Apps directory.*

name, but nobody else needs to. Ask the user to suggest a pattern of characters that she'll find easy to remember and others will find obscure.

- Whether there will be a password, and if so how the server will set it and the user know it.

Step 2. Do not give the users the reports that the Installation Aid generates for them. Instead, generate something similar of your own, including the network name the user will need to know rather than the name of the directory on your machine.

Setting Up Automatic Start for the Server and Each User

Basically, the task is to generate an appropriate Autoexec.bat file on the server machine's fixed disk and on each user's start-up diskette. You could let each individual do this herself. (That's what the *User's Guide* assumes.)

If you prefer to give novice users a diskette with everything already prepared, proceed as follows:

- Start the server (or servers) that the users will use. (Detailed instructions on starting are in Chapter 2.) At each server, offer to share all the resources that the users will need.
- Within the PC Network menus, select the option *Save your network setup.* That writes an Autoexec.bat file on the server's fixed disk. At subsequent start-ups, all the offers you just made will be repeated.
- On another machine, take each user's diskette in turn, reset (with Ctrl-Alt-Del), start the network, and request to use all the facilities the user will need regularly.
- Within the PC Network menus, select the option *Save your network setup.* This writes an Autoexec file on the user's diskette. At subsequent start-ups, all the requests you just made will be repeated.
- Take out the diskette and give it to the user, along with instructions about what it contains, passwords, and so on.

The procedure just described is simple but has some drawbacks. It assumes the server machines are already running anytime the user starts her machine. It assumes the user should start her day requesting to use all the things she'll need. Those assumptions may not always be reasonable. Some refinements to Autoexec files and to application batch files are discussed in Chapter 12.

The Directory Structure Created by the Installation Aid

The files and directories that the Installation Aid creates on the fixed disk of a server machine are listed in Figure 11.16, which shows the structure of the directories.

The arrangement shown in Figure 11.16 is recommended by the *User's Guide* and installed automatically by the Installation Aid. It seems well worth following.

DOS Is Mostly in the Apps Directory

The Installation Aid puts the DOS external commands not in the root directory but in the directory \Apps\DOS, where network users will be able to read them. However, to make sure you can get started with DOS on the fixed disk, it installs the DOS file Command.com both in the root directory and in \Apps\DOS. Since the Installation Aid doesn't erase any files, if you already had DOS in the root directory, as a result of installing it with the Installation Aid you may have redundant copies.

PC Network Is in Both \Network and \Apps\Network

The Installation Aid installs a complete set of the PC Network programs in the server's directory \Network, and another complete set in \Apps\Network.

It is not clear to me why this duplication is necessary. I have tried running PC Network on the server using only the copies in the Apps directory, altering the PATH command in Autoexec so that DOS looks in \Apps\Network rather than \Network. (That causes the printer spool to reside in the \Apps\Network directory, where it is visible to network users, but I did not encounter other problems.)

Prototype User Directory

The Installation Aid creates a directory called User.mdl, which serves as a model for the directory the Installation Aid creates for each user. It creates each directory so that the individual directory has whatever files and subdirectories it finds in User.mdl, including the file Netpath.bat and the subdirectory called Profiles. If you want each user to have her own copy of certain files, save them in User.mdl and the Installation Aid will copy them too when it creates each user directory.

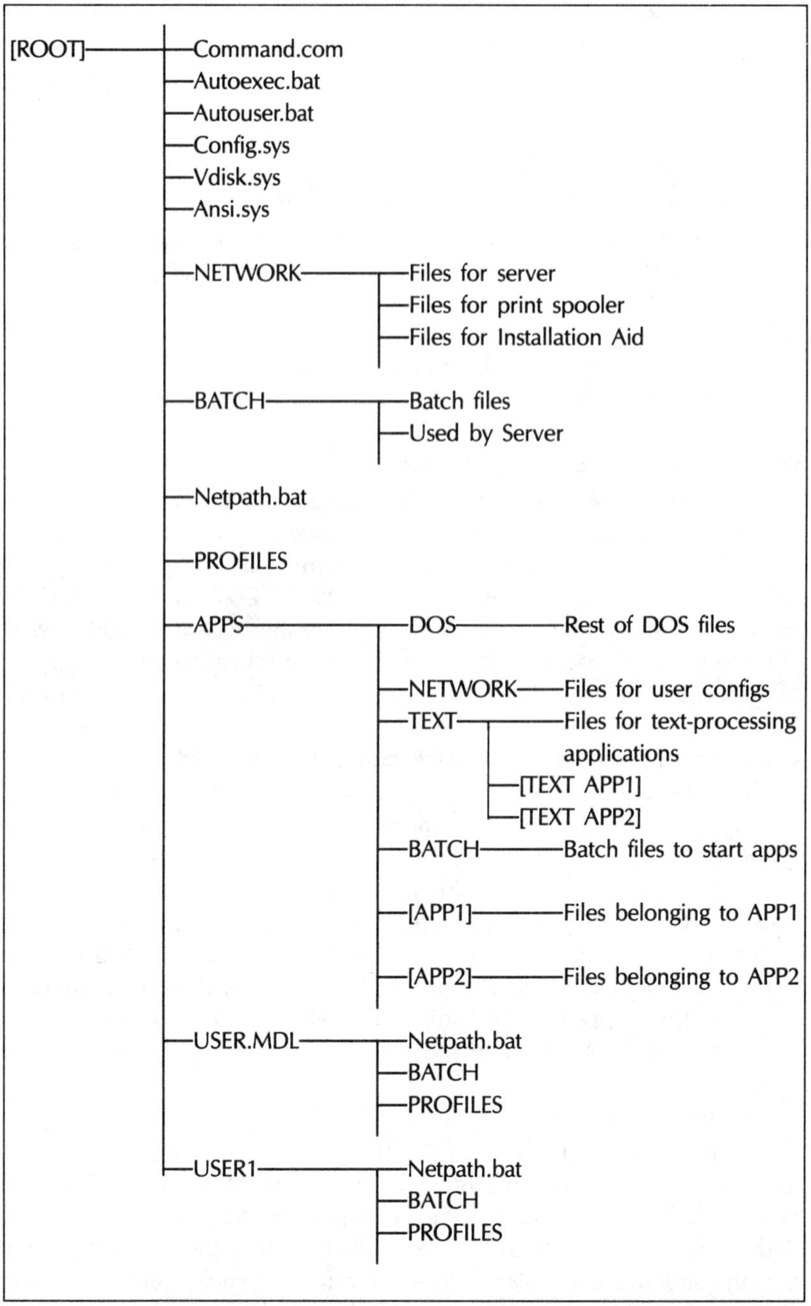

Figure 11.16: *Files and directories created by the PC Network Installation Aid (Note: Files are shown with initial caps, directories in all caps)*

Two Directories for Batch Files

The Installation Aid creates two directories for batch files. (A batch file is a file that can be executed like a command, simply by including its name in what you type at the DOS prompt; it usually provides a convenient way to invoke a program, setting up various conditions so that you don't have to write them each time the program is executed. (See Chapter 12 for further discussion of batch files.)

The directory \Batch is for the server machine's operator, and the file \Apps\Batch for network users. The two versions differ because the user sees the server machine's directories from a different point of view.

The DOS Commands PATH and APPEND in Network Batch Files

Not only would you like to use programs stored outside the directory in which you're currently working, but when you're a network user, you'd like to use programs located on a different machine. The DOS command PATH instructs DOS where to look for the definitions of commands. PC Network takes advantage of that command and also of the recently added command APPEND, which complements PATH.

PATH Rules

When you mention a command but do not state the complete path describing where to find the command's definition, DOS looks in the current directory of the default drive. (I suggest you adjust your DOS prompt so that at each prompt it reminds you what the default drive and directory are; see Chapter 12.)

If DOS doesn't find the file in the current directory, unless you've provided further instructions, DOS assumes it doesn't exist. If it's looking for a command (a file whose extension is .com, .exe, or .bat), DOS reports *Invalid command or file name* (which is its way of saying it can't find a file of that name). If you've asked to write a file, it may assume that since it hasn't found it in this directory, it should create a new file there.

The command PATH gives DOS a list of paths along which to look for the definition of a command if it doesn't find it in the current directory. Here's what a path looks like when displayed:

PATH = \BATCH;*n:*\BATCH;*n:*\TEXT;*n:*\DOS;*n:*\NETWORK;\

(Where *n* is a suitable drive specifier.) The various paths are set off from their neighbors by semicolons. (Unfortunately, DOS doesn't permit blanks in this command, which might have made it easier on the human eye.)

The PATH command only affects where DOS looks for existing files that contain the definitions of commands. That is, it only applies to a file whose name ends with the extension .com, .exe, or .bat.

DOS looks through the paths in the order in which you stated them in the PATH command, but stops its search as soon as it finds a match. If a drive or directory on the list doesn't exist, DOS just goes on to the next without complaining.

Watch out: Even though PATH helps DOS find an existing file, it has no effect on where DOS creates a *new* file, and it has no effect on files whose extension is other than .com, .exe, or .bat.

APPEND Helps Find Files that Aren't Command Files

What about other kinds of files? As it executes, a program may read other files, for example files containing data the program needs. When the program refers to a file whose name is not stated as a complete path (that is, without the initial drive name and \), DOS interprets the name with respect to whatever directory is current at the time DOS gets to it. Especially when you use the network to run a program that was written some time ago, there's a risk that it contains names that are going to be interpreted in a context different from what the author assumed.

IBM distributes with PC Network a new DOS command: APPEND. (Presumably it will show up in DOS a bit later; it comes with PC Network because that's where it's particularly needed to install programs that were not originally intended for networking.)

APPEND works like PATH, but tells DOS where to look for any kind of file, not just a file whose extension is .com, .exe, or .bat. (However, APPEND affects searches done by some DOS function calls but not others, so whether it is in fact effective depends on how the particular program is written. APPEND is effective for function calls *FCB file open, handle file open,* and *get file size,* but not for *find first* or *find next,* so a program that relies on them is not helped by APPEND.)

As part of a command to set things up for work on the network, PC Network routinely includes in the Autoexec that it generates the command *APPEND *, which tells DOS to try the root directory of the default drive.

Manually Installing an Application for Public Use

The Installation Aid will install only programs that are on its menu of eligible (IBM-supplied) applications. It isn't hard to install other applications by carrying out by hand the procedure that the Installation Aid does automatically. Assuming that the application comes to you on one or more diskettes, the steps are as follows.

Step 1. Find out what subdirectories (if any) the application uses. You can do that by putting the diskette in drive A and executing the DOS command *TREE a:*.

Step 2. Find out the agreed-on drive name by which users refer to the server's Apps directory. You may already know what the drive is. You also have the option to look it up. At installation, the Installation Aid records it in the file c:\Network\Sys_IDS.NIA. That file contains the name of the server machine and the network name for the Apps directory, separated by the ASCII control character for line feed.

Step 3. Create a subdirectory within Apps to contain the application. Suppose the application is to be called Fungo and will use a subdirectory Funref. Suppose you have the application diskette on drive A. You can do what's needed by carrying out the set of DOS commands listed in Figure 11.17.

Step 4. Create batch files for invoking the application, one in \Batch and the other in \Apps\Batch. A batch file is a handy way of invoking a program. A batch file's name consists of the word that you write to invoke the application, plus the extension *.bat*. DOS can find the batch

c:	Make C the default drive.
CHDIR \Apps	Select the Apps directory.
MKDIR Fungo	Create the new subdirectory.
CHDIR Fungo	Select the new directory just created.
COPY a:*.*	Copy all files from the diskette root directory. (Doesn't copy subdirectories.)
	If there are no subdirectories, skip to End.
MKDIR Funref	Create a new subdirectory.
CHDIR Funref	Select the subdirectory.
COPY a:\Funref*.*	Copy all files for the subdirectory.
CHDIR ..	Return to the application's main directory. Repeat these four steps as needed for other subdirectories.
CHDIR \	End: Return to root directory.

Figure 11.17: *Creating a directory for a network application*

file because it's in a directory where DOS always looks (having been told where to look by a PATH command). The batch file tells DOS where to find the application itself. The advantage is that the user doesn't have to change directories to find the application, and she doesn't even need to know where the application itself is stored.

Figure 11.18 shows the essentials of a batch file to be used directly by the operator of a server machine, and Figure 11.19 shows the corresponding version for a user. The two versions differ only in the way they refer to the directory where applications are found. Where the server version says *c:\Apps,* the user version has *n:* instead.

These batch files assume N is the drive name the users have agreed to call the server's Apps directory, and E is the drive name the user has assigned to her private directory on the server machine. Of course, a user who calls either of these something else needs different letters in the batch file. (*Note:* On page 10-57 of the first edition of the PC Network *User's Guide,* they forgot to replace *c:Apps* by *n:*)

ECHO Off	Optional preliminaries.
CLS	Clear the screen (may not be wanted or needed; the application may do it itself).
APPEND > Savepath.bat	Create a file in the current directory, and write in it the current APPEND path.
ECHO c:\Apps\Batch\ Cleansav >> Savepath.bat	Add to the text already in Savepath a line that invokes the batch file Cleansav.bat so that, when executed, Savepath will be erased. [The PC Network *User's Guide,* page 10-56, also resets the PATH here, but doesn't preserve or restore the former PATH.]
APPEND c:\Profiles;c:\ Apps\Fungo	Set a new APPEND path pointing to the application's directory and the Server's personal Profiles directory. (Replaces the former APPEND path.)
c:\Apps\Fungo\Start	Invoke the application (assuming that its command to do so is Start)
Savepath	Invoke the batch file set up earlier. It restores the former APPEND path, and then calls Cleansav to erase itself.

Figure 11.18: *Batch file to invoke a network application from the server on which it is located*

The batch files described here are consistent with the ones that the Installation Aid generates for the programs it installs. In Chapter 12 are some suggestions for minor improvements to these batch files; they might apply equally to the automatically generated batch files.

Step 5. Set the read-only attribute for each such file by *ATTRIB +r* followed by the name of the file.

ECHO Off	Optional preliminaries.
CLS	Clear the screen (may not be wanted or needed; the application may do it itself).
APPEND > Savepath.bat	Create a file in the current directory, and write in it the current APPEND path.
ECHO n:\Batch\Cleansav >> Savepath.bat	Add to the text already in Savepath a line that invokes the batch file Cleansav.bat so that, when executed, Savepath will be erased. [The PC Network *User's Guide,* page 10–57, also resets the PATH here, but doesn't preserve or restore the former PATH.]
APPEND e:\Profiles;n:\Fungo	Set a new APPEND path pointing to the application's directory and the server's personal Profiles directory. (Replaces the former APPEND path.)
n:\Fungo\Start	Invoke the application (assuming that its command to do so is Start).
Savepath	Invoke the batch file set up earlier. It restores the former APPEND path, and then calls Cleansav to erase itself.

Figure 11.19: *Batch file to invoke a network application for a remote user machine. It differs from the batch file of Figure 11.18 by replacing references to c:\Apps by N: and references to c:\Profiles to E: (the presumed drive for the user's private profiles on the server machine).*

Automating with Batch Files

Twelve

Batch files give you a way to make operations automatic and convenient. You write in a file the steps you want DOS to take each time you reset the machine or each time you use a command name that you create.

A batch file is a sort of program. The entire file is text, divided into lines in the usual way. Each line is a DOS command, consisting mostly of commands you might have typed from the keyboard, but augmented by a few commands that DOS recognizes only when it finds them in a batch file. When you type the name of a batch file, DOS takes each line in turn, interprets it as a DOS command, and executes it.

The language of batch files is a pretty limited medium in which to write programs, but it is nevertheless a convenient way to automate a variety of simple tasks. This chapter suggests some of the possibilities by offering as examples a few recipes I've found helpful with PC Network. They may be useful to you directly or inspire you to write others of your own.

Batch Files as Commands

A batch file (like any other file) can have any name you like within the DOS eight-letter limit, provided the name isn't already in use for something else. It's common to assign a name that reminds you what the file does or perhaps looks like an English verb. For example, if you have a program that revises some data, you might give it the name Revise and define it so that the name of the file you want to revise comes after it. Thus, to revise a file called Smith.ltr, you write *Revise Smith.ltr.* The definition of the batch file Smith tells DOS the details about where to find the program you want to use and what else must be done.

Although a batch file's name must end with *.bat,* when you use the batch file's name as a command you omit the final *.bat.* (You aren't actually required to omit it, but you may and people usually do.) When you enter a word at the DOS prompt, DOS looks for a file that has that word as the main portion of its name, followed by one of the three extensions *.exe, .com,* or *.bat.* When DOS doesn't find a matching file whose name has the extension *.exe,* or *.com,* but does find one ending in *.bat,* it executes it.

A batch file consists of ordinary ASCII characters that can be written or revised with any text editor. The characters spell out commands in a language with which you're already at least slightly familiar: the DOS command language. Thus, writing a batch file offers you a handy way to record various details of the way you want a program to run without having to write them each time you use the program. For the same reason, each of the programs installed in the Apps library comes with a batch file that makes it easier to use.

As an example, this book was written with a text editor called PCWrite. Its main function Ed was installed in the directory \Apps\Text\PCWrite on a machine called Server2. But to start PCWrite, I didn't have to type or remember *\\Server2\Apps\Text\PCWrite\Ed.* Nor did I have to repeat various details about where I keep *profiles.* I simply typed PCW and the name of the file to be edited. That's because when I installed PCWrite on the server machine, I set up a batch file called PCW.bat. Whenever I type the command PCW, the file PCW.bat supplies the needed details.

Every Time DOS Starts, It Executes Autoexec.bat

By convention, each time the operating system starts, it looks for a file called Autoexec.bat and, if it finds it, executes it. Thus, to tell DOS what you want it to do automatically each time you start the machine, you have only to write the commands in a file with that name. As explained in Chapter 2, PC Network rewrites Autoexec.bat so that its last line is *Autouser.* That causes DOS to execute a batch file called Autouser.bat. The effect is that, with PC Network, you have *two* batch files executed automatically each time you start the system: Autoexec.bat and Autouser.bat.

One Batch File Can Invoke Another Only as the Last Thing It Does

One restriction to note: DOS keeps no *stack* for batch files in execution. If a command in one batch file invokes a second batch file, control passes irrevocably to the second file. DOS doesn't keep a record of how or where the first file was invoked; when execution of the second batch file ends, control does *not* return to the first one. (Too bad. There'd be marvelous things you could do if control did return.) So one batch file can invoke another batch file only as the last thing it does.

A Batch File Begins by Default with ECHO On

ECHO On means that DOS displays the DOS prompt and the command it finds on each line of a batch file, just as it would if you were typing those lines from the keyboard. If you include *ECHO Off* as a line of your batch file, it suppresses further display of the prompt and the command. Each batch file needs its own ECHO Off, since one used earlier doesn't apply to another batch file.

Error Level Set by NET Commands

Each of the PC Network commands sets the DOS error level to 0 when it executes successfully and to 1 otherwise. (You'd think with all those numbered error messages that the error level might be more informative, but it isn't.) The DOS batch-file subcommand *If* can test the error level, as illustrated in the first of the batch files in this chapter, shown in Figure 12.1.

Reviewing Your Current Use of the Network before Saving

The menu option *Save your network setup* writes the batch file Autoexec.bat so as to reproduce the present situation of the network. Before saving the setup, you might want to review what the setup is.

The batch file called Status.bat might help (Figure 12.1). The test after line 1 is intended mainly to catch the error reported when PC Network isn't running, which results in the message *NET500: Network not started* and sets the error level to 1.

Alternatively, you might want to store the resulting reports in a file whose name you enter to the right of the name of the batch file in your command. Statfile, shown in Figure 12.2, permits that. For example, to store the result in the file Status.rpt, you'd type:

```
Statfile Status.rpt
```

However, when you just wanted to see the report without saving it, you could write *Statfile* with nothing after it.

Including the Current Directory in the DOS Prompt

DOS commands and programs are frequently context dependent. That is, the files a command or program refers to may depend on what

```
net name
if errorlevel 1 goto end
net share
net use
net log
:end
```

Figure 12.1: *Batch file Status.bat to report the network setup*

```
if %1 ~= =~ goto nofile
net name > %1
if errorlevel 1 goto end
net share >> %1
net use >> %1
net log >> %1
goto end
:nofile
status
:end
```

Figure 12.2: *Batch file Statfile.bat to report the network setup and, when a file name follows the command, store the report in a file. For the case when you don't name a file to receive the result, this definition invokes Status.bat, shown in Figure 12.1.*

directory you're in. Working with a network increases the likelihood that you'll shift between directories. It's important to remain aware of the current directory. A valuable reminder is to have DOS include the name of the current directory in its prompt. (Unless you specify otherwise, the DOS prompt includes the default drive but not the current directory.)

By inserting the lines shown in Figure 12.3 in the first part of Autouser.bat, you set up a DOS prompt that shows you the date and time followed by the default drive, the current directory, and finally the > sign followed by a blank. The characters $h indicate a backspace; the three backspaces cause DOS to write the drive name on top of where it writes the milliseconds (because milliseconds may be more than you wanted to know about the time). On a machine that keeps track of time while the power is off, omit the lines that say DATE and TIME.

Automatic Netpath for a Remote User

When you start the network in a user configuration, you need to establish a path to the server machine. The Installation Aid has set up a batch file Netpath.bat for you and saved it in your private directory on the server machine. By inserting the lines shown in Figure 12.4 as the last lines of your file Autouser.bat, you can get your machine to execute Netpath automatically as part of the start-up. (They must be the last lines because Netpath is a batch file, so when DOS executes it, control will not return to these commands.) When Netpath is executed, it displays a message saying what it has done.

An alternative approach is to copy the contents of the file n:Netpath.bat into Autouser.bat so that its statements become statements in Autouser.bat. This has one important advantage: it sets the path so that DOS will try to look for commands on drive N but does *not* require you to start using drive N at once. That's preferable when you defer the request to use a network directory until you have specific need of it.

```
echo off
date
time
prompt $d$a $t$h$h$h$a $p$a$g$a
```

Figure 12.3: *Lines to insert at the front of Autouser.bat to reset the DOS prompt*

Saving and Restoring the PATH and APPEND Environments

When you mention a file without saying what directory it's in (and it isn't in the current directory), DOS can't find it without help. You help it by setting up what is called the DOS *environment:* a list of directories in which DOS should look. The environment may contain two lists. The list set by the PATH command tells DOS where to look for an executable file. The list set by the APPEND command tells it where to look for a file to use as data.

The PC Network Installation Aid sets up batch files for the applications it installs, and the *User's Guide* shows a batch file for applications you install by hand. Those batch files use both the APPEND command and the PATH command to specify two new lists of directories in which DOS should look. They do that so the various programs within the application can find any files they need.

When you use the PATH command to set a new list of directories, it erases any list set by an earlier use of PATH. Similarly, when you use the APPEND command to set a new list of directories, it erases any list set by an earlier use of APPEND. The network batch files use both PATH and APPEND. Although the PATH and APPEND commands help DOS find files needed for the application, they also destroy the environment that was in effect before the application started.

The batch files set up by the Installation Aid ingeniously save the list of directories established by a previous use of APPEND. They do that by displaying the list and saving the display in a batch file. When work on the application is over, the batch file written at the start restores the former environment. Curiously, although the network batch files save and later restore the APPEND environment, they do nothing comparable for the PATH environment, even though they often use PATH to create a new environment, which destroys any former one. I'm not sure why they were written that way; I suspect an oversight. The same

```
if not exist e:netpath.bat goto end
e:netpath
rem Since Netpath is a batch file, we never return to this line
:end
echo NOTE: Netpath has not been executed
```

Figure 12.4: *Final lines of Autouser.bat to automate execution of Netpath*

mechanism could just as well save and subsequently restore both the PATH and the APPEND environments.

A batch file for a remote user, revised to save and restore the earlier PATH along with the earlier APPEND, is shown in Figure 12.5. It is an extension of the example on page 10-57 of the PC Network *User's Guide,* which invokes a program called Start in directory \Apps\App1. By convention, the user calls the server's Apps directory drive N, and calls her own private directory on the server machine drive E.

The added line to preserve and restore the PATH command is marked by italics.

Deferring the Request to Use until Specifically Needed

In Chapter 3, I remarked that servers should make their offers as soon as possible, but users should take up the offers as late as possible. The PC Network menu facility to save the network setup unfortunately includes both offers to share and requests to use in the Autoexec file. The underlying assumption is that everybody makes all the requests at the beginning of the day, and then makes use of the resources as needed.

An alternative approach is to make no request until you invoke an application that actually needs the resource. You defer your request to use by making it part of the batch file that starts the application. Since the batch file must be accessible to your machine before it has requested to use a shared resource, the batch file necessarily resides on the user machine.

```
echo off
cls
n:\dos\append > savepath.bat
n:\dos\path >> savepath.bat
echo n:\batch\cleansav >> savepath.bat
echo Setting up to run Application 1
n:\dos\append n:\app1;e:\profiles
n:\dos\path \batch;n:\batch;n:\app1;n:\dos;n:\;\
n:\app1\start
savepath
```

Figure 12.5: *Amending a network batch file to save and restore both PATH and APPEND commands*

The batch file shown in Figure 12.6 is called PCW.bat. It resides on the user's machine. Its job is to invoke the network batch program \Apps\Batch\PCW.bat stored on the server machine. The first statement is intended to decide whether the user has a drive N; it does so by testing whether any files exist in the \Batch directory of drive N. When the answer is no, the program requests to use Server2's Apps directory as drive N. However, when files are found on drive N, the batch file goes ahead and invokes n:\Batch\PCW. The %1 beside the name n:\Batch\PCW tells DOS to pass along whatever name may appear after PCW in the user's command.

When work on the application is over, this approach leaves drive N still in use over the network. It might be preferable to discontinue use of drive N at the end. However, once the batch file has invoked another (as this one invokes n:\Batch\PCW), control never returns to it, so it does no good to include a command to discontinue use.

An alternative approach is to use the same technique that the Installation Aid uses for restoring the use of APPEND: to build a batch file called Savepath.bat. That batch file can also include the command to discontinue sharing (see Figure 12.7).

Because PCW2 includes commands to clean up after the main program has been executed, it can't simply invoke the server's batch file \Apps\Batch\PCW.bat. (If it were to do that, control would not return to it.) Therefore, this version cannot invoke n:\Batch\PCW. Instead, it includes the commands that are in n:\Batch\PCW.bat (which make this version considerably longer than the version in Figure 12.6).

Notice that in the batch file of Figure 12.7, the user machine must make a local copy of the server's file Cleansav.bat because, after drive N has been deleted, it will no longer be possible to refer to the server's copy.

```
if exist n:\batch\*.* goto ok
rem When no files in n:\batch, try NET USE
net use n: \\server2\apps
if errorlevel 1 goto tilt
:ok
n:\batch\pcw %1
:tilt
rem Unable to execute \Batch\PCW on server drive N
```

Figure 12.6: *Request by the user's batch file PCW.bat to use a network directory, but not until the user starts the application. When NET USE has been successful, the user's batch file PCW invokes the server's batch file PCW, which takes over the job from there.*

Warning of Held-over Jobs When Starting a Print Server

As mentioned in Chapter 9, if you're the operator of a machine that shares a printer with the network, as soon as you offer to share your printer the print manager starts at once to print any files remaining in the queue that were not explicitly marked *held*. If this is inconvenient, you can prevent printing by doing something that the print-manager program will experience as an error (for example, turning off the power to the printer that the print manager is using). After that, you can hold the job that the print manager has impetuously started and any others for which you are not yet ready. That done, turn the printer on.

```
echo off
if exist n:\batch\*.* goto ok
rem When no files in n:\batch, try NET USE
net use n: \\server2\apps > nul
if errorlevel 1 goto tilt
:ok
:       Make a local copy of cleansav.bat
copy n:\batch\cleansav.bat > nul
:       Build Savepath.bat to restore environment
:       and delete the network directory when all is done
echo echo off > savepath.bat
path >> savepath.bat
append >> savepath.bat
echo net use n: /d >> savepath.bat
echo if not errorlevel 1 echo Drive N deleted >> savepath.bat
echo cleansav.bat >> savepath.bat
:       Set environment for the application
path n:\text\pcwrite;n\dos;n:\network;n:\batch;\batch
append e:\profiles
:       At last! This is what we came for
n:\text\pcwrite\ed %1
savepath
goto end
:tilt
Rem Unable to execute PCW on Server drive N
:end
```

Figure 12.7: *Batch file PCW2.bat. Like PCW.bat (Figure 12.6), its request to use a network diectory is deferred until the user starts the application. Unlike the version in Figure 12.6, this one deletes the network directory when the application has finished.*

The lines shown in Figure 12.8 are intended to warn you when this may be necessary. A batch file isn't able to tell whether files left in the spool are held, but it can detect their existence in the spool, and that is the basis of the warning this program generates. These lines should be included in Autoexec.bat ahead of the line of asterisks that marks the start of the network portion (see Chapter 2).

When these commands in Autoexec.bat find that there are files in the printer spool other than PQ.spl (which is the queue table), they display the directory listing for those files and a message asking whether you wish to turn off the printer. You'll have time to do so if you want, because right after this the network Autoexec pauses to ask whether you want to start the network, so you can attend to the printer before answering the question about the network.

```
:* * * Network Batch File * * *
echo off
rename \network\pq.spl spl.old
if not exist \network\pq???.spl goto spoolok
echo Files in print spool:
dir \network\pq???.spl
echo Turn off printer before starting Network?
:spoolok
rename \network\spl.old pq.spl
:* * *
```

(Autoexec.bat continues)

Figure 12.8: *Autoexec.bat file segment to warn printer operator of jobs held over in the printer spool*

Tuning the Start-Up Parameters

Thirteen

Each time you start PC Network, you have the power to set the value of each of 18 different parameters that affect the space or time allocated to various network functions, and thereby the performance of the network. It's a list of daunting complexity. Fortunately, if you ignore them, PC Network assigns default values to all those parameters, and you can get started. Fairly soon, however, your particular usage or circumstances are likely to conflict with the default assumptions, and you need to set values more appropriate to your special conditions.

The Variety of Controls

With so many different parameters, it helps to have some basis for classifying the possibilities and grouping together those that apply to a particular situation. The sections that follow briefly describe some broad groups of parameters, as an introduction to the more systematic description of each.

Names and Tables

One group of parameters establishes the sizes of the various tables used to refer to network computers or their devices, or to exchange messages. The sizes of the tables remain fixed during a session and limit the number of machines that can take up your offers to share or whose offers you can accept. They also limit your ability to receive messages forwarded from another machine or to adopt alternative names under which to receive messages.

Space for Buffers vs. Space for Programs

The largest group of parameters comprises those that regulate the allocation of space to buffers in the computer's main memory. Buffers reduce the work of the processor by providing convenient temporary storage for data that is in transit, and hence speed up the flow of data. But because buffers take their space from main memory, they compete directly with the space used for applications. You're forced to pick the best trade-off between the speed of data flow and the loss of main memory that could otherwise be used for applications.

Time for Background vs. Time for Foreground

A computer on the network divides the attention of its processor between work for the local machine—usually, the person at the keyboard—and work for the network (passing data, receiving messages, and so on). The parameters not concerned with the allocation of space to buffers are concerned with the allocation of time between background and foreground tasks.

Commands vs. Menus

Of the 18 start-up parameters, six can be set in the start-up screen headed *Change defaults for starting the network* (see Chapter 2). The others are set only when you execute the NET START command. However, when you subsequently use the screen *Save your network setup* to generate an Autoexec file, any parameters to which you have given nondefault values are included, not just the ones set from the menus.

Parameters for User Machines versus Parameters for Server Machines

Some parameters are relevant primarily to the user machine, others to the server, yet others to both. Start-up parameters that affect your machine only in its role as server are summarized in Figure 13.1. Start-up parameters that affect your machine only in its role as user are shown in Figure 13.2. Start-up parameters that apply to both the server and the user configurations are shown in Figure 13.3.

Parameter	Effect	Limit
SHR	Number of offers you can make to share disks, directories, or printers on your machine.	Default: 5 Min: 1 Max: 150
RDR	Number of different machines that can use resources on your machine at one time	Default: 10 Min: 1 Max: 29

Comment: The menus permit RDR to be no more than 25, but the value may be as high as 29 when you use NET START and set USN and SRV to their minimum values. For RDR, a machine that uses several resources on your machine still counts as one.

Parameter	Effect	Limit
REQ	Number of network-request buffers. This determines the number of data transfers the server can handle concurrently.	Default: 2 Min: 1 Max: 3
RQB	Size of each network-request buffer.	Default: 8k Min: 0.5k Max: 32k

Comment: The product REQ × RQB must not exceed 48k.

Parameter	Effect	Limit
TSI	Time spent on either network or local processing before switching to check for work on the other. (The meaning of the numeric codes is explained in the text.)	Default: 54 Min: 00 Max: 99

Figure 13.1: *Parameters that affect the server role*

Parameter	Description	Values
PRB	Size of buffer used for transferring print requests from spool to printer.	Default: 512 bytes Min: 512 bytes Max: 16k
PRP	Relative priority of printing from spool vs. other local tasks. (High priority to the printer is 3.)	Default: 3 Min: 1 Max: 3
SHB	Size of buffer used to track files opened for shared read/write use.	Default: 2k Min: 512 bytes Max: 60k
SHL	Number of entries in the table of locked ranges within files. Each entry in the table of locked ranges requires 14 bytes.	Default: 20 Min: 20 Max: 1000

Comment: SHL and SHB are relevant to applications that permit concurrent updates to shared files.

Figure 13.1: *Parameters that affect the server (continued)*

The rather inconsistent acronyms that have been coined for these parameters conceal the correspondence between some that concern the user configurations and others that concern the server. I find that grouping the corresponding parameters together helps me to keep them straight. Figure 13.4 arranges several parameters so user and server parameters that roughly correspond to one another appear on the same line.

CMD and SES: Parameters That Affect NETBIOS

Two parameters affect the way the computer uses the network adapter. The parameter CMD sets the number of NETBIOS commands that can be active in the network adapter at one time; the parameter SES sets the number of network sessions that the adapter can be involved in at one time. A *session* is a sequence of related exchanges between machines, for example to transmit the various segments of a file and receive an acknowledgment of receipt.

These parameters instruct the adapter on allocation of space within its own memory. The space available for handling each one is limited, so when you permit a large number of concurrent commands and sessions, the adapter is forced to break transmission into a large number of small segments, requiring more back-and-forth between the adapters and reducing overall speed.

Network performance is optimized when SES and CMD provide for only as many concurrent sessions or commands as are really needed. Most of the time you don't need to set those parameters. When you don't mention them, the NET START command computes them automatically. Large values of SES and CMD may be required for some interactive programs designed especially for the network, but the installation instructions for those programs should include instructions on how to set the needed values.

Parameter	Effect	Limit
SRV	Number of different computers whose resources you can use at one time.	Default: 2 Min: 1 Max: 31
ASG	Number of different network devices (printers, disks, directories) that you can use at one time.	Default: 5 Min: 1 Max: 32
NBC	Number of network buffers on your computer. It is desirable to have at least as many buffers as simultaneously open files.	Default: 3 Min: 1 Max: 64
NBS	Size of each network buffer.	Default: 512 bytes Min: 512 bytes Max: 32k

Comment: The product NBC × NBS may not exceed 32K.

Parameter	Effect	Limit
PB1 PB2 PB3	Each of these three sets the size of a buffer used for sending jobs to a server for printing. PB1 is for LPT1, PB2 for LPT2, PB3 for LPT3.	Default (PB1): 1024 bytes Default (PB2 and PB3): 128 bytes Min(Each): 80 bytes Max(Each): 16k

Comment: The sum of space in all three network print buffers may not exceed 16k. Notice that the default values for PB2 and PB3 are very low.

Figure 13.2: *Parameters that affect the user role*

Buffers: A DOS Parameter That Affects the Network

DOS itself assigns buffers for the movement of data between main memory and disks. Each buffer has space for 512 bytes of data being transferred and 16 bytes of information describing what the data is. Transactions often make repeated reference to the same information on a disk. Keeping the data in a memory buffer saves the time to read it each time from the disk. (Reading from memory is many times faster than reading from a disk.)

By referring to network directories for data, a user machine may actually decrease its use of its own disk, so its use of DOS buffers should decline or remain the same compared to stand-alone use. But a server machine makes heavy use of the DOS buffers because it is continually storing and retrieving data on its fixed disk on behalf of others

Parameter	Effect	Limit
USN	Number of names in addition to your own computer name that can receive messages at your machine (by NET NAME or NET FORWARD).	Default: 1 Min: 0 Max: 12
MBI	Size of the buffer used to receive incoming messages. (Not applicable to the redirector or the receiver configuration.)	Default: 1750 bytes Min: 512 bytes Max: 60k
Comment: Needs space for all unread messages.		
CMD	Number of concurrent NETBIOS commands. Config: *Rdr* *Rcv* *Msg* *Srv* Min: 1 3 3+USN 4+USN+REQ *or configuration minimum, whichever is greater	Default: 8* Max: 32
SES	Number of concurrent NETBIOS sessions. Config: *Rdr* *Rcv* *Msg* *Srv* Min: 1+SRV 2+SRV 2+SRV+USN 2+SRV+USN+RDR *or configuration minimum, whichever is greater	Default: 16* Max: 32
Comment: CMD and SES are usually of concern only when special applications require greater than default values, as indicated by their installation instructions.		

Figure 13.3: *Parameters that apply both to the server and the user configurations*

on the network. Requests to the server contain interleaved requests from different users, and it becomes increasingly useful for DOS to keep separate buffers for the separate transactions.

The number of DOS buffers is set by a value that DOS finds in the file Config.sys when you start the machine. When you change the value written in that file, it takes effect the next time you start DOS. On a stand-alone machine with floppy-disk drives, the default number of DOS buffers is two. On a stand-alone machine with a fixed disk, the default is three.

When you install PC Network on a server machine, the Installation Aid rewrites Config.sys and increases the number of DOS buffers to ten. (From then on you're running with ten buffers whether or not you use the network.) For a machine that experiences very heavy use as a server (for example, a dedicated server), IBM recommends raising the number of buffers to 20 for a PC/XT server and 30 for a PC/AT server. Simply change the line in the file Config.sys that reads

```
Buffers = 10
```

replacing 10 with the number of buffers that you want.

Flow of Data through Network Buffers

To understand how the parameters are related, it's useful to consider a diagram representing the various buffers in a user machine and in a server machine (see Figure 13.5). Recall that a server is also a user; everything found in the upper box (user) also exists in the lower box (server).

The two outer rectangles represent main memory; the user machine has less total memory and so is represented by a smaller rectangle. The rectangles within them represent buffers. They're drawn inside the main-memory rectangle to show that they use space otherwise available to main memory.

User		Server
ASG	Number of resources used/shared	SHR
SRV	Number of machines used/served	RDR
NBC	Number of buffers	REQ
NBS	Size of each buffer	RQB
PB1	Size of print buffer	PRB

Figure 13.4: *Corresponding parameters for server and user roles*

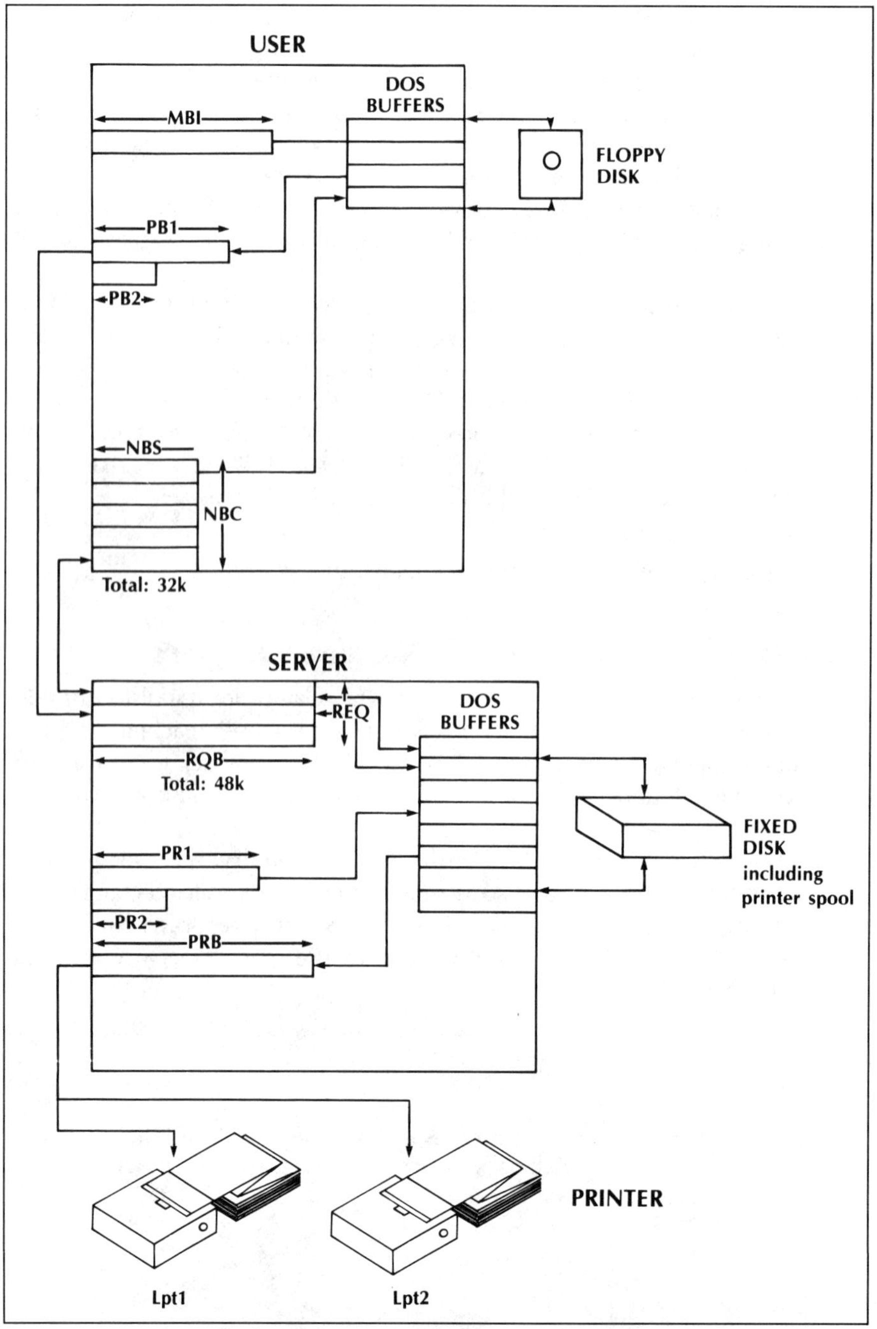

Figure 13.5: *Schematic representation of buffers in user and server machines*

The server's request buffers handle all network data flow except incoming messages. The total space available to request buffers is represented by the shaded area, which is the number of buffers (REQ) times the length of each buffer (RQB). The area may not exceed 48k.

The user machine's network buffers form a similar rectangular area in its memory. Its area is the number of network buffers (NBC) times the length of each (NBS). The area may not exceed 32k. The size of a request buffer or a network buffer has to be a multiple of 512 bytes; you can specify an intermediate value, but NET START rounds it to the next higher multiple of 512.

Flow of Data to Print a User's Job on a Server's Printer

As you can see in Figure 13.5, the user machine has a separate print buffer for each of the printers to which it may send jobs. Their default sizes are different. A print job moves from a print buffer on the user machine to one of the server machine's request buffers, which handle all file transfer both into and out of the server, whether or not they're related to printing. The server machine stores the job in the printer spool on its fixed disk, so the job passes through the DOS buffers on its way to the fixed disk.

Later on, the server's print manager transfers the job from the spool, through the DOS buffers, to the server's print buffer PRB, and from there to whichever printer was requested. Note that although the user machine has separate buffers in which to handle its requests for printing, the server machine that actually does the printing has only one print buffer, from which it sends data to the printer that was requested. This last phase of printing, from spool to printer, takes place entirely within the server machine, and is therefore considered a local task when adjusting TSI, the time slices for local and network tasks on the server.

Matching Buffer Size of Data, User, and Server

When a file is transferred from one machine to another, unless it is small it has to be broken into a series of separate transmissions, each of which is called a *frame* on the token ring or a *packet* on the broadband system. Each frame or packet is a segment of the data, accompanied by additional information that identifies it to the network adapters. When each frame is small, many frames are required, and the "overhead" of transmission time is increased. From that point of view, large buffers make network transmission more efficient. On the other hand, there's no point in making the buffer larger than the files that actually pass through it.

Three things limit the size of a frame or packet: it can't be larger than the buffer from which it is sent; it can't be larger than the buffer to which it is destined; and of course it can't be larger than the entire message. The effective limit is the minimum of those three.

This means that it is *never* useful for a user machine to set NBS, the size of a network buffer, larger than RQB, the size of the corresponding buffer on the server. The same applies to the buffers through which a user machine exports print files: it never helps to make them larger than RQB. Here's a matter for the network administrator to coordinate.

NBC and NBS: Number and Size of Buffers for a User

A user machine usually needs more network buffers than a server does. That's because the user machine is likely to process its data, and sometimes—perhaps frequently—look back at it. To be able to refer to the data just transmitted without having it sent over the network again, the user machine needs a separate buffer for each open file.

A server machine doesn't need buffers any larger than the largest records it commonly sends and receives. When you know that the machine's work involves large numbers of files each (or mostly) involving small records, you want to set NBC, the number of buffers, to a large value (a little over the anticipated number of concurrently open files). At the same time, you can afford to let NBS be fairly small, if a small size can nevertheless handle most records in a single packet. This may be characteristic of some data-base applications. PC Network limits the product NBC × NBS to 32k (of course, you may not want to let it climb that high, since any space you save is available to the application).

Text-processing applications tend to the other extreme. They may keep few if any files open concurrently, but they occasionally transfer large files. A machine doing that kind of work needs only a few buffers, but as large as possible—as long as they're not larger than the server's RQB.

REQ and RQB: Number and Size of Buffers for a Server

The server doesn't have the same problem of looking back at the data just transmitted. For one thing, the server is only transmitting, not analyzing the data. And if it does need to fetch the data again, the server doesn't have to use the network.

The server must set REQ, the number of buffers, to a number sufficient to support the number of files that its network adapter may be concurrently transmitting. IBM suggests two buffers for moderate service, three for a busy server.

Like the user, the server needs buffers no larger than its data. Unlike the user, the server has to cope with several users, and their needs may vary. The server needs to set RQB, the size of each buffer, to a value large enough to serve the users who transmit the largest files. In practice, this means the server needs buffers as large as the largest buffer of its users.

For a busy server with three request buffers, the maximum buffer size is 48k divided by three, which is 16k. Of course, if no user can afford buffers that large, the server doesn't need them either.

A Major Opportunity for Adjustment

IBM has set very small default values for NBC and NBS, the number and size of a user's network buffers: three buffers of 512 bytes each. When NBC is smaller than the number of open files, the user machine must repeatedly reassign the buffers. When NBS is smaller than the data transmitted, both user and server machines must break each transmission into segments that fit. Setting NBC and NBS to match the user's pattern of work can dramatically improve response.

PB1, PB2, PB3: Size of Buffers for Sending Jobs to a Print Server

For each network printer you use, you have to assign a print buffer. Four issues govern the size of those buffers: the amount of main memory that can be diverted to them; the size of the jobs you transmit; the frequency with which you have jobs to send; and the size of the server's buffers to receive the jobs (RQB). These issues are essentially the same as those for data files. However, print jobs are usually less frequent but individually larger than other transactions.

PC Network provides separate buffers for printing, which gives you the opportunity to set their size separately. The defaults provide only a modest buffer for LPT1, and an extremely small buffer to other network printers. Presumably, the idea is that you use the others rarely, so you'd rather have an inefficient transfer than tie up space for a larger buffer. For a user that frequently transmits jobs destined for the other printers, larger buffers speed up both the transfer from memory to the buffer while preparing to transmit, and the subsequent transmission to the server.

MBI: The Message Buffer Must Contain the Whole Message

The buffer that holds incoming messages for the messenger and server configurations is unlike all the other network buffers. For all the others, a buffer smaller than the data being transmitted forces the network to break the transmission into smaller packets. It doesn't do that for messages. As much as will fit goes into the incoming-message buffer, and any excess is lost. If you expect long messages, you have to give MBI a value large enough to accommodate them.

The number of bytes required to receive a message is somewhat larger than what the sender types, because of the addition of a header showing the origin of the message, and control characters at intervals. The length of the original text is increased by 85 bytes of header, and 5 bytes of control characters for every 128-character segment of the message.

Dividing Time for a Server

The network adapter card handles communication over the network at the same time that the PC's central processing unit (CPU) does other things. For many tasks, their operation is concurrent and independent. Nevertheless, as network messages and files arrive at a machine, the CPU has to get involved in interpreting and responding to them. It has to interrupt its service to the person at its keyboard and go tend business arising from the network. (The CPU is somewhat more involved in handling network requests on a token-ring system than on a broadband system. That's because many NETBIOS activities are handled on the broadband adapter card, whereas on the token-ring version the adapter doesn't include NETBIOS and depends on the CPU instead; see Appendix B.)

At a user machine, you don't notice the fact that the CPU is spending some of its time on network activities because almost all such activities arise from what you requested at the keyboard; they're not distractions, but part of your work. However, when you're working at the keyboard of a server machine, the situation is quite different. Many, perhaps all, network activities are generated not by what you're doing but by the work of other users on the network. When the CPU is sufficiently busy that there's contention for its services, it appears to be distracted, as it must turn away momentarily from processing your work to process something else coming from the network. It has to divide its time between local tasks (originating on the same machine) and network tasks (originating elsewhere). From your point of view at the server's keyboard, local tasks are the *foreground* partition of work and network tasks are the *background* partition.

TSI: The Time-Slice Interval

The CPU must shift its attention back and forth between the foreground and background partitions. To make the switch, it arranges to interrupt itself a short time in the future. When the interrupt time arrives, it checks to see whether there's something pending for the other partition (for the background when it's working on foreground, for the foreground when it's working on background). If it finds the other partition has something for it, it puts aside what it has been doing and switches to the other partition.

PC Network permits you to regulate the balance between the foreground local partition and the background network partition by setting the *time-slice interval* (TSI). The time slice is how far in the future the CPU sets the next interrupt. The CPU checks whether to switch either when it finishes what it's now doing or when the interrupt time arrives, whichever comes first.

For either partition, when the CPU has continuous work to do, it is the time slice that determines how long it can keep going before it's obliged to let the other partition have a turn.

The interval until the next interrupt is measured in *timer ticks.* A tick is 18.175 milliseconds. PC Network permits you to select from a set of ten possible intervals. You select an interval for the foreground and an interval for the background. You indicate your selection by a two-digit number that accompanies parameter TSI. The expression */tsi:54* doesn't denote the number 54. It selects interval number 5 for the foreground time slice, and interval number 4 for the background. The possible intervals are shown in Figure 13.6.

The default value of TSI is 54. That selects a time slice interval of 11 ticks for the foreground, 7 ticks for the background. That means when

TSI Number	Ticks	Milliseconds
0	1	18.175
1	2	36.35
2	3	54.525
3	5	90.875
4	7	127.225
5	11	199.925
6	15	272.625
7	21	381.675
8	28	508.9
9	36	654.3

Figure 13.6: *TSI numbers, timer ticks, and milliseconds. The argument of TSI is a two-digit number whose first digit selects the time slice for local work and whose second digit selects the time slice for network services. (The expression /tsi:00 has a special meaning; see text.)*

the CPU starts a task for the foreground, it can keep going for 11 ticks (about a fifth of a second). At the end of that time (or sooner if its task ends sooner) the foreground must yield to the network if the network has something waiting. When the CPU starts on a network task, it can keep going for 7 ticks (about an eighth of a second). At the end of that time (or sooner if the network task ends sooner) the network must yield to the foreground if the foreground has something waiting.

Setting a time-slice interval of an eighth of a second doesn't mean all activity will be delayed that long. When the machine isn't busy, a request gets immediate attention, regardless of the partition from which it comes. A computer often spends much of its time idling, waiting for a network request to come in or for you to press the next key.

The act of checking on the other partition takes a little time itself. Setting longer time slices means a busy CPU spends less time checking because the checks are required less frequently. However, a large TSI makes response uneven or "lumpy." Adding one character to the screen display when you press a key is a task handled by the foreground; people find an uneven response to their keystrokes disconcerting.

Strategy for Choosing Alternative TSI Settings

A setting such as */tsi:91* means the network can keep the CPU for only interval number 1 (two ticks) before it has to yield, whereas the foreground can keep the CPU for interval number 9 (36 ticks) before it has to yield. When you have a CPU-intensive request in the foreground, that setting favors you at the expense of the network.

Conversely, a setting such as */tsi:26* means the network won't have to wait for you for more than interval number 2 (3 ticks), whereas you may have to wait for interval number 6 (15 ticks) for the network.

Settings such as */tsi:11* and */tsi:99* appear even-handed, since they give the local user and the network equal slices. But the situations are not really symmetrical because the activities involved are quite different. Network activities for remote users are almost entirely transfers of files, or parts of files, in response to requests to use them. The routine handling of input and display is done at the remote user's own machine, without involving the network. When you're at the keyboard of a server machine, your situation is quite different. Your foreground partition involves not only your access to files, but also the immediate management of keyboard entry and screen display. Erratic response is more painfully obvious to you than it is to remote users. (Perhaps that is as it should be: in your role as operator of a server machine, you *should* be made aware of an increasing load on the server.)

My judgment is not to give a large time slice to the foreground. Forcing the network to wait seems contrary to the service role that the server should play. I favor a large time slice to the network when the server is not really being used for local work (perhaps little more than a few messages or adjustments to the print queue). Selecting a time-slice strategy goes back to an issue discussed in Chapter 10: Who should sit at a server machine? Doing what? There I suggested that the server be used for tasks that are not CPU intensive, but may require interaction at the keyboard. In that setting, the foreground does not make protracted demands on the CPU, but the human user needs a quick reaction from the machine. To me, that suggests a low value for both sides, perhaps */tsi:11* or */tsi:22.*

Special Meaning of TSI:00 for a Dedicated Server

PC Network gives a special interpretation to the start-up parameter */tsi:00.* That gives absolute priority to the background. The foreground can start only when the network has no activity. Then the foreground gets just one tick before it must yield whenever the network has a new request. This is clearly the setting appropriate to an unattended server.

Need for Experimentation and Adjustment—and Dynamic Adjustment

So many variables are involved in setting the time-slice interval that it seems essential to experiment. The physical load, the work patterns of the users, the psychology and politics of response time to users and the server operator, not to mention the effects of buffer size and the number of buffers: all affect the situation.

I wish experimentation were easier. As it is, to select a different value for TSI you have to reset the server machine and start PC Network again. It seems a great pity that PC Network doesn't provide a way to set this parameter dynamically.

Watch Out: Some Commands Don't Heed the Timer Interrupt

Unfortunately, there are some activities that refuse to heed the interrupt set by the timer. Once started, they run their course until completion, regardless of the time-slice interval or activity on the network. The PC Network *User's Guide* specifically warns against the DOS command FORMAT and the use of COPY for a large file; the server operator should be aware that using them may cause a noticeable pause on the network. The manual also mentions that application programs may contain instructions that make them fail to respond to time slicing (but doesn't identify the specific causes).

PRB and TSI: Flow to the Server's Printer

Jobs are transferred from the spool on the server's fixed disk to the printer by PC Network's print-manager program. When you're at the keyboard of the server machine, printing seems like a background task because it runs on its own, intermittently, while you do other things. But as far as the TSI parameter is concerned, printing is one of the local activities that it considers part of the foreground. A value of TSI that favors the network background facilitates the submission of print requests, but a value that favors the foreground facilitates the actual operation of the printer.

The parameter PRB sets the size of the buffer used for transferring data from a file in the printer spool to the printer. Having a large buffer means the print manager doesn't have to go back and replenish it as often. That gives the CPU more time to do other things, but usually makes no detectable difference to the printer's speed. Assigning a large buffer really depends on what other uses you have for main memory. On a dedicated server, you might as well let the printer have the extra space if the CPU will otherwise leave that space idle.

PRP: Printer Priority

Within the set of local activities that TSI treats as foreground, the parameter PRP controls the priority of the printer relative to commands entered from the keyboard. The setting must be one of the numbers 1, 2, or 3; three indicates high priority to the printer.

The operating speeds of printers vary widely. Some are so much slower than other network devices that the printer is rarely if ever waiting for other components of the network. But with a fast printer and a large volume of requests, printer priority may become an issue.

Demands on the printer may depend on the daily or weekly rhythm of print requests, the amount of space you can afford to allocate to print jobs in the spool, and the impatience of your users. Perhaps a fast printer operated at high priority could get the work done in four hours. In eight hours, you might get exactly the same output from a slower printer or one running at lower priority. Do you have the disk space to let print jobs accumulate in the queue? If you have the space, do your users have the patience to wait? You may satisfy users more effectively by juggling the queue than by increasing the printer's relative priority.

Printer priority is something that should be dynamically adjusted. It's a pity that PC Network at present lets you set it only by a start-up parameter.

Temporary Log of Network Errors

PC Network records in a temporary buffer those network error messages that are not otherwise delivered. The buffer has room for 512 bytes of text—room for about six messages. When the buffer is full, the older messages are discarded as newer ones are added.

The error buffer is useful for checking on messages that may have been concealed while an application controlled the screen. The buffer also provides a note of the time and some details not always included in the displayed message. For example, Figure 13.7 shows an error log that contains messages generated by the print-queue manager. At the time these events occurred, the menu screen showed only *Print file error* opposite the job number. However, the error log records the time, the nature of the error (the print manager was unable to gain access), and the complete name of the file (\Network\PQ137.spl).

Checking the error buffer may be a useful source of information when you suspect an error or a user reports an error on your server machine. It might be instructive to check it regularly. Note that the error-message buffer does not survive system reset.

It's a pity PC Network at present provides no way to log these error reports in a file.

NETBIOS Traffic and Error Statistics

The PC Network software does not include a report on the volume of traffic over the network or the occurrences of errors. However, both the token-ring and the broadband network adapters keep records of their own operation. The records are cumulative since power was turned on at the PC or the adapter was reset, but do not accumulate further than that.

NETBIOS includes a command to read an adapter's operating and error statistics. You can make the request for your own machine, but you can also send a request over the network for a report on the status of another machine.

The reports are parallel for the two adapters, although the detailed contents differ because of differences in the nature of the transmission

```
Sat 1985-12-07 16.55.07 C:\> net error
Error Status
------------------------------------------------------------

16:22:20.54 UNABLE TO ACCESS C:\NETWORK\PQ136.SPL
16:49:55.45 UNABLE TO ACCESS C:\NETWORK\PQ137.SPL
Command completed successfully
```

Figure 13.7: *Report generated by NET ERROR command*

and the adapter cards. Each report includes:

- The hardware ID of the adapter card
- Number of minutes since reset or power was turned on
- Number of successfully transmitted frames or packets
- Number of successfully received frames or packets
- Number of aborted transmissions
- Number of frames or packets that failed a validity check
- Number of transmissions sent that timed-out without acknowledgment
- Number of times the adapter exhausted resources needed to handle an incoming transmission
- Number of various hardware-specific errors (such as framing errors in the token-ring system, alignment errors and collisions on the broadband system)

Clearly, the network collects a lot of data about its own operations. Detailed descriptions of the form and content of the reports may be found in the publications *IBM Token-Ring Network Adapter Technical Reference* and the PC Network *Technical Reference.*

The traffic and error reports are useful both for locating specific problems and for plotting the network's growth over time. It's valuable to have a technical person working with the network administrator to collect reports regularly and accumulate, store, and periodically analyze them.

It seems a pity that such reporting is not now provided by PC Network itself, nor is there yet a guide to their interpretation when you have them. However, the network administrator should be aware of the possibilities and on the lookout for opportunities to make use of these reports.

The Universal Naming Convention

Fourteen

You can see in PC Network the beginnings of a new and much more general approach to naming files. At present it's a minor option, of little practical consequence to the way you use the network. But it's a forerunner of things to come, and PC Network is where you saw it first.

Virtual Drives vs. Network Paths

Each time a server offers to let you use a network directory, you have a choice of two ways to refer to it. One way is to give it a device name and treat it as a drive on your machine. In the menus, this is your only option. The screen headed *Start using a network disk or directory* asks you for a drive letter and won't accept your request without one.

You can choose a drive name with the NET USE command, too. When a machine called Server2 has offered to share a directory it calls Apps, you can assign Apps a drive name by typing *NET USE e: \\Server2\Apps.* That has the same effect as using the menu. But NET USE gives you an alternative. You can type *NET USE \\Server2\Apps,* leaving out the drive name. By doing so, you establish a path to a directory on another machine without the fiction that it's an extra drive on your own machine. That's called a *network path.*

What's the point? Why do that?

The Significance of Network Paths

At present there's hardly any reason to leave out the drive name. The only DOS command that currently recognizes a network path is TYPE. If you execute

```
TYPE \\Server2\Apps\Batch\Cleansav.bat
```

your machine displays the file called Cleansav.bat from the Batch directory within the directory called Apps on the machine called Server2. You've just used a network path. That's all you can do with a network path today, because in current releases of DOS, commands other than TYPE don't yet support network paths. But times change.

A network name is longer than the sort of names you use when everything is on your own machine. It's a bit like requiring telephone users to add area codes or even country codes to phone numbers. That became essential as it became easier to call across great distances. So too with names in computers.

Network paths embody two trends. First, they move away from the specifics of devices. You want to say what something is called, not what drive it's on. Second, network names refer not just to the individual or the machine, but to the community that networking makes possible.

Evolution of Directory Names

Version 2 of DOS introduced tree-structured directories. They were essential to permit many independent applications to reside on a single disk. The server machines use directories a great deal, and familiarity with them is essential to work with PC Network.

With tree-structured names, the files on a disk are grouped in *directories.* Instead of just one list of files, a disk may have several directories. Each directory contains its own list of files. To name a file unambiguously, you have to state not only its name but which directory it's in. When you mean *the file called Data in the directory called Dept8,* you write *\Dept8\Data.*

A directory may contain other directories. Perhaps the directory called Dept8 is itself part of a directory called Acctg. In that case, the full name of the file is \Acctg\Dept8\Data.

As with phone numbers, you don't have to spell out the whole thing when the general area is already understood. If you're already in the area you're calling, you can make a call without dialing the area code. Similarly, if you've told DOS your current directory is \Acctg\Dept8, it can find the file called Data without the "area code."

Machine Names

With DOS 3.10 and PC Network, naming goes further: you can include the name of the machine as well. For example, if the file \Acctg\Dept8\Data is located at a machine called Server2, its full name is \\Server2\Acctg\Dept8\Data. The double backslash indicates a machine name. Names in that form are something new: PC Network uses them extensively to describe offers to share disk space, but DOS hasn't digested them yet, and still requires you to refer to the same facts in other ways.

Eventually, as networking becomes universal rather than an exceptional circumstance, you're likely to see much more use of network paths. The concept isn't limited to machine names. As networks are interconnected, you may need another level of qualification. If the machine called Server2 is on a network called WestHQ, you may at times need to spell that out in full (for example, for someone using it from a different network):

\\\WestHq\\Server2\Acctg\Dept8\Data

Names in that form haven't shown up yet, but that's the direction in which things are evolving. This approach to naming is called the *universal naming convention.*

Two Opposite Developments in DOS

Earlier versions of DOS permitted you to tell it which disk drive you meant. Drives were assigned the names A and B; that was subsequently extended to C, and so on through the alphabet. To specify the file \Acctg\Dept8\Data on drive C, you'd write *c:\Acctg\Dept8\Data.*

In the universal naming convention, drive names are passé. The operating system is supposed to keep track of where things are without having to be told what's on which disk.

At the moment, DOS is evolving in two opposite directions:

1. You can treat a separate drive as if it were part of a larger directory, without having to state a drive name. That's what

the DOS command JOIN does. With it, you can treat all files in your machine as part of a single tree structure, making no reference to drives.

2. Conversely, you can treat a directory as if it were a separate drive. That's what the DOS command SUBST does. When NET USE assigns a drive name to a network directory, that's the network equivalent of SUBST.

JOIN is the wave of the future. Drive designations are on the way out. They'll be replaced by an all-embracing directory structure. That won't force you to type long names all the time; you can still use PATH or APPEND to tell DOS where to look for names that you don't spell out in full; you can still use CHDIR to make a distant directory current.

Commands such as SUBST are a rearguard action, a temporary convenience, a concession to old ways of doing things. They make it easy to run old programs that know about drives but don't know about tree-structured directories.

PC Network lets you have it both ways. It supports the new-style path names that include the machine name as part of the full name of a file. But it can't possibly rely on them entirely because neither DOS nor the programs you're likely to want to run support the new-style names—yet.

Glossary

Appendix A

* (asterisk)	Symbol used by DOS to mean any name and by PC Network to mean any computer.
? (question mark)	Symbol used by DOS to mean any single character.
. (period)	In the name of a file or directory, character used to separate the eight-character body of the name from the three-character extension.
/ (slash)	Within a DOS command, character used to indicate that what follows is a parameter.
\ (backslash)	ASCII character used to separate a file name from the preceding name of the directory to

which the file belongs—also separates a subdirectory name from the preceding name of its parent. A name starting with \ indicates a name in the root directory.

\\ (double backslash) — Precedes the name of a computer on the network.

access — The act of reading or writing stored data, usually to a file. Regrettably, widely used as if a verb.

access right — Qualification on what a user can do with a file or with all the files in a directory (such as read/write, read-only, etc).

adapter — In a microcomputer, a unit (usually mounted on a card) for communicating between the central processor of the computer and a peripheral or external device.

additional name — In PC Network, a name other than a computer's primary name under which it also receives messages.

Alt (alternate) — A key on the computer keyboard that, while held down, alters the meaning of other keys in the same way as the Shift key changes from lowercase to caps.

append —

1. (v.) In general, to attach new data at the end of a file without altering the earlier data.
2. DOS command to stipulate a list of directories in which DOS may look for a data file.

archive (adj.) — DOS jargon: The attribute of a file for which no backup copy has yet been made.

ASCII (American Standard Code for Information Interchange) — System for representing letters and numbers by a pattern of seven bits defining 128 codes of which the first 32 are for controls and the remainder for letters or characters. Widely used in PCs (but not in IBM mainframe computers, which use a different convention). Extended to languages other than American English by ISO (International Standards Organization).

asynchronous (adj.) System of communication common between computers and low-speed terminals or printers in which synchronization of the partners is not critical (in contrast to synchronous communication, used at higher speeds but requiring synchronization between partners).

AT See PC/AT.

attribute

1. Descriptions of a file stored in its directory, including such information as whether a backup copy has been made, whether users may write in it, and so on.
2. DOS command to set or unset the read-only attribute of a file.

Autoexec.bat Name of a file containing DOS commands instructing the operating system on steps to take as soon as the computer is started or reset.

auxiliary storage Memory that is less accessible to programs than the computer's main memory, but useful because it is less volatile, less expensive, or more easily transported; for example, disk or tape.

back up (v.) To make a backup (q.v.).

backbone link A high-speed link connecting LANs at different parts of a campus (not yet available).

background The portion of a computer's activities to which it returns automatically while not engaged in more urgent work in the foreground (q.v.).

backup (n., adj.) Reserve copy of a file or set of files from which the originals may be restored in the event the originals are damaged or lost.

bandwidth Information-carrying capacity of a communication channel.

base expander An eight-way splitter to which other eight-way splitters can be attached. Used in the broadband version of PC Network.

baseband — Sytem of transmission in which the signal does not involve modulation of a carrier signal and can exploit the entire bandwidth of the medium.

.bat — Last segment in the name of a batch file (q.v.).

batch file — A file containing a program consisting of a sequence of DOS commands, often used to automate the starting of a program.

baud — Unit of data transmission speed, bits per second; named for 19th-century French engineer Eugene Baudot.

binary — The internal form of data and programs, where everything is represented by one of two possible values, 0 and 1.

BIOS (basic input/output services) — Collection of functions built into the PC hardware and software.

bit — Minimum unit of information, either 1 or 0.

boot — Computer slang (from the expression "to lift oneself by one's own bootstraps"): The process of locating and executing the first instructions that get a computer going when power is turned on or the computer is reset. Hence, reset.

break — Signal to interrupt processing (borrowed from telecommunications, where it really was a break in the signal). Indicated on the PC keyboard by Alt-Scroll Lock or Ctrl-Scroll Lock.

bridge — A symmetrical link between two LANs.

broadband — In general, communication by modulating a carrier frequency within one of several radio-frequency bands. With respect to LANs, one of the two systems of transmission used by IBM to link PCs in a network. (See also token ring.)

buffer — Block of memory used for temporary storage while marshaling data for transmission to another part of the computer.

byte Unit of data storage containing eight bits, used to encode one character.

card A set of electronic components mounted on a flat, stiff base so that it can be plugged into a socket inside the computer provided to receive it.

CATV Cable television (originally from community antenna TV, the context in which cables were first used).

clock A computer component that counts at a fixed speed (governed by a crystal). One is used to synchronize internal operations of the computer. Another is used to keep track of the time and date. Some have a battery and are thus able to preserve time and date while power is off; others must be manually reset when the computer is started.

close (v.) Act (by a program) permitting DOS to relinquish use of a file that has been opened. (Action taken by PC Network when a file's user disappears from the network.)

closed (adj.) Status of a file after a program has closed it, that is, relinquished use of it.

closed-circuit (adj.) Radio-frequency signals transmitted through cables rather than radiated through space.

cluster (n.)

1. Informal: Several PCs connected to the same multistation access unit or eight-way connector.
2. Technical: Group of consecutive sectors of a disk allotted to a file by the disk's file allocation table (q.v.).

coaxial cable Cable used for data transmission in the broadband version of PC Network (and for closed-circuit TV) in which a single central wire is surrounded by a tubular conductor.

.com Last segment in the name of a command file, denoting a program stored in binary form and ready for execution as soon as loaded.

command — A word or phrase written from the keyboard to instruct the computer what to do (as contrasted with a menu, where the user selects from among a list of alternatives presented in advance).

CON — DOS reserved name for the keyboard and screen from which the computer is controlled. In expressions expecting input, refers to the keyboard. In expressions involving output, refers to the monitor.

Config.sys — Name of a file DOS consults when first started in order to establish certain parameters.

continue — In PC Network, the act of resuming a suspended network function, thereby terminating a pause (q.v.).

crash (n., v.) — Computer slang: Failure of computer software or hardware; usually, one that requires resetting or restarting the system involved.

create — In DOS, the act of naming and locating a new file. In DOS authorizations, the right to create files also implies the right to erase or delete them.

crosstalk — Interference in one electrical circuit caused by picking up the signal of other nearby circuits.

Ctrl (control) — A key on the computer keyboard that, when pressed simultaneously with other keys, alters their meaning in the same way as the Shift key changes from lowercase to caps.

Ctrl-C — Alternative way of keying *break.*

Ctrl-Z — Alternative way of keying *end of file.*

cursor — The position on the screen at which a character typed from the keyboard will be placed, usually marked by a rectangle or underline, perhaps blinking.

cylinder — All the tracks at a given distance from the center of a disk (that is, on both sides of a two-sided disk, on the four sides of a four-surface fixed disk, etc.).

D9 connector A plug and the corresponding jack having nine pins or sockets arranged in a trapezoidal (that is, D-shaped) pattern.

data connector A special connector used to attach type-1 cables in the IBM token ring.

data-grade (adj.) Suitable for high-speed data transmission; said of cabling. Contrasted with voice-grade (q.v.).

date convention The order on which the numbers representing the date are displayed (year/month/day, day/month/year, month/day/year), inscrutably controlled in DOS 3.10 by the entry COUNTRY= followed by the international telephone code designating that country, stored in the file Config.sys. U.S. dates are assumed by default; mysteriously, Japanese-style dates with year first are obtained by using Sweden's country code.

DATE DOS command to display the current date and permit the user to reset it.

dedicated (adj.) A program or machine that permits no other use of the facilities while it is in process.

default (n., adj.) Value assumed unless explicitly stated otherwise.

Del (delete) Key used to delete from the screen the character at the cursor position.

DEL Abbreviated form (surprisingly) of the DOS command ERASE.

delete (v.) To discontinue the use or offer of a network device.

deselect (v.) Term used by some printer manufacturers to denote the action of setting a switch so that the printer no longer receives transmissions from the computer. (The converse is select.)

device In DOS, collective term for printers, disk drives, the console (comprising keyboard and display). Certain devices have recognized names (such as PRN or LPT1 for a printer, and a single letter of the alphabet followed by a colon for a disk drive).

DIR (directory) — DOS command that reports the size of a file as recorded in its directory entry.

directory

1. A set of files with a common group name.
2. The table for such a set of files, indicating the name, size, date, location in storage where each is found, and certain other attributes.

disk — Flat rotating surface coated with magnetic recording medium and used to record data. Used to obtain large amounts of inexpensive storage. May be fixed or floppy, and mounted in a drive (q.v.).

diskette — A small portable disk, made of lightweight flexible material, on which information is magnetically recorded.

DOS (disk operating system) — Trademark name for a family of operating systems for the IBM PC produced by Microsoft Corporation (MS-DOS) and IBM Corporation (PC-DOS).

down — Computer slang: Not working or turned off.

downstream — On a token ring, the direction in which data circulates.

DRDR (PC Network abbreviation for disk redirection). — Process by which PC Network channels a reference to the name of a file or directory so that access is not to the local machine but to a machine shared over the network. One of the functions that can be suspended by the PAUSE command.

drive (n.) — Device built-in or attached to a computer for reading and writing information magnetically recorded on disks (or tapes).

DS (double-sided) — A diskette recorded on both sides, each side divided into 40 concentric tracks, each track divided into 9 sectors, with a total capacity of 320k.

echo

1. (v.) Practice of displaying on the screen a

	character at the same time that it is typed or transmitted.
	2. A DOS command governing the display of commands from the keyboard or from a batch file while it is being executed.
ECMA (European Computer Manufacturers Association)	International group that publishes standards for computer conventions, including the one underlying the token-ring protocols.
editor	Computer program for accepting and revising the text of documents, programs, and so on.
electronic mail	System for storing and distributing messages and documents through a computer network.
enable (v.tr.)	Computer jargon: To turn on or make ready a device connected to a computer.
end of file	An ASCII control character (hexadecimal 1A) used to indicate that there are no further valid characters in a file.
environment	DOS jargon: A particular table of values to be assumed by default, including the prompt for a new command and the path to a file whose location is not specified.
ERASE	DOS command: Remove a file's name from the directory, making it inaccessible and freeing the space it formerly occupied for other use. Abbreviation: DEL.
error	Computer jargon: Some unexpected or unacceptable condition that the hardware or software can't handle.
error level	DOS jargon: A numeric code left behind by a program to indicate whether it ran OK or encountered various classes of problems.
exclusive use	Access to a file granted when no one else is using it, permitting no one else to use it until the present user has finished.
.exe	Last segment in the name of an executable file (like a .com file, but with certain details left open until execution time).

executable file — A file containing a program, denoted by the extension .exe, .com, or .bat.

expansion kit — An eight-way splitter and length of cable, permitting an additional eight PCs to be connected to the base expander on the broadband version of PC Network.

extension — A group of up to three characters optionally added as a suffix to the name of a file or directory. Certain combinations of letters in the extension have special significance (for example, the extension *.bat* denotes a batch file, q.v.).

F1, F2 . . . F9 — Function keys, located at the side of the keyboard. They have no fixed meaning, but are assigned a meaning by the program that has current charge of the screen and keyboard.

F-connector — Type of connector, standard in CATV, having a single central pin or socket, and a threaded outer ring that secures two connectors by screwing them together.

faceplate — A cover with aperture for a connector that can be attached to the box containing cables, so that a data connector can be built into a wall in the same manner as electrical power or telephone outlets.

FAT — Abbreviation for file allocation table, q.v.

FCB (file control block) — DOS convention by which a program establishes what file is being used, where it is located, how much data is transferred at a time, and so on.

field locking — Application of a lock (q.v.) to a specified portion of a file (a field), as contrasted with applying the lock to the entire file.

file — A sequence of characters stored in a computer's auxiliary memory, containing the representation of a collection of data, program, document, and so on.

file allocation table (FAT) — Table on a disk by which DOS allocates sectors of the disk to files.

file control block — See FCB.

file locking — Applying a lock (q.v.) to an entire file, regardless of the portion of the file actually in contention.

fixed disk — Computer memory based on a permanently mounted rotating magnetic disk, usually in a sealed container.

floppy disk — See diskette.

foreground — The portion of a computer's activities it handles with high priority, before less urgent work (which is called the background).

form feed — The action of moving continuous fanfold paper to a position on the first printable line of the next sheet. Also, an ASCII control character having that significance.

format (v.) — To erase a disk completely and build a new table of the clusters of readable sectors on it, which may then be used to store files. Essential before a new disk can be used; fatal to the data already on a disk.

forward (v.) — Arrange for another computer to receive messages addressed to you or to your computer.

frame — In the token-ring system, the token, labeling information, and data transmitted at one time (comparable to packet, q.v., in the broadband system).

frequency translator — Device to convert signals on one TV channel to another, central to the broadband version of PC Network.

full backup — Process of making a spare copy of everything on a disk (contrasted with partial or incremental backup).

full dump/restore — Process of copying everything from a disk to secondary storage (for example, tapes or other disks), reformatting the disk, and restoring its contents from the secondary storage.

gateway	A communications link between a LAN and a computer external to the LAN.
H (hexadecimal)	Written after a hexadecimal number to make clear that it is hexadecimal, as for example 80H.
handle	Within a program, a number used by DOS as a shorthand designation for a file that is in use.
hard disk	See fixed disk.
hardware	Generic term for the physical components of a computer system (contrasted with software, the programs that operate it).
HC (high capacity)	A format used in disk drives available for the PC/AT that divides a double-sided diskette into 80 concentric tracks, each of which is divided into 15 sectors, with a total capacity of 1.2Mb.
HD (high density)	A diskette whose treated surface permits the HC format.
held	Status of a job in the print queue that cannot be printed until the operator releases it.
hexadecimal	Base-16 numbers, written with characters 0 to 9 and A to F, used by programmers. A byte is described by two characters, written 00H to FFH. The final H means hexadecimal.
host	A computer whose operating system can accommodate a variety of services, perhaps concurrently.
incremental backup	Process of making successive spare copies, each including only those files modified since the previous one.
Ins (Insert)	Key to select the insert mode (q.v.).
insert	Mode in which a character typed from the keyboard appears at the cursor, displacing rightward the characters previously there.
Installation Aid	A program supplied by IBM with PC Network to assist in setting up the network programs and programs to be used on the network.

integrity — With respect to data, protection from changes that might make it wrong or unreadable.

interlock — Process by which several users or programs take turns at reading or writing to a particular portion of recorded data to prevent concurrent uses from losing information.

JOIN — DOS command permitting a disk drive to be addressed as if a directory (converse of SUBST).

jumper
1. A cable used for temporary connection.
2. A small connector that can be moved from one position to another on the broadband network adapter card to establish certain settings.

k — Kilobyte.

kilobyte — 1024 bytes. Abbreviated k.

LAN (local-area network) — A set of computers linked by high-speed communication over a short distance.

letter-quality (adj.) — Attribute of a computer printer whose output equals (well, maybe only approaches) the clarity and resolution of a typewriter.

load (v.) — Computer jargon: Bring a program or data into the part of the computer where it can be used.

lobe — In the token-ring system, the segment of the ring from a multistation access unit to a PC.

local (adj.) — Concerning the computer on which one is working, as contrasted with other computers on the network (as in local device, local name, etc.).

lock (v., n.) — Process by which one user temporarily gains exclusive use of a portion of a file, to prevent loss of information from uncoordinated changes by competing programs.

log
1. (n.) A file in which incoming messages are accumulated.
2. (v.) The act of storing incoming messages in that manner.

LPT1 DOS reserved name for a line printer (that is, a printer connected to a parallel port). DOS recognizes LPT1, LPT2, and LPT3 as names for printers.

mail See electronic mail.

main memory Computer's volatile high-speed storage directly accessible to programs (as contrasted with auxiliary memory, usually on disks).

MAP (marketing assistance program) IBM jargon: An arrangement under which an IBM office may refer customers to an independent contractor for special service or advice related to the sale or installation of an IBM product, in particular for the cabling of PC Network.

Mb Megabyte.

megabyte 1024 × 1024 (= 1,048,576) bytes. Abbreviated Mb.

menu A display of a list of alternatives from which the user points to the one desired (as contrasted with typing a command).

messenger abbreviated MSG

1. One of the four configurations in which PC Network can be started.
2. The function of receiving and forwarding incoming messages, one of the activities that may be suspended by the NET PAUSE command.

mode DOS jargon: The convention regarding line width of display to a video monitor, line width of a monitor or printer).

modular connector A plug and the corresponding jack having six contacts, widely used for telephone connections.

monitor Display screen attached to the computer.

MSG PC Network abbreviation for messenger (q.v.).

NETBIOS A high-level language for the management of the network communications hardware, embodied in a software program in the token-ring version of PC Network, and in ROM on the network adapter of the broadband version.

network administrator Person who manages the participation of people in the network and coordinates their use of network programs and resources.

network name The name by which a computer or person is identified on the network. Also, the name by which you refer to data on another computer.

network request key A combination of keys (Ctrl-Alt-Scroll Lock) which, when pressed simultaneously, invoke the PC Network menus on machines running the messenger or server configuration.

OEM (original equipment manufacturer). From IBM's point of view, a manufacturer other than IBM who sells devices that can be used with an IBM system.

open (v.)

1. Act (by a program) identifying a file and requesting DOS to start transactions regarding it, a necessary first step in making use of a file.
2. (adj) describing the state of a file when a program has requested to open it and has not relinquished (closed) it.

packet Segment of a message, together with labelling information, transmitted over the broadband version of PC Network.

pair Electrical or telephonic engineer's jargon. Two wires used together to provide a circuit.

parallel (adj.) Transmission of data through several wires or channels at once (for example, using separate wires simultaneously, one to carry each bit of an eight-bit byte).

parameter

1. In general, the specific value for which a function is evaluated.
2. DOS jargon: An additional specification modifying the action of a command, marked by a slash followed by further

letters or numbers as the particular command may require.

3. PC Network: One of 18 possible values governing the way in which PC Network is started.

password — A set of up to eight arbitrary characters the person offering a network resource requires users to type when requesting to use it.

patch cable — A cable with plugs or connectors used to complete a connection, but easily moved or connected differently.

path

1. The sequence of names, from general to specific, identifying where a file is to be found by tracing from the machine, to drive and root directory, to subdirectory, and so on.
2. DOS command to stipulate where DOS should look for an executable file when the command that refers to it does not mention the path.

pause — Temporary suspension of one or more of the functions that are part of the network (redirection, printing, receiving messages, etc.).

PC/AT (for "advanced technology") — Model of the IBM Personal Computer based on the Intel 80286, and frequently equipped with a 20-Mb fixed disk.

PC/XT (for "extended technology") — Model of the IBM Personal Computer based, like the IBM PC, on the Intel 8088, equipped with a 10-Mb fixed disk.

peripheral (adj. used as n.) — Component of a computer that is not part of its central processor but attached to it (for example, monitor screen, printer, auxiliary memory, keyboard, etc.).

PERMIT (v.) — PC Network command to initiate a special offer to share a disk or directory so that the machine making the offer becomes a dedicated server of one user machine.

port — Point on a machine at which a communication link is attached.

PRDR (PC Network abbreviation for print redirection).
: Process by which PC Network channels a reference to the name of a printer so that work is sent not to a local printer but to the print queue of a machine shared over the network. One of the functions that can be suspended by the NET PAUSE command.

PRINT
: 1. DOS command to print a file (can't be used at the same time as PC Network).
  2. In NET PRINT, PC Network command to print a file at a network printer.
  3. Action of transferring jobs from a server machine's print queue to the printer; one of the activities that may be suspended by the NET PAUSE command.

print manager
: Term used in this book to refer to that part of the PC Network program which handles the queue of jobs waiting to be printed and their transfer from the print spool to the printer.

printing
: PC Network euphemism meaning the task of transferring a job from the print queue to the printer has been started.

PRN
: DOS reserved name for the printer. A synonym for LPT1.

profile
: File containing specifications for the use of a program, used to tailor the program's function to an individual's needs or tastes.

program
: A collection of characters (numbers, letters, etc.) interpreted by a computer as instructions to perform a task; stored in a file.

prompt (n.)
: A message from the computer following which the computer waits for a reply from the user.

PRT
: PC Network abbreviation for print, as in NET Pause PRT.

PVC
: Polyvinyl chloride. White plastic material used to cover coaxial cables used in the broadband version of PC Network.

queue
: List of jobs waiting to be printed.

RCV — PC Network abbreviation for receiver, q.v.

read (v.) — To copy data from auxiliary memory (such as disk files) to the main memory for processing.

read-only (adj.) — Attribute of a file in which one or more users may read but may not write or erase.

read/write (adj.) — Attribute of a file in which a user is permitted both to read existing data and write new data.

receiver (abbreviated RCV)

1. One of the four configurations in which PC Network can be started (able to receive messages, but lacking the powers of the messenger and server configurations.
2. The function of receiving incoming messages, one of the activities that may be suspended by the NET PAUSE command.

redirection — Process of reinterpreting a computer instruction so that although written to refer to one device or location, it is in fact carried out for another. Within PC Network, the process by which a name in the form used to refer to files or devices on the local computer is interpreted so that it instead refers to a remote one.

redirector (abbreviate RDR) — One of the four configurations in which PC Network can be operated, having the fundamental ability to redirect (q.v.) to other machines, but lacking other powers of the receiver, messenger, and server configurations.

reserved name — A name having a fixed significance to the operating system, and one that therefore cannot be used with any other meaning in a command interpreted by DOS.

reset (verb, adj.) — Process that erases all transient memory and starts the computer from the beginning, as if turning on power for the first time.

resident (adj.) — A program that remains in main memory even when not active, and may be triggered by an external event or a signal from the keyboard.

restore — Process of copying from a backup file to working storage, so as to re-create a file as it was when the backup was made.

RF (radio-frequency) — In PC Network, describing the carrier signal used by the broadband version.

ring-in, ring-out — Names for the connectors by which one multiple access unit is connected to another, preserving the ring topology of the network.

ring sequence — In the token-ring system, the sequence in which each PC relays transmissions to the text PC downstream from it.

root directory — The first directory on a disk, to which all other files and directories belong. The root directory has no name; in the name of a file or directory, it is denoted by an initial back-slash \.

screen — A display of characters or graphics which covers the entire 25-line 80-column display at once, rather than generating it typewriter fashion (line by line).

sector — Arc along a track on a disk, usually containing 512 bytes.

security — With respect to data, protection from unauthorized disclosure or alteration.

select (v.) — Term used by some printer manufacturers. The action of setting a switch so that the printer receives transmissions from the computer. (The converse is deselect.)

separator — Page printed before and after printing job, containing information identifying the job that follows and perhaps control information needed by the printer.

serial (adj.) — Transmission of data one bit after another in time (as over a single channel).

Server (abbreviated SRV) —

1. Generic term for a machine that offers resources to the network.
2. One of the four configurations in which PC Network can be started.

3. The function of processing requests for disk service coming in from other machines on the network, one of the activities that may be suspended by the NET PAUSE command.

shared (adj.) — Said of a file, or of access to a file, that is permitted so that several users can write in parts of it at the same time.

shielded — Cable enclosed in a metallic braided cover to protect the cable from electrical interference.

short name — A synonym coined by a server computer to identify a printer or a dirctory offered to the network.

software — Generic term for the information (programs and data) used to control a computer, so called because it is symbolic and volatile, rather than a physical device.

source — DOS jargon: the file from which data is being copied (contrasted with target).

span (v.) — To extend across an additional area of physical storage; said of a file stored in more than one disk.

splitter — Connecter for radio-frequency signals (such as those used in the broadband version of PC Network which divides the signal among several connectors.

spool — A place of temporary storage for data in transit, derived originally from storage on tape, where the analogy with thread was more obvious; in PC Network, the set of files stored on a server machine while on their way to a printer.

SRV — PC Network abbreviation for server, q.v.

star — Pattern of wiring in which each device is connected by its own cable to a hub, but many devices are connected to the same hub.

streaming backup — Spare copies of working files generated continuously as the originals are written.

subdirectory — A directory (q.v.) within a directory. A relative term.

SUBST (substitute) — DOS command permitting a directory to be addressed as if a disk drive (converse of join).

system (n., adj.) — A vague and relative term implying the entirety of a set of interdependent components, usually referring to the underlying software or hardware

tap (n.) — CATV and electrical jargon: Connector or jack on the main circuit where an individual device may be connected.

target — DOS jargon: The file to which data is being copied (contrasted with source).

terminator — Cap with built-in electrical impedence used to cover a radio-frequency jack that is not in use, to prevent reflection of the signal.

text editor — See editor.

tick — An arbitrary time unit used in measuring the time slice (q.v.).

time-sharing — System by which a large host computer serves many users at remote terminals, working on each task in rapid rotation, giving each the appearance of sole control of a part of the machine.

time slice — The length of time a program may run before checking whether other programs on the same machine need a turn. A tunable parameter that adjusts the balance between local work and network services on a server machine.

token ring — System of communication between computers in a LAN in which messages are passed from one to the next in a circular pattern, and the right to send is circulated by a special message called the token (q.v.).

topology — The pattern of connections, regardless of the shape into which it may be squeezed or deformed.

track One of the concentric circles into which a disk is divided for the magnetic recording of data.

translator See frequency translator.

tree

1. The hierarchical structure of directories in a file, branching from a single root. (Despite the horticultural origins of the term, tree diagrams are usually shown with the root at the top, like company organization charts, or at the left so one reads from left to right.)
2. A DOS command to list the files or directories in the order of their tree structure, starting at the root.

twisted pair Two wires used together to provide a circuit, and twisted together in a spiral to minimize susceptibility to certain types of interference.

type

1. DOS command which causes a file to be interpreted as ASCII characters and displayed on the screen. (Note that this is a form of output and thus opposite to the ordinary English use, which means the action of a user to supply input from the keyboard.)
2. IBM terminology for classes of cable in the IBM cabling system. Types 1 and 2 are shielded data-grade cable. Type 3 is voice-grade or telephone-type cable.

universal naming convention A proposed extension to the scope of names recognized by the operating system so that a user may mention not only the name of a file and the directory in which it is located, but also the machine, and perhaps the network.

up Computer slang: Working, functional.

upstream In the token-ring system, the direction opposite to the direction in which data circulates.

user

1. Generic term for anyone who uses an application program on a computer.

2. In PC Network, the role of a machine that redirects disk, directory, or printer references to a network server machine.

utility (n., adj.)
: Program providing a limited service applicable in a variety of situations, as a tool or component intended to be used with other programs.

virtual device
: A name used as though referring to a device that is physically present when it is in fact something else or somewhere else. A user at one machine may refer to a directory on another machine as if it were a disk drive on the user's own machine.

voice-grade (adj.)
: Suitable for telephone transmission and to some extent usable for data.

volatile (adj.)
: Describing memory from which data is lost when the power is turned off or interrupted. Applies to main memory but not disk memory.

waiting
: Status of a job in the print queue when there are other jobs ahead of it.

wide-area network
: A long-distance communication system serving computers.

wild card
: Computer slang: A character indicating that any character is an acceptable match for part of a pattern being sought; applied to the characters * and ? in DOS names.

wiring closet
: Enclosure where cables from various parts of a building come together and may be connected and access units may be housed.

write (v.)
: To copy data from the main memory to auxiliary storage (such as disk files) for storage.

XT
: See PC/XT.

Token Ring and Broadband

Appendix B

This book's principal aim is to tell you how to use PC Network. PC Network is a program that can run either on a network linked by IBM's *token-ring* system or on a network linked by IBM's *broadband* system—with no difference noticeable to the user. To use PC Network, you don't need to know anything about the inner workings of either token-ring or broadband communication. However, since both systems are quite new and the subject of much discussion, this appendix provides some background regarding these alternative ways of linking computers. The information may bear on your choice of hardware; also, the background may be useful in discussions with technical people, if only as intimidation-insurance.

Overview of Characteristics Common to Both Systems

Despite profound differences in their inner workings, the token-ring and broadband networks are installed in much the same way and look very much alike. Each requires an adapter card to be installed in each PC on the network, and each uses its own cables to connect them (although the cables for the two systems are different).

The Network Adapter Card

In either system, the key piece of hardware fundamental to the network is the *network adapter card.* It fits in one slot inside each PC that's connected to the network. It's what permits the PC to transmit and receive data.

The adapter card manages the considerable work of transferring data to and from the PC at the same time that the PC goes about its regular work. The adapter is a fair-sized computer in its own right. It has its own memory, its own microprocessor, its own communications controller for managing access to the network, and its own serial interface controller.

Much of the effective speed of the network comes from the fact that so much of the communications processing is going on concurrently with the PC's main work. There's a great deal of processing involved in passing data reliably from one computer to another, but the PC's main processor doesn't have to be concerned with that.

NETBIOS

The PC Network software is in two main layers: an underlying level called NETBIOS and the umbrella level called PC Network, which is the subject of this book. The PC Network program, which must be installed in each PC, manages the PC's participation in the network.

NETBIOS is an acronym for NETwork Basic Input/Ouput Services. It's named by analogy with BIOS, which performs a variety of services for the PC's main processor. Just as BIOS provides a set of standard services on several different models of the IBM PC, so NETBIOS provides a set of standard services for programs that use the network. It handles all transfers of data between the PC and the network. It manages all the lower layers of the mechanics of communication, doing such things as noting where data is going, establishing communication with the destination computer, breaking apart data into packets (or reassembling received packets into data), verifying that data have been received, and so on.

NETBIOS exists in two versions, one for the token-ring network and one for the broadband network. The commands they accept and the results they produce are the same, despite the fact that the mechanism by which the two versions do their work is quite different. In the token-ring system, NETBIOS is provided by programs that are installed in the PC and run like other software. In the broadband system, NETBIOS is provided in ROM (read-only memory), which is part of the adapter card.

As a user, you'll never need to know about NETBIOS, and this book is not concerned with how programmers use it. I mention it only as background for the perhaps surprising fact that the same PC Network program manages both token-ring networks and broadband networks.

For the assembly-language programmer, NETBIOS amounts to a high-level language for running network communications. A program written in PC assembler language can pass a command to NETBIOS by preparing what is called a *network control block,* or NCB. The programmer doesn't need to know how it does what it does—only how to ask for it. NETBIOS is thus a powerful tool for software developers who build their own network applications. It's what has made it possible for the same PC Network program to manage networks with quite different physical components. The fact that NETBIOS exists, and that IBM has published the details of the way it works, has made it possible for independent vendors to write programs that exploit the network hardware. Chapter 2 of the IBM PC Network *Technical Reference* gives particulars of NETBIOS.

Where the Adapter Fits

Installing the adapter requires only removing the cover from the PC and plugging the card into a vacant slot. The instructions IBM supplies with the card give a detailed step-by-step procedure, and call for nothing more than reasonable care and a small screwdriver. The broadband adapter is enclosed in a metal cover that shields it to prevent leakage of the radio-frequency (RF) signals that are characteristic of the broadband system.

Once the adapter card is installed, from the outside all you see is the jack, to which you connect the cable that comes with the card. That's your connection to the network. The token-ring adapter has a DB9 jack (like the ones used for the PC's serial port, but of opposite gender). The broadband adapter has a round screw-threaded jack for a coaxial F-connector like those used for cable TV.

The Cables

Each system uses its own specialized cables. In each system, the cable runs from each PC to a connector unit that serves a cluster of up to eight PCs. But the connector units and the cables themselves are quite different.

The token ring uses two types of cable: either *data-grade* (surrounded by a metallic braided shield) or *voice grade* (telephone cable). To connect a PC takes four wires: two to bring the signal in, two to take it out. Each pair of wires is twisted in a spiral, so they're called *twisted pairs.* (The cables often have additional wires, intended for possible attachment of telephone circuits, which are not used in token-ring transmissions.) The data-grade shielded cable is part of the IBM cabling system, a general scheme for computer cables to be installed in buildings in advance, so that many types of computing devices can in future be plugged or unplugged at will. With some restrictions on the range and size of the network, telephone-type cable (type 3 in IBM's nomenclature) can be used to link PCs on the token ring.

Cables for the broadband system are coaxial cables like those used for cable TV. Each contains a single wire embedded in a plastic foam core and surrounded by a metallic braided shield and finally a plastic cover. The cables are about the same thickness but perhaps a little stiffer than the token-ring data-grade cables.

The Connection Boxes

From each PC, the cable goes to a connection box where each PC's cable is linked to the cables from other PCs in the same cluster. The connection box used by the token-ring system is what IBM calls the *multistation access unit.* It is fairly large, about 18 inches long. Sometimes the box is mounted in a wiring closet out of sight; in that case, the cable from the PC usually runs to a special outlet mounted in the wall, and from there through the wall to the access unit. The access unit can also be left on the floor or on a desk or shelf. It does not use any external power.

On the broadband system, up to eight cables from PCs come together at an eight-way splitter. From there, another similar cable links the splitter to the center of the network. The eight-way splitter that connects a cluster of PCs is quite small, about four inches long. It's usually left loose at the point where the cables come together, or it can be fastened to a wall or baseboard. The cables lead to a book-sized box called the *frequency translator,* which is the center of the broadband system. It requires an external power supply and comes with its own little transformer.

PCs Broadcast Their Messages on a Cable They All Share

Each PC has a cable linking its adapter card to the network cable. All the PCs are connected to the same circuit.

In the token-ring system, each PC plugs into a multistation access unit. Superficially, the layout looks like a star, since each set of eight is joined to the same access unit. However, inside the access unit, the wires are connected so that they form a ring. The signal is passed from one machine to the next machine, always in the same direction. Any transmission circulates to all of them within a fraction of a second.

Similarly, in the broadband system, each PC plugs into an eight-way connector. Superficially, this layout too looks like a star. However, inside the cabling and the multiway splitters, the PCs are all connected to the same piece of wire in what is called a *bus* topology. Any transmission is physically present at all PCs simultaneously.

Although the token ring passes a message from one PC to the next, whereas the broadband system broadcasts a message throughout the cable, the effect is the same: all transmissions go everywhere. When a PC sends a message, it doesn't have a direct or private circuit to the machine it wants to talk to. It simply launches its message onto the cable. Part of the message indicates which machine it is intended for. The machine to which the message is addressed accepts it and sends an acknowledgment. All the others simply ignore the message.

Each PC Identifies Itself

When a PC attaches itself to the network, it adopts a string of characters to identify itself. When you're using PC Network, you supply the machine name that your computer will use. You can choose up to 15 characters; the adapter adds a sixteenth of its own. (Each adapter also has a unique 16-character ID built in to it, so applications may rely on that, rather than asking the person at the keyboard to supply a name.) The adapter verifies that no other PC on the network is using the name you've chosen. Once it has established its machine name, the adapter tags anything it sends with that signature.

The adapter also listens for messages addressed to it. It intercepts messages addressed to its machine name, to all computers, or to any of several aliases it may adopt. It ignores (and, in the token ring, passes on) everything else.

The Token-Ring System

In 1982, IBM described a long-range plan for the interconnection of computers and other equipment. It had two main ingredients: the token-ring protocols for circulating data between machines and the IBM cabling system, based on shielded twisted pairs, to carry the signals. PC Network is the first delivered product to conform to the new system.

The token-ring system gets its name from the topology of the connections, which form a ring, and the system for determining who may transmit, which involves a signal called the *token*.

Baseband Transmission over Twisted-Pair Wiring

The system uses baseband transmission over twisted-pair cables. *Baseband* means that the entire capacity of the cable may be used for a single signal (instead of being partitioned among different channels by frequency). While the cable is used for the network, the network has exclusive use of it.

Twisted pairs are the sorts of wires used in telephone connections; the twist reduces their susceptibility to certain kinds of interference. Although the total capacity of a twisted pair is not as great as the total capacity of a coaxial cable, baseband transmission has available the entire capacity of the cable (rather than modulating a carrier signal that is confined to a single band). PC Network on these cables transmits at 4 million bits per second, twice the rate of a broadband channel.

Telephone-Style Cable

As part of its proposals, IBM coined terms to refer to the various types of cables. In connection with the token ring, you'll hear mention of *type 1* and *type 3* cables. Type 1 involves twisted pairs with shielding, and type 3 involves twisted pairs without shielding. (Type 2 is the same as a type 1, but has additional telephone wires bundled in the same cable.) Shielding protects cables from crosstalk and interference, but it is not essential to token-ring operations under good conditions over short distances. This means you can operate parts of the token-ring network on what amounts to telephone wire and, therefore, integrate some of a building's data links with its internal telephone system.

Topology of the Ring

If you look at the diagram in IBM's explanation of communication in a ring, you'll see a huge central ring with computers attached around the periphery, like numbers on a clock face or terminals at some airports. The topology really is a ring, but the cables and connectors disguise that; the ring topology is not apparent from outside. A PC connected to the ring has a single cable coming out of it. The cable leads either to a connector, perhaps mounted on the wall, or perhaps directly to a multiway connection box.

Each PC's cable contains four wires: one pair to carry data in and another pair to carry data out. The connectors are built in such a way that each PC is connected to only two others. It's as though each PC receives transmissions only from the machine to its left and sends transmissions only to the machine to its right.

Disconnecting a PC Doesn't Break the Ring

Inside the multistation access unit, at each connector there's a relay. When the lobe that goes out to a PC is idle or disconnected, the relay short-circuits that lobe. At the same time, the lobe to the PC is not only cut out of the ring but is connected back to itself as an independent closed loop. In fact, when all the devices on a multistation access unit are idle or disconnected, there's nothing left but a short loop that is entirely inside the access unit.

Appearance of the Multistation Access Unit

The IBM 8228 multistation access unit is contained in a box about the size of a PC's keyboard unit, but somewhat thicker. Across the front edge of the unit are ten connector jacks. The eight in the middle are for connecting PCs. The two on the ends are for connecting to other multistation access units.

The multistation access unit has no external power supply. It uses no power other than the minute current sent by the network adapter cards to hold its relays in the position required to connect the ring.

The PCs Can Use Modular Phone Connectors

Although each PC must be connected to the multistation access unit, the connection doesn't have to be direct. The access unit can be tucked away somewhere. From each of its connectors, a cable might go to a modular jack set in the wall. The cable from the PC's adapter card can be four-conductor telephone wire, going into a standard six-conductor modular jack. When unshielded telephone wire is used, the D9 connector to the adapter card must include a low-pass filter to limit radio interference that might be radiated from the cable.

Inserting a PC into the Ring

When a PC's network cable has been plugged into one of the jacks on the multistation access unit, the PC's network adapter can ask to be admitted to the ring. (Before the access unit's relay has admitted it, the PC is connected only to its own closed loop.) The PC's adapter sends a small voltage on the loop, which activates the relay in the access unit and admits it to the ring.

Relaying Transmissions around the Ring

A PC's adapter card receives a signal over the incoming pair. As soon as the message starts, the adapter immediately begins retransmitting it on the outgoing pair. This happens so quickly that the outgoing signal is less than a millionth of a second behind the incoming signal. In this fashion, a message started anywhere on the ring can be circulated throughout the entire ring. It goes all around the ring until it has returned to its originator.

The Token Indicates Who May Originate a Message

A short message called the *token* is in constant circulation. It has two values: *busy* and *free.* Initially, its value is free.

A PC that is ready to send can start a new transmission only when it receives the token and the token's value is free. A PC that receives the free token is said to *capture* the token. It changes the token's value to busy, attaches its message, and transmits a *frame* consisting of the token and a segment of the message.

When the originating PC gets an acknowledging signal from the recipient (along with the busy token), it changes the value back to free and continues to circulate the token. A PC with nothing to send simply passes the token on. The free token continues to circulate (making millions of orbits per second) until it is again captured by a PC with something to send. That PC sets the token to busy, and the process starts again.

The effect is that the opportunity to send continually rotates around the ring. Much of the time, no one is sending and the token is free. But when two or more PCs are ready at the same time, only one gets the free token and sends. By the time the token reaches the other PCs that are ready, its value has changed to busy. Whoever has the free token is assured of being the only PC transmitting a new message.

Range of the Token-Ring System

The range of a token-ring LAN is limited by the time it takes the token to circulate through the total circumference of the ring, including all its lobes. The quality of the cabling (unshielded voice-grade cable versus shielded data-grade cable) imposes further limits.

The maximum separation between PCs depends on three things: the distance from an individual PC to its access unit, the number of separate access units, and the distance between separate access units. Since the signal is relayed from each PC to the next, the critical limit is the distance from one active PC to the next active PC downstream from it. Since PCs may attach and detach themselves at will, the distance from one PC to the next *active* PC depends on which PCs are working at a particular time.

When more than eight PCs are connected, the token ring must have more than one access unit. Several access units that are side by side can be connected, in effect forming one large one. It is also possible to have separate clusters of access units, some distance apart. The link between clusters must be type 1 (data-grade) cable, even for systems that use telephone cable for the link to the individual PCs.

For systems that use voice-grade cable, IBM says there may be no more that two clusters, linked by a single data-grade cable (or two such cables to provide a redundant path around the ring). The distance between the two clusters may not exceed about 400 feet, and the individual PCs should be within 150 of an access unit, although distances up to about 330 feet may be tolerable. That suggests a maximum separation between PCs of about 700 feet.

For systems that use data-grade cable throughout, IBM says there may be up to a dozen separate clusters, each up to 650 feet from the next. Individual PCs may be further from the access units, up to 330 feet (and more may be tolerable). Assuming that clusters are optimally arranged, this may give a maximum separation of several thousand feet.

The long-range plans for the IBM cabling system include a *backbone* link that transmits data between widely separated clusters. However, the backbone does not yet exist. A token ring using voice-grade cables thus has a severely restricted range, certainly confined to a single building. Data-grade cabling extends the range significantly, but without a backbone link still cannot embrace an entire campus. In general, then, the token ring must be confined to a single building.

The Broadband System

When IBM first released PC Network (in spring 1985), the program existed in only one version, running on broadband links, manufactured for IBM by Sytek Corporation. The token-ring version was not announced until fall 1985, for delivery the following spring. The software used to manage the 1985 version, and NETBIOS on which the network software rests, were both carried forward to the token-ring version.

When PC Network was introduced, IBM had not previously used broadband communications. There was some tendency to use the term *PC Network* to refer not only to the software for managing the network but also to the broadband hardware introduced with it. Since this book is about the PC Network software that runs on both physical links, I have been careful never to use *PC Network* to refer to one of the two physical links. However, you should be aware that IBM's literature frequently uses *PC Network* to refer not to the software system but to the physical link, as a contrast to the token-ring. In this book I have always called that alternative link the broadband system.

The Term Broadband

Broadband is a term borrowed from radio and TV engineering. The broadband version of PC Network adopts some standard technology from closed-circuit TV, and uses the same coaxial cables and connectors widely used for cable TV.

Transmissions along a TV cable are partitioned into independent *channels* by what is called *frequency division multiplexing.* Each channel is assigned a particular frequency, or rather a band covering a range of frequencies. When it has something to send, each source on the cable transmits a *carrier* signal in the frequency band of its assigned channel. The information (for example, a computer message or a TV picture) consists of variations or *modulations* of that carrier signal. Tuning devices listen to one band of frequencies and filter out the others. In that way, each receiver can select one program from a cable that is transmitting dozens of different programs at once.

Although the total capacity of the cable used for broadband transmission is large (much larger than the capacity of the twisted pairs used for token-ring systems), each channel gets only a small percentage of the total. The capacity of a particular channel (or band) depends on the difference between its highest and lowest frequency: its *bandwidth.* When channels were standardized for TV, the bandwidth was much greater than had been required for simpler signals, such as telegraphy or radio. They were called *broad.* A TV channel usually has a bandwidth of 6 megahertz. For data transmission, that amounts to a capacity of about 2 million bits per second, which is the data-transmission speed of the broadband version of PC Network.

The Frequency Translator Moves Signals between the Network's Two Channels

The broadband system uses two of the standard cable TV channels: one for sending and the other for receiving. All the PCs transmit on channel T-14 (just below the frequency used for broadcast channel 2) and receive on channel J (just above the frequency used for broadcast channel 13). Both signals go over the same cable.

So that the PCs can receive what is sent, the network includes a *frequency translator.* There is one translator for each network. The translator's job is to listen to everything that any of the PCs transmits on its *send* channel, and repeat it on the *receive* channel so that every PC on the network can hear it. The translator is what CATV people call the *headend* of the network.

The broadband system is built on a bus topology, with all machines connected to a common cable. (*Bus* is the electrical engineer's term for a conductor common to several circuits.) In theory, the translator could be located anywhere on the network. The one requirement is that the translator can hear the signals coming from every PC, and every PC can hear signals coming from the translator. As a practical matter, all the cables run from the translator. The connectors form a tree structure, with its root at the translator. From the translator, the cables fan out in clusters.

The frequency translator is about as big as a moderate-sized book. At one end it has a low-voltage power supply with a small transformer that plugs into a wall outlet, and on the other an F-connector to which is attached a single coaxial cable. All communication in the entire network passes through that cable.

Range of the Broadband System

The range of a broadband LAN is limited by the ability of the translator to hear the PCs on the network and of the PCs to hear the translator. That depends both on the cables and their adjustment, and on the sensitivity and signal strength of the translator.

Coaxial cable suffers from a selective bias called *tilt,* which attenuates some frequencies more than others; to compensate for it, the cables have *tilt compensators.* The amount of adjustment depends on the length of the cable. To facilitate installation, IBM supplies a kit of cables in premeasured lengths, with their appropriate tilt compensators and attenuators. The attenuators reduce the strength of the signal over short cables, to make it more nearly equal with the strength over greater lengths. You screw together the appropriate components to obtain cables that work satisfactorily over several different ranges.

The IBM cable kit can accommodate up to 72 PCs with a maximum separation of about 2000 feet. Individual PCs, each on a cable up to 200 feet long, are clustered around an eight-way splitter. Each eight-way splitter is in turn connected either by a short cable or by a 400- or 800-foot *distance kit* to the translator.

A CATV contractor can install and adjust cables that will work satisfactorily over longer distances. (The PC Network *Technical Reference* includes the signal-strength specifications she will need.) A more powerful translator may also increase the effective range of the network; Sytek claims a radius of up to 3½ miles for its 6050 translator.

A network linked by the IBM broadband cabling kit must generally be confined to a single building or to closely neighboring buildings on a campus.

Sharing the Cables with Closed-Circuit TV

It's possible to have the signals used by PC Network share the cables with closed-circuit TV or with signals used by certain building-maintenance or security systems. That's because PC Network confines its signals to just two of the available CATV channels and neither transmits nor receives on the others. If you want your PC Network signals to share the cables with other systems, you will need both the advice of CATV engineers for the cabling, and a different translator box than the one supplied by IBM (for example, the Sytek 6050).

Avoiding Collisions

The various PCs on a network can only transmit one at a time. The computer industry has several different approaches to ensure that the various PCs don't interfere with each other's transmissions. In the token-ring version, the PC that captures the rotating token is next to transmit. The broadband version of PC Network uses a sort of free-for-all in which each tries to transmit as soon as it has something to send. That's called CSMA/CD (carrier sense, multiple access, with collision detection). Here's how it works.

The receive portion of the network adapter is always listening for incoming signals. When the send portion is ready to send something, it checks first to see whether the receiver detects an incoming transmission. That is, it tries to *sense the carrier,* the frequency on which the translator retransmits all messages. If it hears a transmission (other than the translator's rebroadcast of its own), it waits a moment and tries again. If it doesn't hear anyone else sending, it starts its transmission.

Even though the network is silent much of the time, there's still a chance that one or more of the other PCs will go through exactly the same procedure at exactly the same time. They'll all listen, hear no one transmitting, and start to send. That's a *collision.* As it starts its transmission, each computer continues to listen for a transmission from someone else. If two or more computers start transmitting at the same time, each almost instantly detects that a collision has occurred. Each momentarily transmits a jamming signal to make sure everybody involved has detected the collision. Then they all quit sending, wait a moment, and try again. The length of time that each waits is short but random. It's random because if they all waited the same amount of time, they'd all repeat the collision just as before. When a retry also results in a collision, the computer waits a slightly longer random interval before trying again. Extending the delay time (called *backing off*) helps avoid gridlock when the system is heavily loaded.

The probability of a collision depends on the total volume of traffic on the network: both the number of PCs that are active and the amount that each has to transmit. As the volume increases, collisions become more probable, and the effective speed of transmission drops. Just how severely—or even whether—performance drops off as load becomes heavier is a complicated matter depending on the exact tuning of a great many system parameters. At present it appears that the transmission rates used in PC Network greatly exceed the needs of a small- or moderate-sized network. The performance of really large or very heavily loaded networks is an unknown quantity: there are known theoretical limits, but it isn't clear when they'll be felt in practice. Sytek Corporation, which designed the physical equipment used in the broadband system, has constructed networks having more than a thousand computers. IBM has chosen to limit the standard configuration of both versions to no more than 260 computers, and the standard cabling kit to just 72.

Differences between the Two Systems

From the user's point of view, the fundamental difference is in the cables: how long they can be, what it takes to connect them, what else you can connect them to.

Type of Cabling

The token ring uses special cables and connectors, but the local attachment of a PC can be done with telephone-type cables and modular plugs. The broadband version uses coaxial cables.

Range of the Local-Area Network

The broadband version has a range two or three times as large as the token-ring version based on telephone-type cables. The token ring's range can be more than doubled by using data-grade shielded cable; the broadband version's range can be increased perhaps fivefold or even sevenfold, but only with professionally installed cable and a substitute translator.

Equipment Required

The token ring requires a multistation access unit for every eight connection points. The broadband requires one translator for the network and a distance kit for each cluster of eight connection points after the first. (The translator and the multistation access unit have similar prices; the distance kit costs substantially less.) Hardware costs are about the same for a minimum network, but the broadband version is somewhat less expensive as the network increases in size.

Software Required

The token-ring version requires NETBIOS software and the network adapter handler (a one-time cost) and a permanent consumption of 55k of memory. The broadband version doesn't need extra software because it's included in the broadband network adapter.

Speed of the Network

At first glance, the token-ring version runs twice as fast as the broadband. However, the two versions of PC Network are fairly close in the speed with which data is actually transferred from one machine to another, largely because the adapter for the token-ring version handles communication only up to the *link* layer, leaving the rest to software running on the PC, whereas the adapter of the broadband version also includes processing through the *transport, network,* and *session* layers. (Link, network, transport, and session are terms for layers 2 through 5 of the International Standards Organization's terminology for the seven layers of communication in an open system; see, for example, the article by Denning mentioned in Appendix C.) The result is that the CPU must do more of the work when it uses the token-ring adapter than when it uses the broadband adapter, and the extra work slows down the effective rate of data transfer.

Any comparison of the two systems has to make many assumptions about the configurations of the machines involved and the mix of data they transmit. I have not found an independent comparison of their effective transmission rates. Tests developed and published by Sytek have estimated 0.75 megabits per second for the token-ring system, and 0.68 megabits per second for the broadband system (compared with 4 and 2 megabits per second, respectively, of raw transmission speed on the cable).

Other Uses of the Cable

When IBM released its specifications for a cabling system that could be built into an office building (in 1982), the idea was that ultimately any device from the entire spectrum of office equipment—terminals, displays, order-entry devices, PCs, printers, computers large and small, building controls, whatever—could be connected anywhere in the building, simply by plugging into the nearest data jack. Someday that sort of wiring will probably be widespread; a few buildings have already been constructed with such wiring in place. If you happen to be in such a building or are about to install such a general wiring system, the token-ring version of PC Network can make use of it.

The broadband system also piggybacks on wiring that may have other uses. However, the other uses are more related to television, teleconferencing, or building security than to computers. In principle, the network might also share wiring with other computer uses, but at this point no other such uses have been announced.

Shared wiring isn't practical yet. For the small company or department that is installing PC Network as a stand-alone system, neither of these shared uses seems to me very compelling. Where there is a more general corporate plan for data communications, it becomes more important to remain consistent with the rest of the organization.

Summary List

Figure B.1 lists the various points of comparison noted here. With it, filling in the particulars of your own organization's situation, you can clarify how the differences between the two versions may affect you.

Issue	Token-Ring Version	Broadband Version
Distance		
Radius	From access unit 150 feet (voice-grade) 330 feet (data-grade)	From eight-way connector 200 feet
Maximum run	Between wiring closets 1 run of 400 feet (voice-grade)* 12 runs of 650 feet (data-grade)	From base expander to eight-way splitter 800 feet
Maximum separation	700 feet (voice-grade) ?? 4000–5000 feet (shielded)*	2000 feet
Speed		
Transmission	4.00×10^6 bits/sec	2.00×10^6 bits/sec
Throughput (est.)	0.75×10^6 bits/sec	0.68×10^6 bits/sec

Figure B.1: *Summary of comparisons of the token-ring and broadband versions of PC Network*

Hardware		Translator (one)
		Base expander (if more than 8 outlets)
	Adapter (per PC)	Adapter (per PC)
	Multistation access unit (per 8 outlets)	Eight-way connector (per 8 outlets)
	Patch cable (for each access unit after the first)	Distance kit (for each cluster after the first)
Software	DOS 3.10 PC Network NETBIOS (46k) Adapter handler (7k)	DOS 3.10 PC Network
Cables	IBM type 1, or can use telephone-type	Must be coaxial
Connectors	IBM data connectors; Modular (voice-grade)	CATV type F
Shared use of cable system		Closed-circuit TV (with substitute translator)

**Note:* Cable between wiring closets must be data-grade, regardless of the type used to link the PCs. Overall maximum separation of PCs on the token-ring network depends on the existence of series of wiring closets scattered along the way and of PCs connected to them to relay the signal.

Figure B.1: *Summary of comparisons of the token-ring and broadband versions of PC Network (continued)*

When I compiled the comparison, I was surprised that on balance they seemed much more similar than I had expected. With either, you can install a communications gateway to other systems. With either, devices such as printers are connected to the PCs and indifferent to the way the computers communicate among themselves.

Further Reading

Appendix C

Publications by Individuals

Cooper, Edward. *Broadband Network Technology, An Overview of the Data and Telecommunications Industries.* Mountain View, CA: Sytek Press, 1984.

Davis, Lou. "Application Development Guidelines for the IBM PC Network." *In Exchange of IBM PC Information,* pp.23–31. Boca Raton, FL: IBM PC User Support, August 1985. (Available from IBM-PC user groups.)

Denning, Peter J. "Computer Networks." *American Scientist,* **73** (1985), pp. 127–129 (March/April), pp. 225–227 May/June. Discussion of concepts of layers of network communication.

Manuals, Catalogues, and Corporate Publications

Architecture Technology Corporation (P.O. Box 24344, Minneapolis, MN 55424). *The LOCALNetter Designer's Handbook.*

——. *The LOCALNetter Newsletter.*

——. *Personal Computer Local Networks Report.*

IBM Corporation. (Publications are available through local branch offices.) *An Introduction to Local Area Networks.* SC20-8203.

——. *Building Planning Guide for Communications Wiring.* 8320-8059, 1982.

——. *Disk Operating System Technical Reference,* version 3.10, part 6138536, 1985.

——. *IBM Cabling System Catalog,* G570-2040, 1985.

——. *IBM Cabling System Planning and Installation Guide,* GA27-3361.

——. *IBM PC Network Program User's Guide,* part 6361559. 1984, 1985.

——. *IBM PC Network Technical Reference,* part 6322505 (same book also listed as part 6322916), 1985.

——. *The IBM Token-Ring Network Decision,* pamphlet, IBM 59X7202, October 1985.

——. *IBM Token-Ring Network Installation Guide,* GA27-3678. (Data-grade cabling only.)

——. *IBM Token-Ring Network Introduction and Planning Guide,* GA27-3677, October 1985.

——. *IBM Token-Ring Network PC Adapter Technical Reference,* part 6165876, 1986.

——. *IBM Token-Ring Network, PC Network and Media Alternatives,* pamphlet, IBM 59X-7205, October 1985.

——. *IBM Token-Ring Network Telephone Twisted-Pair Media Guide,* GA27-3714, October 1985.

Texas Instruments, (LAN Products, P.O. Box 1443, Houston TX 77001). *TMS 380 Adapter Chipset User's Guide.* (The TMS 380 is a chip set compatable with the IBM token-ring network adapter card.)

Index

Note: Entries in italics are either screen messages or menu options. Page numbers in italics refer to definitions in Appendix A: Glossary (pages 302–323).

Selections from The SYBEX Library

Computer Specific

IBM PC and Compatibles

THE ABC'S OF THE IBM® PC
by Joan Lasselle and Carol Ramsay
143 pp., illustr., Ref. 0-102
This book will take you through the first crucial steps in learning to use the IBM PC.

THE BEST OF IBM® PC SOFTWARE
by Stanley R. Trost
351 pp., Ref. 0-104
Separates the wheat from the chaff in the world of IBM PC software. Tells you what to expect from the best available IBM PC programs.

THE IBM® PC-DOS HANDBOOK
by Richard Allen King
296 pp., Ref. 0-103
Explains the PC disk operating system. Get the most out of your PC by adapting its capabilities to your specific needs.

BUSINESS GRAPHICS FOR THE IBM® PC
by Nelson Ford
259 pp., illustr., Ref. 0-124
Ready-to-run programs for creating line graphs, multiple bar graphs, pie charts, and more. An ideal way to use your PC's business capabilities!

THE IBM® PC CONNECTION
by James W. Coffron
264 pp., illustr., Ref. 0-127
Teaches elementary interfacing and BASIC programming of the IBM PC for connection to external devices and household appliances.

BASIC EXERCISES FOR THE IBM® PERSONAL COMPUTER
by J.P. Lamoitier
252 pp., 90 illustr., Ref. 0-088
Teaches IBM BASIC through actual practice, using graduated exercises drawn from everyday applications.

USEFUL BASIC PROGRAMS FOR THE IBM® PC
by Stanley R. Trost
144 pp., illustr., Ref. 0-111
This collection of programs takes full advantage of the interactive capabilities of your IBM Personal Computer. Financial calculations, investment analysis, record keeping, and math practice—made easier on your IBM PC.

YOUR FIRST IBM® PC PROGRAM
by Rodnay Zaks
182 pp., illustr., Ref. 0-171
This well-illustrated book makes programming easy for children and adults.

DATA FILE PROGRAMMING ON YOUR IBM® PC
by Alan Simpson
219 pp., illustr., Ref. 0-146
This book provides instructions and examples for managing data files in BASIC. Programming design and development are extensively discussed.

THE MS™-DOS HANDBOOK
by Richard Allen King
320 pp., illustr., Ref. 0-185
The differences between the various versions and manufacturer's implementations of MS-DOS are covered in a clear, straightforward manner. Tables, maps, and numerous examples make this the most complete book on MS-DOS available.